Pr…

SEA PAY

"I foolishly thought I knew everything about the US Navy. *Sea Pay* blasted open a new door of experience and shed light on rarely told aspects of the insanity of life underway. It was very fun to read. I recommend that old salty dogs like Bob and me and especially non-Navy (normal) people enjoy this book. You will learn many things. It's a funny, honest, and sometimes tragic chronicle of the adventure that is the US Navy. I am reminded of the great Willie Nelson when I loosely quote, 'Mammas, don't let your babies grow up to be sailors . . . '"

—Eric D. Atno, SCPO, USN (Ret.)
Author of *Underway: Good Times in Uncle Sam's Canoe Club*

"As an author myself, Bob Dorgan has another 'must-read' that held me captive to the last page."

—Luke Ridenhour, USNA, Attack Pilot USN
Author of *Over the Horizon*

"*Sea Pay* is a must-read for anyone interested in the Navy way of life back when 'sailors had more fun.' The book's title is appropriate because US Navy sailors are paid, even when they are in trouble, much more than the cash they receive on a bimonthly basis. Sailors earn experiences that few others will ever enjoy. Dorgan tells his story as he spins his yarns to the reader as if situated together at a table, enjoying a nice beverage. His tales may seem too tall for some readers, but believe them as they are not fairy tales. As Dorgan qualifies, 'Listen up, this is no shit!'"

—Johnny J. Moye, PhD, MCPO USN (Ret.)
Author of *The Master Chief's Sea Stories*

"Eye-opening and riveting."

—Galen D Peterson, USMA, Tank Commander USA (Ret.)
Author of *Strike Hard and Expect No Mercy*

"Great Read! This book brought me back to my first command while serving as a young sailor onboard the USS Midway CV-41... an accurate view back through the spy glass of time to what day to day life was like Stationed on a Forward Deployed Aircraft Carrier... Every Day was full of Adventure, and Challenges; Challenges that forged us to who we are today!"

—Jeffrey Denny, EMCS(SW/DV), USN (Ret.)

"Your first set of orders says USS *Midway*, Yokosuka, Japan. What mischief and adventure can a young lad get into on a floating city in the Far East? Bob tells his unique story for all to enjoy. This will have seasoned sailors reflecting how they earned their sea pay and the interesting characters they met."

—CWO Larry Fordyce, USN (Ret.)

"Each sailor has his own story to tell and a unique experience to share. In reading *Sea Pay* I realized how my 'tin can' experience aboard several Navy destroyers in my book, *A Sailor's Journey*, was vastly different from what the writer experienced in *Sea Pay*. As a US Navy veteran, I would highly recommend the book *Sea Pay* as a book every sailor should read. Especially those who served on carriers and made West Pac cruises."

—Ray Perrotti, USN
Author of *A Sailor's Journey*

Sea Pay
An Enlisted Man's Naval Adventure

By Bob Dorgan

ISBN 978-1-64663-709-6

Published by

◤ köehlerbooks ™

3705 Shore Drive
Virginia Beach, VA 23455
800–435–4811
www.koehlerbooks.com

SEA PAY

AN ENLISTED MAN'S NAVAL ADVENTURE

BOB DORGAN

VIRGINIA BEACH
CAPE CHARLES

For Virginia:
my best friend, my constant, and my greatest love.
You make the world a better place.

The difference between a fairy tale and a sea story:
A fairy tale starts with "Once upon a time . . ."
A sea story starts with *"Listen up, this is no shit . . ."*

Table of Contents

PREFACE

THE LIFE OF A YOUNG ENLISTED SAILOR at sea is made up primarily of hours and hours of boring, mundane routine interrupted by flashes of intense danger and chaos. At a moment's notice, a sailor can be called upon to perform the duties for which he has been trained to the best of his ability, without hesitation, and often at great risk to his own safety and well-being. This book is about my personal experiences as a young enlisted man stationed aboard the aircraft carrier USS *Midway* (CV-41) during the late '70s and early '80s and recounts how I, along with my shipmates, added adventure and excitement to our tour of duty, both on and off the "boat."

This was an earlier time when many Navy liberty ports of call were still filled with the temptation of vice, sin, and debauchery, as well as dangers that lurked around every corner. Many of us as young sailors often fell into these temptations not realizing the consequences which could and often did accompany them. As I now reminisce with old shipmates from this era some forty plus years ago, we all agree on one common statement: "I can't believe we really did all that stuff way back then. We must have been crazy!"

Out of respect and admiration, the names and nicknames of some of my shipmates and other personnel have been changed to protect their privacy in today's modern world.

As I wrote this story, I tried to be as accurate as possible. There may be some minor inaccuracies regarding naval or historical content, and I hope sensitive readers will forgive my occasional backslide into sailor slang, curse words, mild sexism, and other grievous offenses. This was a time, years ago, when the United States Navy was a true boy's club.

CHAPTER ONE
THE FORGE

WE COULD SEE the distant faint light of approaching headlights through the lightly falling snow from our lookout point at the top of the Press Shop Hill. It was January in southeast Pennsylvania, when the black of night comes early. The season we cadets of Valley Forge Military Academy referred to as *The Dark Ages*.

Each season has its high points, but in this one, they were few and far between. The Christmas holidays were over, and we were settling in for a long stretch, looking forward to the spring thaw and the coming of the Easter holiday, when we could enjoy a break from "the Forge."

Enrico and I had just returned from Managua, Nicaragua, after spending the Christmas holidays with his family. We still had that Central American tan from days of exposure to the intense tropical sun. Enrico's family had sent him to school in the States because of the political and economic problems in his country, then under President Anastasio Somoza. His older brother had been deported and was living in New Orleans after being accused by the Nicaraguan government of being a Sandinista revolutionary. Enrico's family seemed to feel a sense of security knowing their son was thousands of miles away, in a safe environment.

We were roommates and in our senior year at Valley Forge Military Academy. When Enrico invited me to head south with him and his other brother, Ricardo (who was in B Company), for Christmas, my answer, without hesitation, was "*you bet!*" Fortunately, my parents backed me on this adventure with a passport, airline tickets, clothes, and spending money—it is amazing what you take for granted as a teenager.

Following our Amtrack train ride from Philadelphia to Washington, DC, Enrico, Ricardo, and I spent the night at the home of the Nicaraguan ambassador to the United States, who was a friend of their family. Enrico and Ricardo's family, the Targas, owned the Avis car rental office in Managua. In the cold, snowy, twenty-five-degree December morning, we were driven to Dulles International Airport to catch our flight to the land of warm breezes. When I handed the airline attendant my ticket and passport for boarding, she handed it back to me and said, "You have no visa to travel to Nicaragua, Mr. Dorgan."

Fortunately, the Nicaraguan ambassador standing next to me was able to write an emergency vias on the passport with an explanation and her signature. That did the trick. I was allowed on the plane and into Nicaragua when we arrived. Apparently, I was traveling in good company, and I was very lucky.

The headlights grew brighter and closer. There were already almost three inches of snow covering the ground and the Academy roadway, which came off Radnor Road onto the campus of the Forge. This road served as a back entrance and the route up the hill to the junior college. The press shop that the hill we occupied was named for was where cadets took our stiff wool uniforms weekly to be cleaned and pressed. Our vantage point was looking out from inside of a small group of evergreen trees. From there, we could see 200 feet down the steep hill to the snow-covered road, across the creek and then up to the top of Junior College Hill.

Looking to the right, I could see the lit windows of three of the two-story brick cadet barracks buildings: H Company, A and B Company, and C Company. Study hall had been in session for about an hour now. From 1930 to 2130, all cadets had to be in their barracks, in their rooms, at their desks, sitting quietly and studying.

Three hours earlier, from the main phone room, I had called in a hoagie order to the local sandwich shop in Wayne: twenty roast beef, twenty Italian, twenty turkey, and ten clubs.

"Any tuna?" the guy on the other end of the line asked.

"Hell no!" I replied.

The past fall, I was almost busted because a couple of guys in B Company wanted tuna hoagies and the smell had alerted the faculty study hall monitor. Luckily, they had devoured all the evidence before the TAC could find any of them. The only evidence was that lingering smell of tuna.

"You're going to military school!" To this day, those words from my mother's lips still ring in my ears.

After an on-again, off-again marriage, my parents called it quits when I was eight. After that I lived with mom, who did her best to provide a good, stable home for us both. Between her and my grandparents, I felt like a normal, fairly well-adjusted kid. Then, one morning when we were visiting my grandparents when I was eleven, I overheard her tell them, "Tex asked me to marry him, and I said yes."

Tex? I didn't remember her going to Texas. Hell, I didn't even know she was dating anybody! A month later, on a snowy winter morning, we all trotted over to the justice of the peace for the official ceremony.

That January, Mom and I moved in with Tex. He had a nice house in the country backing up to a big farm and orchard. I changed schools again, for the sixth time in seven years. We all settled into a normal routine. Then, late in my eighth-grade year, Mom and Tex were not very happy with the way we were—or were not—getting along. As a teenager, I guess I was learning how to push their buttons. They began talking with me about going to see other schools to consider attending for high school. We visited several on weekends. What really caught my attention was all the girls I noticed living at the different boarding schools. With no parents around? Wow! What a great concept! Maybe this would not be too bad after all.

Well, you guessed it. The straw that broke the camel's back was an argument that blew up between me and Mom about a girlfriend she did not want me seeing. Boom! And that, as they say, was that.

That fall they loaded me up, footlocker and all, and dropped me off at Valley Forge Military Academy. VF was steeped in tradition, and I could tell immediately this was not going to be summer camp.

Mom and Tex told me, "If you do well this year, next year you can choose any school you would like to go to."

Well, for me, that was a challenge. I took quickly to the military life of rules, regulations, and responsibility. During my plebe year, as well as performing well academically and earning several honors, I was awarded the coveted Superintendent's Award as the best new cadet in C Company for that year.

Yup, you guessed right again. When I went home for summer vacation that year, Mom and Tex said, "Bob, we are so proud of you and how well you have performed at VF this year, you will be going back there again this fall."

––––––––––––––––––

Economics was my favorite class and was taught by Colonel Quinn. It did not take long for me to understand the finer points of the basics of supply and demand. When I look back on that class, I believe a risk and reward chapter should have been added to the year's textbook.

The food served during third mess at VF was generally tolerable, to say the least. After about two hours of evening study hall, it amazed me how much young cadets would pay for a fresh hoagie sandwich, delivered to their room. I found it was quite simple for me to more than double my money, for a little risk. I was hooked on the lure of easy money.

We developed a delivery routine for the hoagie run. The driver from the sandwich shop drove in through the service gate, up the road, then cut off his headlights when he was close to our pickup spot at the bottom of the hill. He would then proceed another 500 feet to the fork in the road, then turn around and head back to meet us. By that time, we would have had time to make our way down from the top of the hill, where we were anxiously waiting. This plan had worked time and time again, without fail.

That snowy night after Christmas seemed routine. With one last look around, I motioned to Enrico, and said, "Let's go." We started down the hill toward the car. By this time the snow was really peppering down. I headed down as fast as I could, doing my best to keep my footing on the slick, snow-covered hillside. Through the darkness and the falling snow, I could see the driver had stepped out of his car, opened the trunk, and was unloading our delivery. Then, boom! As my legs were knocked out from under me, I fell backward on to Enrico, who had lost his footing on his way down the hill. He took me out like a bowling pin. Like a two-man bobsled, we were gaining speed, headed straight for the driver unloading our sacks of hoagies from the trunk. *Bam!* He went down too, and hoagies scattered everywhere.

Funny? No! This dude was not laughing.

Philly is well known as being the best area of the country to get world-class hoagies. An Italian family ran this sandwich shop. It was the best around. This guy had delivered to us a couple of times in the past. He seemed to be in his late forties. He was a big, heavy-set, no-nonsense kind of guy. He could have passed as an enforcer for the Italian mob. Always made me a little uneasy when he delivered.

I jumped to my feet and tried to help him up. But he wouldn't have any part of it.

"Give me the money you fucking clowns!" he bellowed out.

As I dug into my coat pocket for the envelope of cash, he got up out of the snow and stuck out his hand.

"This is my last trip," he said as he turned, jumped into the car, and sped off into the snowy night, leaving us there with a mess.

At this point, Enrico was sitting on the cement curb at the side of the road.

"Are you okay?" I asked.

"Yeah, but my foot is killing me," he replied. "I think I sprained my ankle or something."

"Let's get these hoagies up. We gotta get going," I said.

Just then, I looked up to see the headlight and amber flashing roof lights from the Campus Cushman Security Cart coming down the road from JC Hill, heading straight for us.

"Come on! Grab those bags!" I yelled to Enrico.

We both grabbed what we could and started running. To go back up the hill we just slid down would be suicide. We would never make it and surely be caught, from the top or the bottom of the hill so we headed straight down the road, in the opposite direction of the security cart coming our way. As we veered to the right, off the road and up toward the path leading to our C Company barracks, I looked over my shoulder to see the cart stopping at our point of disaster.

"Hoagie and pizza runs were a longstanding tradition passed down through the years at VF. I can remember back in my plebe year, the smell of fresh, hot pizza interrupting the quiet of evening study hall. Pizza was a much tougher product to deliver successfully. Keeping it hot and level, and getting a fast delivery was too complicated. In addition, that unmistakable smell was tough to hide from the faculty.

During my junior year, Jeff Landau introduced me to the hoagie business and his contacts. Right away, it clicked in. I had guys in other barracks who would be standing by in the evening to receive my delivery for their company. I gave them hoagies. They gave me cash. The system was working well.

The faculty at VF knew the business went on and frowned on it.

As we ran toward the side entrance door of our barracks huffing and puffing, the thought went through my mind: *this is not going to turn out well.*

I quickly made it down the corridor and back to my room to find Major Martin, his back to me, standing in front of my window on the opposite side of the room, staring out the window.

"It is really coming down out there now, isn't it, Lieutenant?" he asked without turning around.

Major Martin was a graduate of Valley Forge. He was our C Company TAC officer my plebe year, during the time we were housed in Hamilton Hall. He was later promoted to the rank of major and helped oversee the entire academy. Major Martin seemed to always look favorably on me. I am certain, my promotion to cadet second lieutenant, regimental staff, was partially his doing, even after being busted down to private from master sergeant the year before when Pete, Joe, and I skipped out of the Dunnaway reading assembly. It was tradition that all those who had earned the Superintendent's Award would, in their senior year, be promoted to the rank of cadet officer.

"Yes, sir," I replied.

The major and I had always gotten along well over the years. However, a visit, especially during evening study hall, was quite unusual.

"Had a busy evening, Dorgan?" he continued, as he passed by me, heading for the door.

I stood there speechless in my room trying to slow down my rapid breathing from our run up the hill.

As Major Martin left, I had the feeling, he wanted to say more, but did not. A sense of relief passed over me, but it was to be short-lived.

The next couple of days passed by normally—marching, meals, classes, assemblies, marching, physical training, marching, and study hall—until the evening I was summoned to Lee Hall, the office of the commandant of cadets, Brigadier General Mataxas. I thought that by then the events of our botched hoagie run a few days earlier were but a bad faded memory. *Ugh, was I wrong!*

General Mataxas was a member of the faculty whom I never wanted to spend much time around. We all gave the general a wide berth. He was a towering man, built like a barrel, with a full chest of campaign ribbons and medals. His Army dress hat covered his shiny bald head. He was an intimidating figure, with veins that bulged out when he was riled up. His voice commanded the attention of anyone within earshot.

It was after dark when I entered the office of the cadet officer of the day. The snow was again coming down hard, covering the blacktop of the main arena between Wheeler Hall and Lee Hall. The officer of the day told me to sit on a nearby chair until General Mataxas returned. The longstanding procedure in the military has always been to hurry up and wait.

After what seemed like an hour, I was led into the conference room, where I was told to sit in a chair about halfway down the length of the big wooden conference table. After sitting there alone for another thirty minutes, our C Company TAC, Lieutenant Rapp, entered the room. He sat down across the table from me, slid a yellow tablet over to me and said, "Dorgan, I need for you to write down the events of your day as they occurred from beginning to end on Tuesday of this week." That was it. He then stood up from the table and left the room.

Well, now I was getting a bit uneasy. I began writing. Another thirty minutes went by. The door opened again. This time Major Martin walked into the room. "Hello, Bob," he said as he took the yellow tablet away from me. "There are some events which have recently come to light that need to be dealt with."

He then gave me another blank yellow tablet.

"I need for you to write down the events of your day, Tuesday, from beginning to end," he continued.

As the major got up to leave, he looked at me and said, "I am sorry, but this is out of my hands now."

Sitting there alone, late into the night, in the dead quiet of the conference room, I could hear my heart beating in my ears.

When are they going to let me go back to my barracks? I wondered.

After another thirty minutes or so, the conference room door opened again. In walked Lieutenant Rapp, Major Martin, and right behind him was General Mataxas. For all three of them to be here, this late at night could only mean one thing. *I was in deep shit*!

After another thirty minutes of interrogation, they all left the room. Shortly thereafter, the officer of the day came to get me.

"You will be spending the night here in Lee Hall—upstairs," he said. I followed him out of the conference room, up the stairs, and into a small room with a cot.

The night in that cold, dark, tiny room seemed to take forever to pass.

———

A knock at the door woke me. It was early the next morning and there was light outside. The cadet officer of the day said, "Come on, it's time to go."

I followed him down the narrow stairway to the first floor. The office was bustling with activity. Apparently, the snowstorm had continued all night. Snow shoveling this morning was the priority of the Corps of Cadets. I was guided into the office of the commandant, who sat behind his huge cherry desk. Sitting across from him was my mother.

The conversation that went on after that was a blur. The next thing I remember, I was walking off the campus of Valley Forge Military Academy, trudging through the newly fallen snow, for the last time. That car ride home was the quietest ride of my life.

After arriving home, I expected to never hear the end of how I had ruined my life and disappointed my family for being kicked out of school. To my surprise, the subject was never brought up again.

Now the only question was, "Bob, what are you going to do with your life?"

I have always believed life is what you make of it. But at the age of seventeen, without a high school diploma, my options and future looked limited. We scheduled a time at a nearby high school to go in on a Saturday and complete the standardized test to earn a General Educational Development (GED) diploma.

Mom and Tex did their best to smile day to day. However, the dinner table was often stressful. One evening, Mom perked up and said, "I picked up some information today on training available through the Navy."

The United States Navy. Now that caught my interest.

"Today I visited the local Navy recruiter's office," she said. "They have training available in many different fields that could lead to a good career. They provide three meals a day, medical coverage, travel, and even tuition for college."

Compared to what I have going on in my day-to-day life right now, that sounds pretty good, I thought.

The next week we took a trip to downtown Philly to see the Navy recruiter. I completed some tests, took a physical, and looked over a few career training choices.

Just like that, I enlisted and was sworn in to The United States Navy. This was the delayed entry program. The electrician's mate training program was the one that interested me. However, there was not an available class opening for several months. *This is a skill I could get a good job with when I get out.* I thought. *Electricians are always in demand, and they get paid well.*

We went home and began the waiting process. For the past couple of years, when I was home, I worked part time for our neighbor

Jimmy Woodward, who owned the farm behind us. During the dead of winter there was not much outside farm work to be done, but the chicken eggs had to be gathered from the huge chicken house once a day, cleaned, and sorted. I made a little money with that, and it kept me busy. In addition, it just so happened that my parents had quite a few household painting projects, both inside and out, that needed completion. The experience of painting our barracks at VF had prepared me well for this—it seems like we were always putting a coat of paint on something.

CHAPTER TWO
BOOT CAMP

IT WAS MAY 2. The bleak, snowy winter of 1977 was finally over. I was summoned to the Military Entrance Processing Station (MEPS) in downtown Philly. After another brief physical, I was given my orders, a big brown envelope with my Navy personal records inside, and a train ticket. Destination: Basic Training, Recruit Training Center, Great Lakes, Illinois, otherwise known as boot camp.

Once again, Mom took me, driving me in the car this time. She dropped me off at Philadelphia's Pennsylvania Station for a one-way trip. I am sure she was relieved that I was on my way to the next chapter in my life. I never moved back home again.

Boarding the train, I met a couple of other new recruits with the same destination. Each of us seemed a bit reserved, with our own quiet anticipation of what lay ahead. It was a long, peaceful trip. With the rocking and swaying motion of the train cars passing through the Pennsylvania countryside, I had no trouble napping, especially with the warm sunshine pouring in through the huge glass picture windows.

By the time we reached Pittsburgh, it was dark outside. We paused briefly in the switch yard while the crew attached additional sleeper cars. After our stop at the main train station in Pittsburgh, I was assigned a berth in one of the newly added cars. It was a nice setup, with bunk beds and a little washbasin area, plus a window with an adjustable blind.

Just as I was making myself at home in what seemed to be my private stateroom, there was a knock at the door. The conductor popped his head in the door. "You've got company," he said, moving aside to show another passenger in, "a fellow sailor to join you."

I thought, *Well, my days of privacy are over for a long, long time.*

———————

Looking out the window in the early morning daylight the next day, the scenery gradually changed from wide-open, uninhabited spaces, to populated neighborhoods. Soon the view became dense, urban sprawl and then industry, smoke, and pollution. It was easy to tell we were arriving in Chicago.

As the train began to slow as it neared the station, an announcement came over the public address system, "All passengers, please prepare to disembark at our final destination, Chicago Station." I gathered up what little I had brought with me.

The recruiter had said, "Do not take anything with you to boot camp but the clothes on your back. The Navy will issue you everything you need."

I did bring a deck of cards, my address book, a toothbrush, and my Social Security card. We were all told, "Your Social Security number will be your identification number. You must know it by heart." I spent most of the trip running that number through my head again and again, committing it to memory.

Chicago Station seemed to be a mass confusion of people going in every direction, and all in a hurry. After locating the information desk, I asked to be pointed in the right direction. The train ticket I was issued had me catching a connecting train north to Great Lakes, Illinois. Looking around, seeing other young men carrying large brown envelopes and no luggage, I knew we must be headed in the right direction.

This train was not like any I had ever traveled on. It was a double-decker. Each train car was tall, with a second area of seating on the upper level that overlooking the lower seats. As a commuter train, it made regular stops all along the way north.

"Highland Park, Fort Sheridan, Lake Forest." The conductor went through his calls. "Lake Bluff."

Suddenly, he called out in what seemed like an extra loud voice,

"For all of you new Navy recruits, this is the end of the line, Great Lakes Naval Training Center. Good luck and God bless you!"

As the train slowed to a stop, all of us young men grasping the envelopes began getting up out of our seats and heading toward the exit door. That's when the comments started coming out from those remaining on the train, "Boys, your life as you know it is over!" some called out. "Last chance—stay on the train!" others offered, with a chuckle.

When the train stopped, we all shuffled down the steps and onto the platform.

The train station at Great Lakes was not very big. We followed the signs west to the base. It was a clear but chilly early spring day. After walking a short distance, we arrived. Facing the main gate, we stopped to read the huge sign: *United States Navy Recruit Training Command.* The voices on the train were right; once we entered that gate, our lives would never be the same.

For some, boot camp was tough to get accustomed to. Most everyone was older than me, ages eighteen to twenty-eight. Many were guys who had floated from one dead-end job to another after high school. For most, this was an opportunity to get out of the rut they had found themselves in.

Some had problems with authority and taking orders. Overall, although we were from many different parts of the country, we all tried to get along together. One reason was that we never knew when we would need to rely on one another.

Getting into the military routine again came easy for me. Many fellow cadets at VF would be moving on to the service academies following graduation. Whether it would be West Point, Annapolis, or Colorado Springs, Valley Forge was well known as an excellent military prep school. The daily Navy training routine of marching, breakfast, marching, physical training, marching, lunch, marching, classroom, marching, dinner, marching, and hit the rack, was a breeze.

With almost four years of marching experience at VF, it was no surprise Chief Danforth selected me to be the Company 925 guidon to carry the company flag on a pole. The guidon is first on the blacktop for every formation. The entire company, of about sixty recruits, lines up in formation based on where the guidon is standing. The guidon then leads the company, lined up in four squads, marching on to the next destination.

———————————

A destination none of us were looking forward to in week one was the medical clinic for our shots. There were of course 101 rumors about the inoculation process and worst of all, the dreaded "A" shot. Unavoidably, that day came much too soon.

"Attention on deck. Company nine two five, muster outside on the blacktop!" yelled our recruit petty officer in charge (RPOC), "Bacon."

Bacon had a loud, resounding voice that was easily recognizable. His distinct Boston accent was unmistakable. "Hey Dorgan, grab your guidon and get 'em formed up," he commanded, pointing toward the door.

With that, we all scrambled in the same direction toward the door, each determined not to be the last recruit in formation.

"This is it Dorgan—A-shot day, buddy!" whispered "Alabama" in his thick Southern accent as we formed up on the blacktop outside of our barracks.

"Yeah, not a day I've been looking forward to," I replied.

"Quiet, or I'll make sure you get two A shots today!" barked Bacon. And with that, we were on our way, marching off to the clinic.

The company scheduled before us was just finishing up as we arrived. One by one they exited the building, each recruit rubbing their hip, some with a slight limp.

"Look over there," said Alabama, pointing in their direction. "That doesn't look good!"

"Shit, I hate shots!" I heard someone else behind me say.

We formed a single line and, one by one, we apprehensively entered the building.

As we reached the door to the inoculation room, I tried my best to peer around the guys in front of me to see what was going on.

It was a system all right. Each time a recruit moved forward in line and stepped between the two corpsmen, he received a shot just below the shoulder in each arm, made with an automated inoculation gun.

"Next!" I heard the corpsman say, and suddenly it was my turn.

Ca-chunk, ca-chunk.

That was it? Not too bad, I thought.

"Next!" another corpsman yelled, as I stepped around the corner to the next station.

In front of me was a recruit pulling up his pants and moaning as the corpsman at this station turned toward the table at his side to prepare another syringe for the next victim.

"Drop your pants boot, this won't hurt a bit!" he said as he turned toward me with a large, loaded syringe in his hand, poised to thrust its long, sharp needle tip into my butt cheek.

I unlatched, unsnapped, unzipped, and dropped 'em, exposing my bare ass for the unavoidable.

"Yeeoww! *Shit!*" I blurted out after the sting of the cold needle pierced my skin and muscle.

"Walk it off. Just keep moving and you'll be alright," he said with an evil grin. "Next!"

I pulled up my pants and moved on, anxious to get out of the building. Now it was our turn to be the ones staggering out, rubbing our sore butts.

"Company nine two five—fall in!" yelled Bacon. "We're going for a little run."

From there we all marched over to the main parade field ran in formation at least two miles. We moaned and groaned and felt the pain every step of the way. But, I would hate to imagine how we would have felt if we had not kept moving.

The Navy's goal with boot camp, as we saw it, was to gather young men, take away everything we possessed, and break us down to the basics. Then, provide us with only what we needed—clothing, food, shelter. From that point, we would be taught the Navy way. There was an old saying: *If the Navy doesn't issue it to you, then you don't need it.* In other words: *Is that Navy issue, sailor?*

One routine most of us fell into easily, was writing letters home. We were all issued Navy stationary, envelopes, and a pen. Our first week at boot camp, we were given fifteen minutes one evening to write a letter home. Everyone had to turn in a letter to be mailed. Until we sent letters out to our family and friends, nobody would know our mailing address to send letters to. That made sense.

Bringing a little pocket address book with me to boot camp proved to be a great idea. Writing letters was already a habit from my experience at boarding school. Mail call was always the highlight of the day, or at least it was for those who received a letter. There was no price you could put on the excitement of receiving a letter from home during mail call. It was an acknowledgment someone out there in the real world thought enough about you to make contact. We would keep these letters in our lockers and read them over and over again. For those who did not receive a letter, mail call was a downer.

Christmas vacation to Nicaragua with Enrico had been great fun. While there, I observed what seemed to be more of a two-class system in his country, the well-off and the poor. Fortunately, we partied with the well-off—and partied and partied.

One evening after dinner, Enrico said, "Bob you ready to go party?"

Well after about a week of this nightly holiday routine, I was considering staying in for the night. I was glad I didn't. After a little persuasion from Enrico: a rum and coke, and a bit of coca (the little white line kind), I was ready to go.

Enrico, Riccardo, and I headed out in their red Toyota Land Cruiser to a big party at the home of the minister of agriculture. They were good friends with the minister's son. When we pulled up to the estate's front gate, Ricardo stopped the truck. We were met by three huge men carrying semi-automatic weapons. After a flurry of Spanish back and forth, the double-wrought-iron gates opened inward. We drove between the huge entrance columns and up the driveway toward the huge white two-story stucco estate house. As I looked around, I could see the vague figures of other armed guards in the moonlight throughout the tropical landscaping.

With the brewing revolution going on within the country, the well-to-do families took every precaution with security. I felt safe in that compound for the evening.

As we entered through the front door of the home, we received a warm welcome, complete with hugs and kisses, and were told to make ourselves at home. Of course, we headed straight for the bar. Rum and coke was the drink of the night.

We walked into the spacious family room and on through the arched doorway out to the open-air patio. White Christmas lights were strung in every direction, crisscrossing over our heads. The lighting gave an elegant glow to the warm tropical evening. After ordering drinks from the bartender, who had set up shop not far from the disc jockey, I felt an elbow nudge in my left rib cage.

"Bob, let me introduce you to a girl I went to grade school with," Enrico said.

I followed him over to a group of girls who were standing on the other side of the disc jockey's stand.

"Carolina," Enrico called out.

I quickly realized how he was able to recognize her so fast out of the crowd of thirty or so on the back terrace. As his tall, slender Nicaraguan friend spun around, in her skin-tight, short, black cocktail dress, I couldn't help but notice that she had the longest, straightest, shiniest black hair I had ever seen. It flowed all the way down her back.

After they shared a friendly hug and exchanged a few words, they both turned to me.

"Bob, I'd like you to meet my childhood friend, Carolina," he said.

I was spellbound. They may have been childhood friends, but this girl was no child now!

Carolina was twenty. Her parents owned several fabric shops throughout the country. She was on Christmas break from the University of California at San Francisco. The rest of the evening, I tagged along with her as if I were a puppy dog and she was wearing a bacon necklace. Fortunately, she didn't seem to mind my company.

So far during my two-week stay in Nicaragua, I had learned more Spanish than during two years in high school. However, it was still not very good. Carolina was one of the only people there that night with whom I could speak English fluently.

We saw each other a couple of other times before we all headed back to school. She and I exchanged addresses and phone numbers. We agreed we would write, and we did.

———

For me, mail call during boot camp was usually not a downer. I had become a fairly good correspondent. I received mail from Mom

and Tex, my grandparents, my aunt and uncle, and the occasional
friend. However, regular letters from Carolina came like clockwork.
When the company clerk handed out the mail and mine smelled like
perfume, that's when I really got roughed up by my buddies. But I
didn't mind. We all had a laugh. It seemed the other guys may have
been just a little jealous.

Basic training was designed to last about nine weeks. The Navy
had developed an excellent system of preparing us to be either
shipped out to the fleet to our first command or, if we were lucky
enough, to a pre-scheduled "A" School for further training in a
specific skill.

As enlisted men, we were all pretty much at the bottom of the
barrel. The very bottom level was known as a seaman recruit E-1.
Then came the next level, seaman apprentice E-2. After that was the
seaman E-3. The higher the rank, the higher the pay grade.

In addition, there were three different classifications, which
meant what type of work you would end up doing when you arrived
aboard ship. An airman wore a rank on his left arm of three green
stripes at a slanted angle. The airman, or airdale, worked in various
types of service to aircraft. Usually, the airman's next destination
was an aircraft carrier.

A fireman wore a rank on his left arm of three red stripes at
a slanted angle. The fireman rate worked in the ship's engineering
department, which was responsible for keeping the ship going.
Everything from creating high-pressure steam to running the main
propellers, which move the ship through the water, to creating fresh
drinking water from seawater through the evaporator systems.

The seaman served in all the other classifications, from cook
to postal service. There is a huge list of jobs that fall under this a
category.

Most who enlisted in the Navy went in at the recruit level.
Usually, when basic training is completed, the promotion and pay
raise to apprentice is included.

Fortunately, due to my years at VF attending ROTC Training,
I went in as a fireman E-3. I had the fireman rate because I was
scheduled to attend the electricians mate A School after basic
training.

Basic was the Navy's cram course. Classroom training and

hands-on exercises included: lifesaving, firefighting, swimming, riflery, physical training, and nuclear, biological, and chemical warfare preparedness and countermeasures. *The Bluejacket's Manual* became our bible and was never far from reach.

Finally, the day came for our graduation ceremony on the main parade arena. After all the congratulations and hand shaking was completed, we headed on to our next assignments. Some were headed to the fleet. Some were headed to additional schooling. Most of us had about a week or so off before we were required to check in to our next command.

My next duty station was just across the railroad tracks from Recruit Training Command, Great Lakes Naval Training Center. When time came to check in, I would be assigned to a barracks, and attend the US Navy Basic Electricity and Electronics School.

During the past nine weeks I had saved up quite a few paychecks while confined to RTC. With my fully packed seabag I headed to Chicago O'Hare International Airport. Next stop, you guessed it. San Francisco, the City by the Bay.

Carolina picked me up at the San Francisco International Airport. She had a high-rise hotel room reserved for us downtown. Before I knew it, a week had passed and I was at the airport heading back to Chicago. I don't know where the time went and I don't remember seeing much daylight, other than when room service delivered but, it sure was fun. I remember smiling like the cat that just ate the canary.

After leaving the strict, disciplined routine of basic training, life at my new duty station felt like that of a college campus. No one was looking over my shoulder telling me when to be where. The Basic Electricity and Electronics School (BEE) was a self-paced, ten-week school. Each student was assigned a computer, in a row, of rows of computers. That is all I did all day long. Sit in front of that black and white computer screen and read subject material, then test out. I was a sponge, there to absorb basic electrical knowledge.

The mess hall on base served four meals a day. We went to school Monday through Friday then we had the weekends off. I was introduced to the four-section duty system at my barracks. It was simple. Every fourth day, you could not go anywhere other than the barracks, except for class and meals. In other words, someone had to stand watch at the barracks all night. Duty at school was pretty simple.

One thing that caught my attention and seemed odd was Iranian sailors, in uniform, on our base. Going to school in our schools. Eating in our mess hall. Learning all about our Navy. That never did sit well with me.

My schedule was busy that summer. Between classes, meals, working out at the gym, and a little partying, I had completed BEE before I knew it. Next stop, electrician's Mate A School.

This also meant a change in barracks. Again, I packed up my seabag with all my worldly possessions. Most of my bag, of course, was only what the Navy felt I needed to possess, plus a few civilian clothes.

Arriving at my new barracks, I was impressed. The housing compound was made up of a group of ten, two-story, dark brown brick buildings with black trim. They were much cleaner and more modern than the last barracks. The buildings were connected with enclosed walkways. There were common areas with couches, TVs, and ping pong and game tables.

I was assigned to a room with two other fireman apprentices and one fireman, Mike. Mike was back from the fleet for training and had a car. The room had a separate area for each of us, complete with a locker, study desk, and single bunk. Down the hall were common bathroom and shower facilities. That it was so modern, neat, and clean was what impressed me most.

On Monday, EM A School began. Each week a new class formed. All students who passed that week's study materials and hands-on lab training were passed on to the next class level the following week. If you did not pass the class, you repeated it the next week. This is how I met Wilken. Wilken didn't pass his first week's class and was held back, which landed him in my class. Wilken was one of these guys you couldn't help but like, even though he asked a million questions in class. He seemed to make things more complicated than they really were. Although everybody enjoyed picking on him, in fun, he seemed to take it well.

Classes started early for us and not everyone took the time to eat breakfast. It didn't take me long to notice that many of my classmates got pretty hungry by about ten o'clock. There wasn't any food in the school and the next meal, served at noon, was a five-block walk.

Leaving the barracks each morning, I noticed there was usually a snack truck parked by the curb out on the main road. One morning as I was headed to class, I stopped and picked up a bag of doughnuts from him.

When I broke out the bag of doughnuts at ten o'clock, my classmates practically threw money at me, wanting doughnuts to satisfy their midmorning hunger.

The next day, I asked the guy at the snack truck for a full box of doughnuts. Once again, my classmates ate them up. After a few days of that, I had much more cash in my pocket than I had started out with. This became a routine of mine, but I didn't bring doughnuts every day. I remembered what Colonel Quinn at VF had taught me in economics class: keep 'em guessing, always leave them wanting more, and don't be too predictable.

Soon summer faded and with fall, the days became cooler and shorter at the big training base on Lake Michigan. Graduation day came quickly and everyone in our class, even Wilken, was promoted and ready to be sent on to the fleet as electrician's mates.

Several weeks earlier during class, we were all required to fill out our *dream sheet.* This was our opportunity to request where we would like to be stationed and what type of ship we preferred to serve on.

"Wow! This is great, Wilken! Anywhere I want to go," I said.

"Don't get too excited, Dorgan. Wait till you see where they send you," he replied.

Several years earlier, after Mom married Tex, my grandparents had decided to retire, head south, and leave the cold winters of northern Delaware behind. After traveling the Sun Belt, from Florida to California, they settled in sunny San Diego. My cousin, Peter, and I visited one summer during high school break. Sun, surf, sandy beaches, and *California Girls*. We had a blast! Now *that's* where I could see myself settling.

Dream Sheet. This will be easy, I thought, looking over the choices. It didn't take long: I found a coastal minesweeper home ported out of San Diego, California on the list. *Perfect. I can go along the coast during the day to sweep for mines, be home on the weekends, and hit the beach—party time! Carolina will be just a short trip up the coast for a visit anytime. Yeah! What a life! I will even have my grandparents nearby, who I have always been close to. This is going to be great! I love the Navy!*

School days passed quickly, and along with graduation came our orders to our next duty station. As our names were called, we each went up to the front of the class to receive our orders. As our classmates read their sheets of paper, breaking the news to them of where they would be spending the next two years of their lives, reactions were mixed. "Yay!" was a reaction I did not hear much that day. Mostly it was, "Shit. Son of a bitch!" along with a flurry of other curse words. Some classmates were silent, speechless.

My eyes read the words typed across my orders page twice, carefully, my brain working in slow motion to comprehend their meaning. *Surely there has been a mistake*, I thought. *This was not in my plans at all!*

I had been assigned engineering division aboard the aircraft carrier USS *Midway*, based out of Yokosuka, Japan.

"Yokosuka? Japan? What the fuck?" I bellowed. "No way! I think I got somebody else's orders here. There must be a mistake."

With that one sheet of paper, all my great plans for fun in the sun and good times had burst like the poof of a fart.

"Hey, Wilken, where are you going?" I asked.

"San Diego, bro," he replied with a grin.

My stay at Great Lakes was over and it could not have been timed better. I arrived in early spring, at the end of a very snowy, bitter winter. My departure was early in the morning, the day before

Thanksgiving. The first snowfall of the season had begun to fall as I exited the main gate.

The flight from Chicago O'Hare to San Francisco was nonstop. I was glad about that and anxious to arrive on the West Coast. Carolina was picking me up at the airport. She said she had *plans* for me and I was looking forward to helping her to be successful with her plans.

By this time, I was resigned to the fact I was heading to Japan for two years. So far, the Navy life had been pretty good to me. Over the summer, I had turned eighteen. I was receiving an electrical education and having fun, too. With free meals and housing, my paycheck money was building up. Between paid travel days and vacation days, my orders didn't have me due at my new duty station for about three weeks, so I was determined to live it up.

After a week with Carolina, I pried myself away from her and took a flight to San Diego, where Mom, Tex, Buck, and Susan (my stepbrother and stepsister) were visiting my grandparents. My grandfather, Fred, had served as president of the National Rifle Association in the early 1970s. He was still very active in the organization on the executive committee and traveled east at least once a year. This year, with me leaving for Japan, it was agreed we would all meet up in San Diego.

We all celebrated Christmas early that year in San Diego. As we said our goodbyes and I headed off to the San Diego airport to board a flight back to San Francisco, thoughts went through my mind of how I would not be seeing my family for a long time. At the time I did not realize how long it would really be.

The last week in the City by the Bay went by way too quickly. Suddenly, I was saying goodbye to a tearful Carolina and boarding a bus with my seabag, headed for Travis Air Force Base, east of Oakland. My life was about to change in so many ways and it would never be the same.

The chartered bus was full of military personnel: sailors, marines, soldiers, and airmen. The US military had contracted with *the Flying*

Tigers airline, to fly service men and women all over the world. We were all headed to Travis to catch a flight somewhere.

As we approached the base, the word going around the bus was, "They will search the bus with dogs at the main gate. If you have any pot, better get rid of it."

Sitting there toward the back of the bus, I considered the quarter ounce of pot I had in a baggie in my peacoat pocket and sat up at attention. There in the dark, as the bus began to slow near the entrance of the main gate, I ate every bit of that bag of pot without anyone seeing. No evidence here!

It was not until we were all off the bus and inside the airport terminal that it hit me. Or, should I say, that is when it first started to creep up on me. I was successful at checking my seabag, getting on the plane, and finding my way to my seat, and then it *really* hit me. I was stoned. Soon I was out like a light.

Oh, and by the way, there were no dogs.

CHAPTER THREE
CULTURE SHOCK

THE TOUCH OF THE STEWARDESS'S HAND on my shoulder woke me from my deep sleep.

"Excuse me, sailor, the pilot is beginning his descent for our landing in Japan. Please return your seat to the upright position and prepare for arrival," she said in a soft but authoritative voice.

Opening my eyes, I tried to focus. It seemed as if I was in a fog. A ten-hour flight and I had slept through most of it. Well, I guess it was just as well. Crossing the Pacific Ocean at night, I'm sure I didn't miss much.

It was early morning. The fresh new sunlight of the day came streaming in through the windows all the way along the left side of the cabin. By now, others were also preparing for our destination: the Land of the Rising Sun.

As the pilot brought the airplane lower and lower, we could see through our small cabin windows what seemed like unending urban sprawl. Tokyo, Japan—one of the most densely populated cities in the world. Highways and roads seemed to spread out in every direction. There were no straight lines or patterns, just city as far as the eye could see.

The cabin shuddered suddenly as the pilot banked the plane sharply into our final approach of the landing strip. The roofs of thousands and thousands of homes and buildings surrounding the airport were like a patchwork sea of blue, white, and silver shapes. *It looks so crowded down there*, I thought.

We landed safely and I stepped off the plane and into the airport terminal. As we waited for our bags to be unloaded, we learned we would be going through the normal customs processing. However, only one out of every five travelers would be required to have their bags inspected.

The customs processing went smoothly. We were required to listen, as a group, to a short thirty-minute *Welcome to Japan*, presentation. This was a crash course on etiquette and proper behavior while living in Japan. Those of us heading to the US naval base at Yokosuka, then boarded what seemed like a miniature bus.

Our bus, loaded up with sailors and a few marines, headed out of the main gate of Naval Air Facility Atsugi and into the public streets of Japan. I had a window seat on the left side of the bus about halfway back. My first thought was, *Wow, they drive on the opposite side of the road here.*

My second thought was, *These buildings, cars, trucks, and people are really close to my window!*

It amazed me how our driver was able to effortlessly maneuver the bus through the winding, narrow, busy streets with such ease and confidence. I had never seen anything like it.

The sights and sounds were fascinating too. All the people outside of my window were so short and they all had black hair. I felt almost removed from it all, as if I were peering through a TV screen.

The ride to Yokosuka seemed to go quickly. There was so much to take in. As the bus headed down a hill, I could see the dark blue of a large body of water to the left. *We must be getting close*, I thought.

Shortly after, the bus driver made a slow left turn into a wide roadway with many traffic lanes across. There were US Marine guards stopping all the vehicles. Above the lanes of traffic was a wide sign that read: *United States Naval Base Yokosuka*. I knew we were in the right place.

A young marine guard boarded the bus and checked everyone's IDs. After he stepped off the bus, another guard waived us through the main gate.

The bus proceeded on along the main road of the base. To our left were large, plain industrial buildings, many without windows.

On our right were tree-covered hills. From my seat on the left side of the bus, I could see we were approaching the waters of Yokosuka Bay. There was a row of ten or so gray tugboats along the wharf. Just beyond the tugs was a massive, gray flat-topped ship tied up to the pier with huge mooring lines. This was the largest ship I had ever seen in my life.

As our driver turned the bus toward the left to drop us off alongside our destination, I read the name painted in big black letters across the back of the ship, just below the fantail: *MIDWAY*.

The USS *Midway* was the lead ship of its class. Her keel was laid down on October 27, 1943, in Newport News, Virginia. She was commissioned eight days after the surrender of Japan—September 10, 1945. From the lessons of World War II, this carrier version (CV) was built on the planned Montana class new hull design to make her more maneuverable than previous carriers. *Midway* was the largest ship in the world until 1955 when the USS *Forrestal* was commissioned. *Midway* was the first ship in the world too large to fit through the Panama Canal.

The *Midway* was known as the Navy's Tip of the Sword for the American military's foreign policy. As the longest serving aircraft carrier in the fleet, she had a long history of answering the call when trouble brewed around the world.

In 1965, aviators from the *Midway* shot down the first two MiGs by US forces in Southeast Asia. In addition, the last plane shot down of the Vietnam War was by a *Midway* aircraft in 1973.

On October 5, 1973, *Midway* docked in Yokosuka, becoming the first forward-deployed carrier task force home ported in Japan. This move would allow the families of *Midway* sailors and marines to live in Japan.

April of 1975, when the North Vietnamese overran South Vietnam, *Midway* participated in Operation Frequent Wind, evacuating hundreds of US personnel and Vietnamese after the fall of Saigon to the North Vietnamese.

There I stood on the pier in my dress blue uniform, with my seabag next me, looking up. I had to tilt my head all the way back to see the top of the ship. Its size was overwhelming. It looked to easily be 100 hundred feet from the waterline up to the flight deck. There was activity and noise all around. Trucks unloading. Welders welding. Shipyard workers and sailors everywhere. It was midafternoon. Two large overhead steel cranes towered over the flight deck level. The one on steel rail tracks running parallel to the ship and was loading and unloading equipment from the flight deck and the ship's deck-edge elevators, which were in the lowered position.

The *Midway* had just returned two days earlier, December 21, from a four-month Indian Ocean cruise. There was plenty to do.

Just then, an alarm sounded. The huge wheels of the crane near me began moving. "Hey Boot Camp," I heard someone yell. "Over here."

Boot Camp, I thought. *Wow, do I look lost or what?*

A sailor in faded Navy dungarees on the edge of the pier near a large steel walking ramp leading up to the ship motioned to me. "This is your new home, shipmate," he said as he pointed up the walkway.

Walking up that brow for the first time was an intimidating experience. Here I was, in Japan, on an aircraft carrier with a crew of 4,500 men, as well as hundreds of ship repair facility (SRF) workers scurrying about, and I didn't know a soul.

Fortunately, there was another sailor ahead of me who stepped onto the ship at the hanger-bay level. I watched him.

He stopped, faced the American flag and the officer of the deck, stood at attention, and saluted. "Permission to come aboard, sir?" he smartly asked, as he showed his Navy photo id card.

"Permission granted," replied the OOD, with a sharp salute.

I followed his lead and did the same thing.

The OOD looked at my ID card, then at me with my seabag and brown envelope in my other hand.

A big grin spread across his face. "You'll need to wait over there to the side," he said.

First of all, my ID card did not have a USS *Midway* sticker on it, identifying me as a crewmember.

Secondly, seeing I was a new arrival, he knew I would be completely lost in a matter of seconds without a guide.

I headed to a waiting area a few feet away, where I saw a couple of other sailors from the bus ride. They too had their seabags and brown envelopes. We were replacements for sailors who had completed their tour of duty aboard *Midway*. Those sailors who had done their time would be transferring on to another duty station or back to their hometown to be separated from active duty.

A few minutes later, another petty officer on duty at the after brow came over to us and asked to see our orders.

He opened mine and said, "Engineering department, E Division." He then yelled to another sailor nearby, "Coccia, here's one for you! Take him to E Division berthing, will you?"

I followed Coccia (sounded like "Cochi") through the hanger bay, down a stairway (ladder), along a hallway (passageway), past the aft galley, across the aft mess deck, through another passageway, down another ladder, through a doorway, and into the E Division berthing compartment.

He showed me to what would be my rack. It was a middle. There was one metal rack above me and one below, at floor level. The top rack did not have much room to the ceiling. I was provided with a mattress about two inches thick and a pillow not much thicker, along with two sheets, a pillowcase, and a gray blanket.

For storage, I was assigned a two-foot by two-foot metal locker with a door on the front—the bottom one in a stack of three. For hanging clothes, I had a metal locker that was about eight inches wide and about three feet tall and in a row of three. Both of my lockers had a hasp, to be locked with a padlock. Coccia advised me to keep them that way—locked.

"Welcome aboard. I'll be back to check on you later," Coccia said as he turned and left.

I began unpacking and making myself at home.

After stashing away my gear, I began to look around my new berthing compartment.

The berthing for E Division was roughly in the center of the ship, as measured from the bow to the stern. The hanger bay was deck one. Below that was deck two. We were the next deck down, deck three. Our compartment straddled the centerline. There were about forty-five men bunked on one side and forty-five on the other. In between the two sides was a small lounge area about fifteen feet square. There was a television hanging on the wall, a stationary game table and about ten stackable chairs.

The overhead was low and cluttered with pipes, electrical cables, ductwork, and florescent lighting. Anyone over six feet tall would be constantly hunched over for fear of knocking their head on low hanging obstacles. I was just six feet tall.

Just behind the wall of the TV lounge, there was a workshop area with electrical tools and equipment. This was known as E Division Power Shop.

"Dorgan, you want to eat?" I heard Coccia call out. "Come on."

We headed up to the hanger bay and back aft again, to the area near where I came aboard, the after brow. There was a line of about twenty men standing by a hatchway, ready for their turn to step down the ladder.

"Chow line," said Coccia. "It's not too bad today here in port. Wait till you're in it at sea, with the full crew of 4,500 aboard, it winds out the hatch and along the edge of the hanger bay."

As the line moved along, we headed down through the hatch, past the door to the aft bake shop.

"That's where they bake all of our bread," said Coccia. Next, we stepped into the starboard serving line area of the aft crew's galley. There we picked up our stainless-steel trays from a stack at the front of the line. As we slid our trays along the metal rails, the mess cooks on the other side of the counter spooned the evening's meal out to us.

I followed Coccia through another passageway, which opened into into a large room with about twenty-five round tables—the aft mess deck. There were sailors sitting around most of the tables eating. On two opposite sides of the room were dispensers for what we called *bug juice* and milk. We each grabbed a plastic cup, filled it with crushed ice from the ice machine, and topped it off with juice. After sitting down at a vacant table, it didn't take us long to polish off our meal. In our early days at boot camp, we learned that dining in the military is not a leisurely activity. Hurry up and make room for the next man.

Coccia told me there wouldn't be much going on the next few days for us. It was Friday evening, December 23, the day before Christmas Eve. For a crew who had spent the past four months at sea, anyone who could leave was off the ship tonight.

I couldn't help but ask, "Why are you still here?"

"We are in a four section duty rotation. I'm on duty today. Can't leave the ship," Coccia replied.

As we left the aft mess deck, we dropped off our trays at the scullery window. Heading forward toward the port side passageway, we passed the ship's US Post Office and down the ladder to E Division berthing.

With a full belly and drained from the long day of travel, jet lag, and new experiences, I headed for my rack. My head hit my pillow, and as my eyes closed, I tried to retrace in my mind how to get back to the aft galley and mess deck for my next meal. I began to realize, *I have so much to learn.*

As I awoke Christmas Eve morning the thought went through my mind, *I probably need a shower. . . where is the shower?*

There was a sailor standing in the aisle near my rack.

"Can you tell me where the showers are?" I asked.

"Through that door, up the ladder, to the right, then take a left at the passageway and you'll see it," he replied, heading off in the opposite direction.

I grabbed my shaving kit and towel and headed for the door.

When I arrived at the head, I found there were four sinks, four showers, three toilets, and three urinals. *Wow, this is going to be tough when everyone is trying to get in here at the same time.*

My first time in a shipboard shower was a learning experience. Since freshwater on a ship at sea is produced by running seawater through an evaporator system, drinking and bathing water is a precious commodity. Salt water is used for toilets and urinals. The water handles are spring loaded, so when the handle is released, the water shuts off. *No thirty-minute showers here.* A sailor learns how to do everything with one hand—everything.

After returning to our berthing and getting dressed in my blue work uniform, the same one I had worn through boot camp, I found my way to the chow line, galley, and mess deck—a routine I would be doing three times a day, seven days a week.

Later in the day, while sitting in the E Division lounge, Coccia came walking through. "Hey Dorgan, Sully and I are going to do laundry on base, then to the chapel for Christmas Eve service. Want to go?"

"Sure," I said. More of my clothes were dirty than clean, and it sounded better than spending Christmas Eve on board. I packed up my laundry bag and we headed out.

When we stepped off the brow, we walked across the crane rails and jumped in a cab. "Sully" Sullivan was lean and tall, about six foot three, and was one of those who had to duck and walk hunched over through much of the ship. It was a squeeze getting into the cab. He was from Massachusetts and had a thick northeast accent.

After a short stay at the on-base coin laundry washing, drying, and folding, we headed over to the base little white chapel. By the time we arrived, the sun had long since set. There was a chill in the air from the moist evening fog drifting in from Tokyo Bay. I pulled my peacoat collar up around my neck.

The chapel was full. Every seat was taken. There we stood, the three of us, standing in the doorway. We looked in, straining to see and hear the preacher's words as we anxiously awaited the celebration of the birth of our Lord and Savior, Jesus Christ.

I thought, *This is a much different Christmas than a year ago in Nicaragua.*

CHAPTER FOUR
POWER SHOP

FOLLOWING THE CHRISTMAS HOLIDAY, I received my assignment to the E Division shop where I would work for the next six months.

The responsibilities of we electricians (EM) and interior communications electricians (IC) of E Division covered practically every bit of the *Midway*, top to bottom, bow to stern—everywhere there was electricity and electric cables.

We were responsible for creating electricity through the eight ship's service steam-powered turbo generators and two emergency diesel generators and routing it to all sections of the ship with the use of four electrical power distribution switchboards, which were manned twenty-four seven.

In addition, we ensured all the equipment operated by electricity kept functioning, from ventilation motors and galley equipment to deck-edge aircraft elevators and aircraft lighting on the flight deck. This was a big responsibility. Electricity powered everything.

We electricians were divided up into six workshops: Lighting, Flight Deck Lighting, Safety shop (tools, portable equipment, and the *movie booth*, which was responsible for crew and officer movies), Distribution, Aviation and Ordnance, and Power Shop. The IC electricians had two shops: Telephone Exchange and Forward

Gyro. There were about ten or more men assigned to each of the E Division shops.

My assignment was to Power Shop.

Every morning by 0800, we were required to report to our assigned workshop for muster. The plan of the day was reviewed, and we were all assigned repair jobs or planned maintenance subsystem (PMS)—which was basically routine preventative maintenance—to complete.

Chief Kusano was in charge of Power Shop. He was a short man of Japanese descent, a quiet type of leader who knew his electrical skills well. Second in charge was Petty Officer First Class Dunca who was fairly tall for a Filipino. He was a no-nonsense type of man. Petty Officer Second Class Galace was the motor rewind expert. Galace was not only a very knowledgeable, hands-on electrician, he knew all the textbook stuff—formulas and everything. He had the gift of gab and didn't mind explaining how things worked. Steve, a third-class petty officer, had been on board a long time too. He didn't get worked up about anything.

I was introduced to everyone in the shop, all twelve, including Sully and "JoJo," issued an electrician's tool belt with a basic set of hand tools, and assigned to work with a third-class petty officer named Lenny.

Lenny was a quiet, no-nonsense, dry humor kind of guy from New York. He had a thick New York accent and could come off as a little coarse sometimes, but he always had that little bit of extra patience that was needed when training those of us with less experience.

Lenny picked up our work order and said, "Come on Dorgan, you're with me today."

We headed out of the shop, up the ladder and aft toward the galley.

"We've got a grill that's not working," said Lenny, in his thick accent.

When we arrived at the door to the galley, Lenny grabbed two paper mess-cook hats from a box and handed one to me.

"Anytime you are in the galley, you've gotta have a hat on," he said. "Capisce?"

We put our hats on and headed toward a row of flat, commercial electric grills, each with a metal surface about three feet square.

"They said the temperature dial is not working right," Lenny said. "See if you can sit down underneath the grill and pull the fuses out and I'll check the dial."

I got down on the floor. There was just enough room for me to scoot in under the grill and sit down, with my legs crossed in front of me. At that point, I was facing a covered metal box, which held the control circuit for the grill. I removed the cover. Inside was a maze of wires and a set of fuse blocks. I grabbed the fuse pullers from the tool pouch hanging from my belt. The fuse pullers were like a set of insulated pliers. If you happened to touch anything that was *hot* (live) with them, you wouldn't get electrocuted.

Reaching in with my fuse pullers, I grabbed the first fuse and pulled it out. The second fuse didn't come out so easily. The fuse popped out but got hung up and fell between some of the wiring. I reached in with my other hand to grab it and *zap*!

I felt the tingle go through my arm as fast as lightning! The surge of electricity jolted me. I spontaneously tried to jump up to get away from the panel and knocked my head into the bottom of the steel grill.

"Shit! *Motherfucker!*" I shouted. "Yeeooww!"

After Lenny saw I was going to be okay, he started laughing. "First day on the job and you almost kill us. I'm gonna have to keep an eye on you, Dorgan."

Yup. First day on the job and I got my first jolt of AC voltage. Not a good way to start out. Now I really did feel like a "Boot Camp."

Lenny finished up the job as I observed and learned a thing or two about troubleshooting galley equipment. We grabbed a couple of trays while we were still in the galley. Lenny seemed to know everybody working in there. They filled our trays with a little extra of the day's lunch.

"Beats waiting in line," Lenny said as we turned to leave. "It helps to get to know people."

I made it a point to volunteer for electrical trouble calls in the galleys, mess decks, bake shops, and food supply departments. It wasn't long before I got to know a lot of people, all over the ship.

CHAPTER FIVE
HAZE GREY AND UNDERWAY

EARLY ON THE MORNING of January 25 an announcement was heard throughout the ship over the shipboard public address system, referred to as the: "Now set the special sea and anchor detail."

The day starts very early for the crew of the engineering department of the *Midway*. During the past five weeks tied up to the pier, *Midway* was hooked up to shore power, large electrical cables that ran from the pier power source to the receptacles on the side of the ship. These cables supplied all the electricity required to power the huge ship while in port.

Steam was the lifeblood of this mighty aircraft carrier. The boiler technicians of B Division were responsible for bringing our ship to life.

There were twelve oil-fired boilers, which turned water into steam. There were four boiler groups. Each group had three boilers: Able, Baked, and Charlie.

The boilers produced high-pressure steam, 600 pounds per square inch (psi). This steam ran the turbines that turned the four huge propeller shafts. Steam powered the flight deck catapults that shot the aircraft off the flight from zero to 120 miles per hour in four seconds.

Steam also powered the eight Ships Service Turbo Generators, which provided three phase AC power to the ship's four electrical switchboards. Each switchboard always had an electrician on watch while at sea. Below the switchboard, in the generator room, there were machinist's mates from M Division on watch at all times monitoring the two turbo generators.

Liberty was over early the previous day for the BTs who were responsible for firing up the boilers. After the BTs got the steam going early in the morning, the MMs began opening steam valves to start the turbine blades turning in the generator rooms. The electricians on watch on each of the switchboards were standing by to bring the generators online and shift from shore to ship's power.

My sea and anchor station that morning was shore power detail. Our job was to detach the huge electric cables from the ship, kind of like we were unplugging it. At least from there, we had a pretty good view of what was going on. The other shipmates with me had more experience at it, so I mostly tried to stay out of the way.

After we heard the announcement, "Now shift to ship's power," we got the word to do our job and we unplugged the ship. The pier crane then lifted the ramp away that held the shore power cables. Next the crane lifted away the after brow walk ramp. Then the last of the SRF workers scurried off the ship. The crane then lifted away the forward officers' brow. At the same time, the mooring lines were loosened and hauled into the ship.

It was a chilly, damp January morning when we got underway at 0900. The *Midway* was pointed in the direction of the mouth of Yokosuka Bay for a smooth, quick departure. A sense of excitement was in the air. There were friends, family members, and SRF workers all along the pier waving and shouting. I could feel the movement of the huge ship as we began to steadily inch away from the long concrete pier.

The machinist's mates in the four main engine rooms had opened the steam valves and the turbines were turning the propeller shafts. One of the propeller shafts was one and a half football fields long.

As we passed the end of the pier, she began to pick up speed, turning slowly to the right. There ahead of us, I could see the low-hanging gray marine haze over Tokyo Bay. As we steamed further into the bay, the Yokosuka naval base began to fade away behind us. We continued to head south, Chiba to our port side, the Miura peninsula to starboard.

An announcement came over the 1MC: "Now shift to the at-sea uniform. Covers are no longer required."

Wow. I like the sound of that, I thought.

After what seemed like just a few minutes, we were in open ocean water and the land faded away behind us. There was more chop in the water and the ship seemed to sway more from side to side the farther out we went.

"Now secure from the special sea and anchor detail," came the voice over the 1MC again. That was my cue. I headed down to Power Shop to get my work assignment for the day.

The ship was a much different scene now from what it was during the first few days following my arrival. With the full crew on board, including carrier air wing five and the Marine detachment, there were men scurrying about in every direction.

Each time the *Midway* returned to Yokosuka, all the aircraft that could fly were launched and flown to Naval Air Facility Atsugi, west of Yokosuka. After the ship docked, the aircraft support crew left the *Midway* and went to Atsugi, where they could continue to perform their duties in support of the air wing.

Soon, the airdales up on the flight deck would begin the recovery process. All the aircraft would return from NAS Atsugi and land back aboard *Midway*.

We were headed out to sea for an exercise with our escort ships to an undisclosed destination in the Western Pacific Ocean to run drills and flight operations. We called it a doughnut cruise, since we would basically just go around in circles for a few weeks.

When I arrived back at Power Shop, I received my schedule for my assigned underway watch station. The new guys always started out at the bottom with the assignment to After Steering. We were running a four and eight watch rotation. I had the upcoming watch from noon to 1600, which meant I also had the midnight to 0400 watch, seven days a week.

"And when you're not on watch Dorgan, I want you here in the shop!" EM First Class Dunca said. "You're in the Navy now; your ass is mine!"

Next, I proceeded to the aft mess deck to get lunch. It was always required to report to our watch station fifteen minutes early to relieve the off-going watch stander. As I walked across the hanger bay to get in the chow line, I did a double take. The chow line wound around back through hanger Bay Two, toward deck-edge elevator two on the starboard side. *Coccia was right. Plan ahead.*

Waiting in the line was out of the question as I would be late for watch. I headed down to the mess deck through a different hatch and grabbed a couple of grapefruit from the fruit table. (We were freshly stocked up with plenty of good fruit to eat.) Then I made my way toward After Steering, down the second-deck port-side passageway. Just past the aft galley there was a series of *knee knockers*, doorframes about a foot high that you had to step over to go through. Knee knockers were at the beginning and end of each compartment where there was a watertight doorway through the bulkhead, and you had to duck your head and lift your feet up high to get through each opening.

As I started through the second opening, I lifted my leg, but didn't clear the knee knocker. *Bam*! I went sailing through the opening headfirst and landed on the deck, the grapefruit rolling down the passageway.

"Haven't got your sea legs yet, Boot Camp?" said a sailor passing me from the opposite direction, as he turned to his buddy, laughing.

Grabbing my lunch, I got up and continued on my way.

After Steering was located all the way at the stern of the ship, the aftmost compartment. There is a ladder down from a watertight hatch in the ship's laundry leading to it. This third deck machinery space is divided into four compartments. Each of the two rudders have motor room and a steering gear room to each side of the centerline. My watch station was the port-side After Steering gear room. There were two large horizontal hydraulic rams that were joined to a huge cylinder, which pivoted between the two cylinders. The cylinders were the tops of the port and starboard rudders, and when they turned, they determined the direction of the ship.

Three sailors stood watch in each of the two compartments at all times while at sea, twenty-four seven, an electrician's mate (EM), a machinist's mate (MM), and a quartermaster (QM). Normally, steering of the ship was done by a quartermaster from the navigational bridge on the *island*, the tall command center located on the flight deck. In the event the bridge, where the captain sat, was knocked out of commission, steering would be performed by a quartermaster from "Secondary Control, located at the forward most part of the bow, just below the flight deck. That is where the round portholes are.

In the event of a severe catastrophe with both of those options out, steering would be performed by the quartermaster in After Steering by orders over the sound powered phones from Main Engineering Control. At this point, all hands would certainly be at their general quarters battle stations, with all watertight doors and hatches closed and sealed. The EM and MM would be required to keep their assigned rudder functioning for as long as possible.

In other words, this was not a place I would want to be in the event of a catastrophe. The chances of getting out alive would be slim.

Until I learned my duties in After Steering and passed the qualification test, I was required to stand watch with another EM who was qualified. That took about a week, then I was on my own. After Steering was a boring watch station, hot and noisy. The vibration from the four huge screws even made it difficult to catch a nap. (Of course, sleeping on watch was punishable by captain's mast—so don't get caught.)

After my watch was over at 1600, I headed up to hanger Bay Two to get in the chow line. With no lunch and only a couple of grapefruit to snack on, I was getting very hungry.

With my dinner tray in hand, I scanned the mess deck for a free table. I saw Coccia with an empty seat at his table, and he waived me over.

"Hey Dorgan, you want to go up and check out flight ops after dinner?"

"Sure," I replied.

After dropping off our trays at the scullery window, we made our way off the mess deck. I followed Coccia as we headed up the ladders and through the maze of passageways on the starboard side, past the hanger bay level and up through the 02 level, which is the level above the hangar deck. The narrow ladder up through the island brought us to a door. As Coccia opened the door, sunlight poured through the opening, as well as a strong blast of brisk ocean air. I followed him out onto a platform area of the 06 level, facing the bow. There were cables around three sides. We were above the navigational bridge and flight deck control. This was an area known as *Vultures Row.* From our vantage point, we had a good view of the bow and the center of the flight deck.

During the launch cycle of flight operations, this was a good place for those who did not work on the flight deck to watch aircraft as they were launched off the bow from catapults one and two. The flight deck crew was now in recovery mode, bringing aboard all the aircraft that had flown off December 20 to NAS Atsugi.

The trick for the pilots was to fly their plane in at an angle, approaching the stern of the ship, the ramp of the flight deck. As they touched down, the pilot would aim to catch one of the three arresting-gear cables with their tailhook. If the hook caught a cable, once given the signal, the pilot would shut down his engines. If he missed the cables, he would full throttle it, and takeoff again to circle around the ship for another attempt, known as a *bolter*.

We watched a few F-4 Phantoms land successfully. After landing, the flight deck crew lined them up on the bow, along with other aircraft that had already landed. The yellow-shirts and blue-shirts of the flight deck crew moved aircraft around all afternoon as the planes arrived back on board. Some aircraft had already been moved down to the hanger bay on the huge deck-edge aircraft elevators. Soon the entire air wing would be back on board and the *Midway* would be fully ready for duty.

January 25–27 we were scheduled to carry out flight ops in the Pacific Ocean, east of Tokyo Bay. We spent the day of January 28 enroute to the Okinawa area, where we participated in ReadEx 1-78, an exercise against the *Kitty Hawk* (CV-63) and its carrier task group.

It was starting to get cold up there on vulture's row as the sun was setting.

"Let's head down. It's freezing up here and I have the mid-watch," I said to Coccia.

As we headed in through the door, I had no way of knowing this would be my last view of daylight for the next two weeks.

We made our way down to E Division berthing on the third deck.
I figured I'd get a shower and hit the rack for a couple hours of rest
before reporting back to After Steering for the mid-watch (2400 to
0400.).

———————

After taking off my dungaree uniform and hanging my shirt and
pants on the side of my rack, I wrapped a towel around my waist.
Grabbing my shave kit from my locker, I headed toward the showers.

As I attempted to step out through the doorway of our berthing,
I had a tough time getting the door to open. There seemed to be a
huge amount of air pressure against the door. When I finally opened
the door and stepped out into the passageway, the door slammed
shut behind me. It felt like I had just stepped into a wind tunnel of
cold air. At the same time, I dropped my shave kit. As I bent over to
grab it, the force of the wind coming down the passageway ripped
away the towel from around my waist. There I was, standing in the
cold breeze, wearing nothing but my flip-flops.

Below our berthing was one of the ships main boilers, One
Charlie. The boiler technicians had just fired it up and it was sucking
air in from anywhere it could get it. It turned the passageway up the
ladder to the showers into a cold tunnel of rushing air. I could just
imagine how it would feel walking back wet, after my shower.

Turning back around to my right, I saw a BT coming up the
ladder from the boiler room. He had my white Navy issue bath towel
in his hand. When he saw me, he started laughing and held up the
towel.

"Lose something?" he asked, throwing the towel at me as he
passed by chuckling.

"Thanks," I responded, wrapping the towel back around my
waist, covering up my dignity.

After my shower, I climbed into my rack to catch a couple of
hours of rest before my next watch. Sleeping with the lights on in a
noisy berthing compartment with ninety or so other men coming
and going at all times can take a while to get used to. My solution was
to put a pair of socks over my eyes and put my rubber Navy-issue
earplugs in my ears. Worked like a charm.

———————

It seemed as if I had just closed my eyes when there was a tug on my forearm. "Dorgan, you've got the mid-watch, time to get up." It was 2330. I had just fifteen minutes to get to After Steering for my watch.

I jumped up and grabbed my dark blue boot camp pants and shirt hanging on the side of my rack. I got dressed and headed through the TV lounge and up the port-side ladder, then down the passageway to After Steering. Checking in right on time, I was ready to sit for the next four hours.

After shooting the breeze with the other guys on watch for a while, the QM asked the other EM on watch with me, "Is he cool?" pointing to me.

"Yeah, he's cool."

The QM then broke out a little hash pipe he had made and filled it up. After firing it up with his lighter and taking a big draw he handed the pipe and lighter to me.

"Go ahead," the MM said. "It's the real deal—straight from Karachi."

I put the pipe up to my lips and clicked the lighter turning the flame to the bowl. Taking a big draw on the little pipe, I could feel the smoke expand in my lungs.

I burst out in a series of hacking coughs, trying to catch my breath.

"Good stuff, eh?" said the QM. "You'll be set for the rest of the watch."

We all started laughing. He was right.

Before I knew it, four hours had passed and our watch was over. We were all hungry by now. The aft galley had not opened yet, so we headed to the aft mess deck to grab a couple of boxes of dry cereal and fruit to hold us over. We ate up and headed our separate ways. I then headed back to my rack to catch a couple more hours of sleep until breakfast. Then it was time for quarters for muster in Power Shop at 0800 to receive work assignments for the morning, to be completed before heading back on watch again.

This was my daily routine, for the next four weeks at sea. During that time, between working, watch, meals, general quarters, underway replenishment at sea (UNREP), man overboard drills, and sleeping, I was below the hanger bay level and did not see much daylight until we returned to Yokosuka.

After nine days back in Yokosuka, we went out for another short doughnut cruise of three weeks. From March 2–12, we conducted refresher operations while in transit, heading north through the Tsushima Straits between Korea and Japan, into the Western Sea of Japan. Next, we joined up with the Japanese Maritime Self Defense Force (JMSDF) for Team Spirit, the largest combined exercise to date with the Japanese Navy.

For most of us in Engineering, it just meant more of the same. Never-ending workdays and watches, broken up only by the occasional general quarters battle stations drills.

During my first cruise, I came to realize one of the reasons people, even those I did not know, kept calling me *Boot Camp.* The work pants and shirt I had been wearing were my Navy issue working blues, straight out of NTC Great Lakes boot camp. Most of the other sailors on board for a while, wore faded blue denim dungarees (bell-bottomed blue jeans) and faded denim work shirts.

During our nine day stay in Yokosuka, I made it a priority to visit the Navy Exchange on base. There I picked up several pairs of blue, bell-bottomed dungarees and short-sleeve work shirts. I made it a point to ditch that boot camp working blue uniform real quick! My goal was to wash them a few times, fading them, like the jeans I had worn back home. I could finally start to blend in.

Between burning up JP-5 aircraft fuel with the continuous evolutions of flight ops day and night and the consumption of fuel oil in the twelve ship's boilers day and night, *Midway* used up a lot of fossil fuel while steaming. With this high fuel consumption, we needed to replenish our supply regularly while at sea. To do this, a "fleet oiler (a large fuel and dry goods supply ship) would pull alongside *Midway* while steaming through the open ocean in a straight direction.

The oiler would run cables across to us and they were secured to the side of the ship. Then large fuel hoses were sent across those suspended cables and attached to a fuel port on the side of the *Midway*. The pumping of fuel would then commence and continue for hours. At the same time, dry goods and food were transported on board by helicopters and suspended cables between the ships. It was fascinating to watch. It was not fascinating if you were assigned to a working party to pack all the boxes of supplies down into the lower decks and storage compartments.

UNREPS were always an exciting time. Besides fresh food, it also brought the possibility of receiving a letter or care package from family or friends.

Another announcement occasionally heard over the 1MC was, "COD on the ball with mail." This announcement was always followed by a cheer of excitement from the crew.

So far, I was receiving letters regularly during the occasional mail call. I usually received a letter from Mom and Tex and my grandparents, and I could always count on several letters and cards from Carolina back in San Francisco. One stormy evening, the COD landed on a pitching flight deck, carrying a letter from Carolina.

Dear Bob, I have met someone . . .

That was how the last letter I ever received from Carolina began. It felt just like a hatch slamming shut. *Bam!*

One of the first assignments everyone receives upon arrival to serve on board the *Midway* is battle station. The assignment generally has something to do with your rate or specialty. My battle station assignment was Repair Main One. Our space to report to was the middle center passageway, right between the port and starboard main forward and aft passageways on the second deck. We were the main damage control team for the Engineering Department. Our team of about thirty-five was made up of electricians, hull technicians (HT), machinists' mates (MM), boiler technicians (BT), interior communication men (IC), corpsmen, and various other rates in support of firefighting, flooding, and damage control.

Every time we performed a battle station drill, there was some sort of emergency in a main engineering space, like the boiler room, generator room, main engine room, etc. The damage control party responsible for the space where the drill was held would perform their duties. At the same time, Repair Main One would be called in as back up. This meant we were involved in every drill. Every drill. Every fucking drill!

To top that off, with condition Zebra set throughout the ship, with every watertight door and hatch closed and sealed shut, it was hot, stuffy, dirty, and just miserable. I hated my GQ station!

––––––––––––

Following one particular afternoon GQ drill, I arrived back at Power Shop to find several guys in the shop laughing out loud.

Most of the time I did my best to keep a low profile and stay below the radar, as they say. I slipped over to the workbench area. There I had a locked drawer to stow my tool pouch and gear.

"Hey Dorgan, we're getting together tools for the next job. We need you to go down to four Charlie Boiler and get a BT punch."

What are we getting into next? I thought.

For this cruise, I was switched to the 0400 to 0800 then 1600 to 2000 watch in After Steering. There was not much time till I needed to head to my watch station.

"Hurry up, Dorgan. We'd like to get started today!"

Power shop was located on the second deck, adjoining our berthing compartment. I headed out of the shop door on my journey, not looking forward to it a bit. Next left and down to the fourth deck and on down toward the first platform. Below that was second platform. The farther down you go into the engineering spaces of an aircraft carrier, the hotter it gets. The heat and humidity are sweltering. Without even moving a muscle, you sweat like a whore in church.

There is no air conditioning in these spaces. The supply ventilation air blown into these machinery spaces through huge vent motors is outside air. When the ship was operating in a cool temperature area, the air in these spaces might be bearable. When operating near the equator, unbearable would be the description. One hundred degrees was the norm. The men in the engineering department who work daily and stand watches in these extreme conditions, also known as *snipes*, earn every cent of their pay.

Soon, I made it down to the bottom of the steep, narrow ladder of the boiler room. Two BTs looked over at me at the same time.

"I was told to come down here to get a BT punch," I said loudly over the noise in the space.

"Are you from Power Shop?" one of them said to me.

"Yup," I said.

"Come over to the booth, you have to sign it out in the logbook," the other said.

There I was, standing between these two huge barrel-chested BTs, drenched in sweat, who looked like they spent all their off time pumping iron.

"Look here, sign on this line."

As I looked at the white, lined pages of the green, hard backed logbook, I began to reach for the pencil when *pow*! They both hit me in my upper arms at the same time from each side, just like the corpsmen did with the shots back in boot camp. They both stood back, laughing out loud. "There's two BT punches you can take back up to your buddies, sparky!"

Even though I was the joke, we all had a good laugh.

After shooting the shit for a while, one of them asked me, "Smoke a bowl with us?"

I checked my watch. *Man, I'm running out of time*, I thought. *But I can't say no and run off and leave them. That wouldn't be cool.*

"We're in a fucking boiler room. I'm sure you can find a light around here somewhere. Fire it up," I replied with a big smile.

We fired up that bowl and passed it around. The huge exhaust vent we were standing close to sucked that smoke away so fast, you couldn't smell a thing.

I thanked them for the lesson and the buzz as I headed for the ladder to begin my climb up out of the depths of the hot boiler room. As I lifted my arms up along the rails of the ladder, I could feel the blood pumping, swelling each of my arms. My shirt soaked with sweat and humidity and I thought, *How do they survive down here, day in and day out?*

When I arrived back at the shop, the guys who had sent me on my "mission" saw me walk through the door drenched in sweat. They burst out laughing and said, "Dorgan, aren't you supposed to be on watch?"

I checked my wristwatch. Five minutes to get there. I turned around, ran up the stairs and all the way to After Steering, jumping over every knee knocker. Made it, just in time. You don't want to face the consequences of being late for watch.

———————

We arrived back in Yokosuka March 21 for three weeks in port. Compared to eastern Pennsylvania, winter on the Miura Peninsula was fairly mild. We had returned on the first day of spring. With the warmer weather finally here, we all were all eager to get out and about.

On one of our first days back in port, I decided to venture off base to the area just across from the main gate known as the Honcho District. After leaving the base, I found myself walking along through the maze of narrow side streets passing storefronts, bars, and restaurants. After looking at the meals displayed in the many restaurant front windows, I stepped through the front door of one that looked appealing.

It didn't take me long to finish off the steaming bowl of hot udon noodle soup the young Japanese waitress had quickly served me.

Thanking the cashier, I paid for my meal and was on my way once again to browse the *Honch.*

As I walked out of the front door, I turned to my right and began walking down the sidewalk. After taking a few steps I noticed the American voices of sailors walking behind me.

That's Wilken from EM A School, I thought, *that voice is unmistakable!*

I turned around and sure enough, there I was face to face with my old classmate and two of his shipmates.

"Wilken, what are the chances of this?" I said to him with surprise. "What the fuck are you doing here, bud?"

"No shit! Dorgan!" he stammered, equally surprised. "We just tied up to the pier for a couple of days of liberty."

We explained to his buddies how we knew each other as we continued down the sidewalk and into the next *hoppy bar* we came to. There I introduced them to *hoppy beer* and drank the evening away until they ran us out at closing time, and we staggered back to the base.

Since arriving on board, I had made quite a few friends. We made it a point to make our time in port count and enjoy it as best we could. Lenny found out KISS was scheduled to play five shows at the Budokan concert arena in Tokyo.

A group of us had gone to Budokan our last time in port to see ELO (Electric Light Orchestra). Budokan was a huge arena. KISS playing there would be a wild show. We got tickets and a group of us took the train to Tokyo. It was a blast. We found out later all five shows had been completely sold out.

April 4 was another good concert at Budokan. Lenny, Galace, Adamos, and I rode the train to Tokyo to see Foreigner. Wherever we traveled around Japan, we always managed to get stopped along the way by Japanese girls. They had a great pickup line: they all wanted to practice their English— and we were happy to help. It was spring, cherry blossom season, and we were sailors on liberty.

CHAPTER SIX
THE PI

APRIL 11 WE WERE UNDERWAY AGAIN. This time there was an undercurrent of excitement about the crew. After a four-day carrier refresher landing period off Tokyo Bay, the *Midway* battle group participated in a four-day training exercise ASWEX J-78 with the JMSDF.

We then headed south to the Okinawa area for cyclic operations. By the beginning of the third week at sea, we had sailed much farther south. When we reached the area near Taiwan, the air was much warmer and humid. Exercise Bluesky was scheduled against the Taiwanese Air Defense followed by exercise Newboy against the Philippine Air Defense.

———————

We had all gathered in Power Shop for 0800 muster. Chief Kusano was posting the in-port duty roster for our upcoming port visit to Subic Bay, Republic of the Philippines, which we referred to as the PI.

"Dorgan, we are almost there, only five more days till the PI," Lenny said. "Are you ready?"

"Sure, I'm ready," I said enthusiastically.

"Yeah, he's ready to stand in line to get a shot in his dick after we leave PI," said Steve.

"No, he won't be standing in line for a shot, his dick will already have fallen off by then!" said Kenny, laughing.

"No, Kenny, he just has to be sure he only spends time with a virgin," replied Steve.

"Dorgan, just be sure to ask them first. They'll tell you the truth," continued Lenny.

"Yeah, like, 'I love you no shit. Buy me a drink,'" Kenny stammered out.

"More like, 'I love you no shit. My mother's a virgin, too.'"

With Steve's last comment, they all burst out laughing. I had no idea what to expect when we arrived and hit the beach for that first night of liberty in Subic.

Subic Bay was the largest overseas US naval base in the world. Not only was it of huge importance during the Vietnam War in supplying our war efforts in Southeast Asia, but it was also built as a vital rest and relaxation destination for servicemen who needed a break. There were golf courses, bowling alleys, beaches, water skiing, sailing, swimming pools, and tennis, just to name a few of the available recreational activities on base. There were also various restaurants, shopping centers, housing facilities and schools.

Subic was also a ship repair facility with mooring piers, berths, and floating dry docks. There was even a naval air station, Cubi Point, for the aircraft to land and operate out of while we were in port. There was a Pier Alpha adjoining Cubi point, for aircraft carriers to tie up to while in port. However, it made for a much longer cab ride to the main base or main gate from Cubi.

Everyone was anxious to look at the duty roster. We were in a four-section rotation.

"Dorgan, looks like you lucked out," said Steve.

I was scheduled to have the first three days off, with duty not starting until 0800 on the fourth day and then off again on the fifth day. At 0900 on the sixth day, we would be underway again. That sounded like a good schedule to me.

Early on the morning of April 28, the call came over the 1MC. "Set the special sea and anchor detail." This time I was assigned to our shop to be available for any electrical repair jobs that may come up.

We were scheduled to tie up to the pier by 0900. Nothing much was going on in the shop so I decided to head up to the hanger bay level to see what I could see on my first time pulling into Subic Bay.

Subic is a huge bay on the western side of the main island of Luzon, just to the north of Manila Bay, with the Bataan Peninsula separating the two bays.

It was a clear, calm, sunny morning as we began to enter the bay. On each side of the ship there were large mountains that seemed to rise right out of the water up into the sky. Right there in the middle of the entrance to the bay was Grande Island with Fort Wint perched high on top. Built in 1907, the fort had a great vantage point to protect the bay. The ship turned just slightly to starboard, to pass straight between the island and the shoreline.

This large, lush green jungle area to the starboard side was a huge arsenal zone. A puzzle of roads with a complex maze of underground munitions storage bunkers hiding every kind of bomb or missile that you could imagine. Of course, it adjoined the airfield and was strictly off limits.

After passing Grande, we made our way toward the center of the bay, the airstrip of Cubi coming up on our right. Passing Cubi, we continued to turn starboard. I could see the gray outlines of other Navy ships tied up along the pier. By now the land had surrounded us on three sides. In fact, the ocean was no longer visible. It was easy to see why this area made such a safe harbor from the sea, as it was encircled by large mountains on all sides.

As we began to make a sharp turn to port, I noticed several gray tugs coming around that side of the ship. We slowed and they closed in on us to begin their job of guiding us smoothly to Alava Pier, where we would be docked for the next five days. I headed back to the shop, hoping I had not been missed, and nobody would put me to work on a detail. There was liberty ashore to prepare for.

After taking a shower and getting dressed in my civvies, Lenny, "Lite Weight," and I headed up to the hanger bay. We made our way to the quarterdeck.

Lite Weight earned his nickname honestly. After a couple of rounds of beers, anyone could tell the title fit. EM3 Lite Weight was assigned to flight deck lighting. Born and raised in Michigan, he took every opportunity to enjoy these tropical port visits.

"Permission to go ashore," Lite Weight requested as he saluted the OOD.

"Permission granted."

We each followed his lead then headed down the brow and onto the pier.

"Ahh, dry land," exclaimed Lite Weight.

"Come on, let's get a cab and go have lunch at the Sampaguita Club," replied Lenny.

After lunch we bowled a few games at the bowling alley to eat up a little time till we were ready to venture off base to the crazy nightlife of Olongapo.

"Hey Bob, you ready to see the town?" asked Lenny. "Let's go look at a few shops first."

"Let's go," I replied.

We were within walking distance of the main gate of the base, so we hoofed it.

When we arrived at the main gate, the Marine guards were at their post, checking identification cards as people were leaving the base. We showed them ours and they waived us through.

Subic Naval base is more or less an island surrounded by water, the bay, a river, and a canal. To get to Olongapo we had to walk across a bridge about 400 feet long, spanning the river. Much of the raw sewage from the town drained into this canal. You pretty much had to hold your breath walking across it from one end to the other.

As we began our walk across the bridge, on the right side I noticed there were eight or nine small open wooden canoes in the sludge-filled river. Little kids in the boats called out to the pedestrians crossing the bridge, "Peso, peso, throw me peso!"

I had not converted any US dollars to Philippine pesos yet.

"Go ahead, throw them a coin," said Lenny.

There was only a quarter in my back pocket. I had put my wallet in my front pocket, on the advice of my shipmates. "Be prepared for pickpockets," they had all warned me.

I tossed the quarter over the rail toward the boy in the canoe. He snatched it out of the air like a pro. Lite Weight tossed one in just after mine. His coin hit the edge of the canoe then bounced into the brown, stinky water. In a flash that kid had jumped out of his canoe and into the canal after the coin. At the same time, a kid from the next canoe over jumped in too, after the same coin. It would be a race to see who could grab the shiny coin before it sunk to the bottom of *Shit River*.

Shortly after, their two heads bobbed up out of the mire. The second boy had snatched the quarter away. Lite Weight threw another quarter to the first boy's canoe. This time it landed squarely on the floor of his dugout.

"That's some fucked up shit!" said a voice from behind me.

I turned around to see "JT" coming up behind us.

"JT, I'd rather spend three months in a wiring trunk with a needle gun chipping paint day and night before you could get me to dive in there for a gold bar," I replied. "That *is* some shit!"

We all laughed and continued our trek across the bridge.

The moment we stepped off the bridge on the other side, we had entered another world. People came at us from all angles. "Psst! Hey buddy, need a ride? My brother got Jeepney," one told me. "Hey! I got trike—give you ride," said another. I heard another call out: "Hey *Midway* sailor, my sister a virgin, my mother virgin, too."

"Come on, keep moving." Said Lenny, as he headed off down the right side of the road, along the shops and buildings. All the shopkeepers were trying to get us to stop and come into their stores. T-shirts, clothes, furniture, lamps, carvings, wooden salad bowls— there was all kinds of stuff for sale.

"Let's head over to that shop where I got this belt last time, Lite Weight," Lenny said, as he motioned toward the other side of the street.

To me it looked as if we were gambling with our lives, attempting to cross the chaos in front of us.

The most popular means of transportation were old army jeeps that had been customized. They were lengthened and had two bench seats running the length of the back passenger section of the vehicle. There were steps at the end of the vehicle for passengers to get on and off. These were known as *Jeepneys*.

Another popular mode of transportation was the *trike*. A trike is just what you think is would be, a motorcycle with a sidecar. But they were nothing like I had ever seen. There was even a roof and a windshield on it. The driver often carried two passengers—three or four if we were drunk enough.

These vehicles were all over the place, driving crazy, and zipping in and out of traffic. You really had to keep your wits about you.

We followed Lenny across the street and made it to the shop he had in mind. I browsed around, but really was not ready to purchase any souvenirs yet.

After looking into a few more shops, we decided it was time to hit the clubs.

I had never seen so many bars and clubs—California Club, Florida Club, Kong's Club, Oriental Club, Stardust Club, 7 Fleet Club, Wild West Club, Alamo Club, Pussy Cat Club, Sea Horse Club, Twins Club, Whiskey-A-Go-Go Club, 7-11 Night Club—the list went on and on. There were more than seventy-five clubs on Magsaysay Drive alone. When the thousands of sailors and marines from an aircraft carrier task force hit the beach for liberty, you could be sure the town was prepared. There would be many US dollars spent here that night.

We settled into one club for a couple of drinks. Lenny ordered a pitcher of *Mojo*. Never having experienced Mojo before, I was game. The girls immediately swarmed over us. I figured out quickly where the term *bar flies* came from.

"Buy me drink. Buy me drink. You Cherry Boy? I show you good time. You first time? You *Midway* sailor? I love *Midway*." Whatever it took to get your attention, the girls said it.

After a while we all had a girl, or two, who had staked their claim on us, and we had allowed them to stay, after kicking a couple of them out of our social circle. We partied late into the night. There was drinking, dancing, and more drinking. We all ended up in hotel rooms across the street, on the second floor. Now *that* was some wild shit that first night in PI!

———————

It was hot, humid, and muggy when I woke up the next morning in a dingy second floor hotel room. No air conditioning here. *A shower would be nice*, I thought.

This tall, slender, naked Filipina chick was laying there on the other side of the bed, on her side with her back toward me. She had straight, long black hair down to her ass—must have been a phase I was going through.

"Hey, Baby, is there a shower here?" Her name really was Baby. Hell, I think half of the girls in Olongapo were named Baby.

"There's a shower down the hall," she motioned in the direction of the door.

There was a towel on a side table. I grabbed it, wrapped it around my waist, and headed out the door and down the hall. Just before walking through the doorway, I thought, *my wallet, don't leave it behind.* I stepped back in, grabbed my pants, and said, "I'll be back in a couple of minutes." Imagine returning from the shower—no Baby and no wallet.

As it turned out, there was no need to worry about that. She had plans for me.

When I returned to the room, Baby said, "Let's go sightseeing. I will be your tour guide. Today's a good day to go to Manila."

What could I to say to that? With two more days of liberty till I had to be back on the boat, sightseeing with a pretty girl sounded fun to me. We got dressed and left the hotel. As soon as we made it out to the dusty, noisy street, she hailed a Jeepney. I followed her, stepping into the back passenger section to sit on one of the two bench seats. We zipped through the hot busy streets on our way to the Olongapo Victory Liner bus station.

———

The bus ride to Manila was a wild ride as the driver guided the bus along the zigzagging road, up and out of the low-lying Subic Bay area. We crossed through the pass at the crest of the hill, the Bataan Peninsula to the right. To the left was the towering volcano of Mt. Pinatubo. Village after village passed by the bus windows, down the mountain and across the river valley. As we neared Manila, the housing grew thicker, the population denser.

Arriving in downtown Manila, we left the bus and grabbed a cab to the waterfront of Manila Bay. It was a beautiful, sunny afternoon, with a light breeze off the bay when we stepped out of the cab. Picture perfect.

Baby turned to me and said, "Today you get a history lesson on my country, and this is where we start."

After being briefed on the early history of the Philippines and the Spanish influence, we headed across the street to The

Rizal Monument in Rizal Park. Jose Rizal, a hero of the Philippine Revolution, was executed in 1896. The monument also stands as the point of origin or Kilometer Zero to all other cities in the Philippines.

We strolled around the various parks and sights of interest till we came upon a seafood restaurant.

"I'm starving," I said. "This looks like a good place to me."

After a great meal, we left the restaurant and headed for a nearby modern hotel to spend the hot sultry night with air conditioning.

The next day was sightseeing in Quezon City.

But little did I know, there was no actual sightseeing in Quezon City, at least none I would be interested in. It turned out to be a trip to visit Baby's family, who lived in what seemed like one of the most impoverished areas of the huge city. Tin shacks of one or maybe two rooms ran along narrow alleyways. Wastewater trickled along the steamy open street drains. It was hot, humid, and dirty.

We visited a short time and left. I didn't speak Tagalog, but I felt as if I was being introduced as her ticket out.

Arriving that night back in Olongapo after a long bus ride, we spent the night in a hotel on Rizal Avenue. The next morning the shit hit the fan.

Knowing, after three days of liberty, I had to return to boat for quarters at 0800, I was up early to be sure I made it back on time.

"Where you going?" Baby said, as I was buttoning my shirt.

"Back to the ship. I have duty today," I replied.

"*Midway* no leave till Wednesday, so I see you again Tuesday," she said.

"I have plans Tuesday. I want to see what is on base and do some shopping," I replied.

"What? You have another girl? I your only girl?" she shouted out.

"No, I don't have another girl. I've had a good time with you," I said calmly.

With that, she set off on the biggest temper tantrum I had ever witnessed, cussing and screaming words, most of which I couldn't understand, and throwing whatever she could get her hands on.

"I not just your good time girl! I serious girl!" she screamed.

As fast as I could, I made it out the door, down the stairs, and got the hell out of there. *That chick is crazy*, I thought. *That bitch would have cut my dick off if I had stayed in there any longer. Man, that was close!*

Out on Rizal Avenue, I flagged down a Jeepney, jumped in the back and headed to the base. All the traffic seemed to be headed in the same direction I was trying to go. I got out of the Jeepney at the end of Magsaysay Drive, where everyone bottlenecked to get over the Shit River bridge and onto the Navy base.

Presenting my ID card to one of the Marine guards at the main gate, he waived me on. Boy, I was so glad to be back on base. Seemed like I was back in civilization. *Wow, what a trip those last three days of liberty were.*

After arriving back aboard the *Midway* and changing back into my work dungarees, I made it to 0800 muster in Power Shop without a minute to spare.

———————

The next day, Tuesday, I was off again. There was an E Division cookout planned for the afternoon on the beach over near Subic City. JT and I had been on duty together, so we figured we would head over to the picnic after lunch.

The moment we crossed over the Shit River bridge, Baby was there waiting for me, standing with a girlfriend.

"Bob, we go picnic with you, Subic City," Baby said.

JT looked the other girl over and said, "Sounds good to me. Let's go."

"Seems like these Olongapo girls know more about our schedule than we do," I said to JT.

Baby flagged down a Jeepney. We all climbed in and headed along the long, winding cliff-edge road leading along the bay to Subic City.

The afternoon on the beach went smoothly. A lot of shipmates from E Division were there, some with PI girls, some without. We ate, drank beer, and swam in the smooth calm of the bay water through sunset. It was really a beautiful tropical setting.

We sat there in the water just past the edge of the sandy beach watching the sun setting across the bay. One of my E Division buddies, Dimmock, with a PI girl in his lap, turned to me and said, "Living the dream bro. Living the dream."

Yeah, living the dream, but I hope this psycho chick doesn't freak out again and this turns into a nightmare, I thought.

When the party was over, most of us took advantage of the Navy bus that was chartered for the picnic for a ride back from the Subic City Beach to the base. We all said our goodbyes to any girls who were still around. I waved to Baby from the bus window and that was it.

"Whew, I hope I never see that chick again," I said to JT.

"You just never know bud; you just never know," he replied.

CHAPTER SEVEN
ORE

TRAINING. EDUCATION. DRILLS. Teamwork. Practice. Repetition. In my early days at Valley Forge, I learned these were the key principals in making any organization successful in its mission. The US Navy is a prime example of that.

The call came over the 1MC to set the special sea and anchor detail early on the morning of May 3. Nobody was happy about it, but we were headed out of Subic Bay and back to sea again anyway.

Steaming north toward the Okinawa area, day and night flight operations were on the agenda from the third to the twelfth. Beginning May 13 and running through May 16, we participated in Multiplex 1-78. This exercise was designed to see how well the carrier task group could defend itself against surface and air units.

Woven in to Multiplex 1-78 was the operational readiness evaluation (ORE) May 12 through the 20. No one was looking forward to ORE. This evaluation period was designed to test a multitude of fleet exercises and affected every department from the top to the bottom. No one escaped ORE testing!

ORE testing was especially tough on the Engineering Department. With engineering, there was much at stake. Water, steam, electricity—these three components were arguably the lifeblood of the *Midway*. Without these three, she was dead in the water.

This was my first ORE, so I had no idea of what to expect other than longer days and longer sleepless nights, and drills, drills, drills; battle station, battle station, battle station. Additionally, I was promoted up out of After Steering, to the number two electrical switchboard for training to stand switchboard watch. Big changes.

"Psst, hey Dorgan, time to get up."

In the fog of waking up in the middle of a good dream, I heard Kenny's voice.

"Come on, Dorgan, let's get a gut bomb at the forward line before the mid-watch. If you'd hurry up, we'll have time."

There I was peacefully sleeping away for once in my rack. It was 2330. Kenny and I were due to go on the mid-watch shift of our four and eight watch cycle on Two Board.

I jumped up, pulled on my dungarees and boots, and we headed up the ladder to the second deck port side main passageway. Weaving our way through the normal foot traffic, we soon found ourselves at the serving line of the forward galley.

The forward galley served a basic menu from 2200 till 0200 for those of us who needed a bite to eat in the middle of the night— midrats. The hamburgers were not steakhouse quality, but they helped fight off the hunger pains.

Kenny and I both grabbed a burger, slopped on some condiments, and inhaled them as we headed down the ladders to the fourth deck engineering space known as Number Two Electrical Switchboard. Lucky for us, Two Board was just around the corner from the forward crews' mess deck.

Two Board was the largest space of the four switchboard rooms. As you opened the hatch and stepped down a couple of steps into the space, there to the left was the switchboard, which controlled the electrical power produced from the two steam-driven, ships service turbo generators, housed directly below in Number Two Generator Room.

Kenny was relieving Sully, who had the 2000 to 2400 watch. Sully looked like he was glad to see us. I was in training and standing watch with Kenny.

"Hey, Sully, what's happening?" Kenny sung out, in his normally smooth, easy-going manner.

"Two Charlie boiler has been given everybody in engineering fits. It's on again, off again," said Sully. "I don't think you'll be getting any sleep tonight."

Two Board also served as the main control board for E Division over the other three switchboards, After Steering, and the emergency generators. The electrician supervisor of the watch stood his watch at a large desk, directly behind the switchboard console. To the right and the left of the switchboard operator were floor to ceiling banks of gray circuit breaker enclosures, with switches all along the front. The entire room hummed from the sound of the current running through the breakers and vibrated from the steam-powered turbo generators in the engineering space below. If not for the air conditioning cooling the space, it would have been brutally hot.

In addition to the supervisor of the watch, the trouble-call watch electrician operated out of Two Board and reported with his tool belt on. For the next four hours, if there were any emergency electrical problems within engineering, it was the prerogative of the engineer of the watch in Main Propulsion Control, to be able to call on the supervisor of the watch at Two Board to send the trouble call. He usually sat in a chair in front of the supervisor's desk, when not out on a trouble call.

EM2 Galace was on trouble call tonight, and he was one of the best.

EM1 Dunca was supervisor of the watch from midnight to 0400. It seemed like a pretty skate job, but he had to keep on his toes for any calls from Main Control or problems in any of the other groups.

We had several forms of communication on the switchboards. The switchboard operator wore a sound-powered phone headset at all times. There was a squawk box mounted to the side of the switchboard console. This was electrically powered and had several different lines connecting us to other locations such as Main Control, generator rooms, other switchboards, After Steering, Damage Control Central, etc. There was also a telephone on the switchboard console and on the desk of the supervisor of the watch. We had all the bases covered.

Kenny sat down in a chair next to the switchboard console, handed me the headset, and said, "Here. You got the watch. I gotta do my hair."

Kenny was well known for taking pride in his hair. We had limits on how much hair we could grow, and the ship's barbershop did get a lot of business but, it was the 70s and hair was *in*.

He pulled out his pick and started running it through his course curly afro from back to front, as if he were getting ready for a hot date.

Dunca called out to me, "Hey, Dorgan. Do a board check."

Every so often, Two Board would call for a phone check to be sure all the board operators' sound-powered phones were working. I think it was mostly to make sure everyone was awake. Ask any switchboard operator if they ever fell asleep on watch.

"All boards—Two Board—phone check," I spoke into my handset.

"Three Board—aye—loud and clear."

"One Board—aye—loud and clear."

"Four Board—aye—loud and clear."

One by one, each responded, "Phone check complete; all checked in," I reported back to Dunca.

"Alright, let's hope this watch is quiet," he replied.

Watch time was Dunca's letter-writing time and he did not like to be disturbed.

After a couple of hours into our watch, my eyelids were getting heavy. There is only so much you can talk about when you are on watch with someone else in the middle of the night.

After you have read every bit of written word within sight, and you're tired of doodling, the eyelids weigh about one hundred pounds.

"HIGH WATER TWO CHARLIE BOILER! HIGH WATER TWO CHARLIE BOILER!" a stressed, cracking voice yelled out over the squawk box.

BOOM! The lights went out in our switchboard room. The room now was completely dark except for an eerie glow of white light coming from the four backup yellow battle lanterns hanging from the bulkheads, barely illuminating the space.

With the warning of "high water," Kenny had jumped to his feet. Using both hands, he had grabbed the controls for both generators of Two Board, throttled them down and opened the two breakers that fed Two Board from the generators, averting a catastrophe.

High water in the boiler meant there could be water going

through the pipes from the boiler heading to the generator's turbines instead of steam. Water in the turbines instead of steam could result in a huge explosion of the turbine and generator, sending turbine blades and all kinds of parts in all directions, and up through the floor we were standing on.

With Two Board out of commission, much of the forward portion of the *Midway* was without electricity, including one of the catapults for launching aircraft. Some of the highly vital equipment such as radar and sensitive electronics gear were wired into automatic bus transfer (ABT) switches. In the event of loss of their primary power supply, these units would automatically switch to a secondary source of power. They switched over immediately.

"Parallel Two Board and Three, Kenny!" yelled Dunca.

"Three Board, Two Board—paralleling Three and Two Board," Kenny said through the sound powered phones.

"Three Board—aye. Standing by to parallel Three and Two Board," replied the Three operator, who had seen the two indicator lights for two able and two baker SSTGs go off, knowing what would come next to restore power.

Kenny then closed the port and starboard bus tie circuit breakers, putting Three and Two Board in parallel, using Three's generators to restore power to Two Board.

With that, our lights came back on. It all happened quickly, but it seemed like slow motion.

"Good job, Kenny," I said.

"Shiiit man . . . leave it to a brother to stay cool under pressure," he replied.

With the ORE testers aboard, it was pretty much like this for the next two weeks until we arrived back in Yokosuka May 23. Testing day and night, under all sorts of circumstances—fire, flooding, high water, low water, chemical and biological attack, mass casualty—you name it. All departments scored high in every evolution during ORE. *Midway's* performance was judged as outstanding. The exceptionally high exam scores of ship's company and CVW-5 air wing was a credit to all personnel in the command.

Every effort is made to avoid a fire aboard a ship, especially at sea. Whenever there is any sort of hazardous work being performed aboard ship, a fire watch is required to be present at all times. The duty of the sailor on fire watch is to be present on the site of the work with a CO_2 fire extinguisher, prepared to extinguish any fire so it does not spread.

This type of continuous training makes one respond automatically when the actual event happens and sometimes it does.

We headed back to port in mid-May. During the second week back in Yokosuka. I was fortunate to be off duty for the day and had decided to do a little sightseeing.

The Great Buddha statue is in the small beach town of Kamakura. Kamakura had once been the capital of Japan hundreds of years ago, before it was wiped out by a huge tidal wave. The city was just a short train ride from Yokosuka, so I decided to check it out.

When I returned to the *Midway*, there was an unusual amount of activity, and the strong smell of smoke in and around the ship. I soon learned there had been a large fire in one of the ventilation exhaust uptakes of Three Able Boiler. Apparently, the fire was caused by a welder and quickly got out of the control of the sailor on fire watch.

Back in boot camp, firefighting was one of the most important weeks of training, both in the classroom and hands on. All sailors must successfully complete firefighting training and extinguish several types of fires inside structures and outside.

Drills and practice produce good fire fighters. Thanks to our rigorous training and testing, such as ORE, this uptake fire was quickly brought under control. *Midway* was well known for the proficiency of our crew.

CHAPTER EIGHT
SUMMER IN JAPAN

AFTER RETURNING TO YOKO on May 23 from our visit to the PI, we settled into a casual in-port summer routine. We did go out to sea for two doughnut cruises of about two weeks apiece. We performed routine flight ops off Northern Japan and in the East China Sea. The rest of the time we were in port and made every effort to do what young sailors do best: enjoy time off.

After being stationed aboard *Midway* for about five months now, I was beginning to develop some good friendships. I felt fortunate that some of my shipmates, many who had been there longer than I, included me in their lives off the boat.

While the average age of a *Midway* enlisted sailor was about nineteen, there were older men who had served on other ships and commands prior to their assignment to *Midway*. With their previous experience and time in service, they were usually assigned to leadership positions, depending on their rank. Usually these were chief petty officers, first-class petty officers, and second-class petty officers.

Chief Kusano was a short fellow, soft spoken and even tempered, but you didn't want to piss him off. He treated us fairly and we respected him for that. The chief knew most of us were far from home and family and he made it a point to involve us in activities off the ship while we were in port. (Chief had helped organize the Subic beach picnic back in PI.)

One morning we were all sitting around in Power Shop for morning muster, waiting for the chief to arrive with the plan of the day. After he arrived and read through the plan, he looked at us all and said, "It's my birthday Saturday. We're having a party at my house, and you're all invited."

Cool. The only reason not to go to the chief's house for his birthday party was if you had duty and I didn't have duty Saturday. "I'll be there," I said, as did everyone else who didn't have duty.

Saturday afternoon arrived and we all met up over at the chief's home.

Chief Kusano, along with his wife and two young daughters, lived in base housing. Their apartment was in a two-story building in one of many rows. The front door faced the street. The back sliding-glass doors opened out from the living room into a small backyard, enclosed by a tall, wooden privacy fence. There was a gate in the fence that opened out to an off-street parking lot behind the apartments. The apartments were modest yet cozy.

The weather was sunny and pleasant that day, so we spent most of the afternoon in the backyard around his picnic table. Chief was in charge of the grill, so the rest of us all drank a few beers while he and his wife served up dinner. We, of course, helped when we could, and . . . helped ourselves to another beer.

After dinner, the chief's daughters, who were about eleven and twelve, were doing a lot of giggling and pointing at me. For some reason they took a liking to me and decided to name me "Mr. Cool."

It didn't take long for my shipmates to pick up on that title. The rest of the party, I took a ribbing and became known as Mr. Cool, a nickname that stuck.

Sure enough, at Monday morning muster in Power Shop, everyone had a good laugh about it and made it official during roll call. "Hey, Mr. Cool."

The next summer outing the chief organized for us was a weekend camping trip in the mountains.

On Friday afternoon we loaded up a pickup truck with tents,

camping gear, hot dogs, hamburgers, and beer, and headed out for an adventure. Chief drove the truck and we followed along in cars, vans, and on motorcycles.

Tanzawa National Park is about 100 miles west of Yokosuka, in the mountains leading up to the famous quiet volcano, Mt. Fuji. The park is well known for its many streams, rope bridges, and waterfalls.

We spent the next couple of days hiking, swimming, and jumping off the waterfalls—in other words, forgetting all about Navy shipboard duty. Lenny, Lite Weight, Kenny, Jojo—we all had a great time. Those mountain streams were icy cold, even in the middle of summer. Jumping in that water made you feel rejuvenated. Chief Kusano knew how to show us a good time and make us feel appreciated.

Most sailors who went off base went by taxicab, bus, and train. Japan's public transportation system is first class and very convenient. A few sailors, who had been around for a while, did have a car or a motorcycle. Several of my buddies belonged to the Yokosuka Road Masters motorcycle club.

The motorcycle club was sanctioned by the base. On the northeast point of the base, fronting the bay, there were two buildings: a wood frame single story building and a Quonset-style hut style metal building. The metal building was for storing and working on motorcycles. The other building was set up as a clubhouse. The front section of the clubhouse building had a kitchen area and a bathroom. There was a pool table, couches, chairs, and tables. There was a back room with several bunk beds for members who wanted a night off of the boat.

Both Lenny and Lite Weight had motorcycles. They introduced me to the club, and it didn't take me long to realize how much I would enjoy having a motorcycle.

Summer just wouldn't be summer without some time spent on the beach. We had that covered too.

Roughly twenty miles west of the Yokosuka naval base, on the other side of Miura Peninsula, is the small beach village of Hayama.

The village also contains the summer beach compound and home of the emperor of Japan. The small, sleepy town rises from the beach through dense housing to high mountaintops. Generally quiet in the winter, this beach area really gets hopping in the summertime, when thousands of Japanese from the large cities flock to the beach on vacation.

The previous year, several of my E Division shipmates pooled their money and rented a house in Hayama, just across the road from the public beach. This was a grand house, as home sizes go in Japan. It was two stories and the main level had a kitchen and small dining area, as well as two large rooms, each separated with sliding doors. The tub and shower room was also on the main floor. (Toilets and tubs are usually in separate rooms in Japan.) The second floor also had two large rooms. There was a toilet room on both floors.

Lenny, Lite Weight, Sweeney, and Kenny were the official tenants. However, with each having the right to invite company, the Hayama house soon became *the party pad*.

Even though it didn't take much persuading from my motorcycle club buddies that I would enjoy having a motorcycle, my money situation did not agree. Since I had been assigned to sea duty on the *Midway*, I received a little increase in my biweekly paycheck, with the addition of my usual sea pay. It helped, but it wasn't changing my lifestyle.

One day while in port, several of us decided the next best way to get around would be by bicycle, so we went over to the Navy Exchange and bought ten-speed bicycles, all of them lime green. We were soon nicknamed "the Green Hornets." We could be seen riding all over the Miura Peninsula.

The ten-speed was a great start. I could jump on the bike and zip off almost anywhere with a new sense of freedom. We rode those bikes rain or shine. It is amazing how much you can carry on a ten-speed. With a front and rear rack, you can really load it up.

One Friday, I traded with a guy from Supply Department. After I installed an electric fan on the wall next to his bunk, he took me deep down to one of the freezer rooms onboard and handed over a case of frozen lobster tails to me.

Later that afternoon, after stopping by the commissary, I headed out the main gate on my bike. That ten-speed was loaded down. Strapped on the front rack was a huge brown paper bag full of groceries, including butter and seasoning. On the back rack was a case of beer and a case of fifty frozen lobster tails. When I arrived at the Hayama house, I was met with cheers. "We are gonna party down tonight!"

The beach was just a short walk from the house, across the street and down a little pathway. There was a wall on one side of the path and trees on the other. At the end of the path was the beach. The waterline was about 150 feet from there. On the high side of the beach, where the sand meets the land, vendors set up beach front stands each summer selling everything from food and drink to suntan lotion and souvenirs.

We all headed down to the beach with towels and a few beers for a jump in the water and to see what action was going on. If you think the trains are crowded in Japan, you should try the beach. Long summer days meant plenty of evening daylight on the beach and there were always the girls.

After messing around for a while, Lenny said to me, "Hey Mr. Cool, let's go get those lobster tails cooking."

It wasn't dark yet, but I was getting hungry, too.

After we arrived back at the house, I was filling a big pot with water to boil the lobster tails when I heard Lenny coming down the stairs to the kitchen, smoking a doobie.

"Hey, Mr. Cool, want a hit of this?"

"You bet," I replied.

Now, I hadn't yet figured out why, but Lenny and some of my other shipmates seemed to always have a good supply of pot and I didn't usually ask a lot of questions.

It was potent. After some intense coughing after my first hit I asked, "Lenny, why is it you seem to always have good pot?"

He turned to me with a grin and said, "While you were out there messing around with your PI girl, I was taking care of business."

It took me a little while for that to sink in.

"What do you mean?" I replied. "You were with a PI girl too."

"Yeah, but mine did errands for me," he said.

"What kind of errands?" I asked.

"This is PI pot; how do you think it got aboard?" he replied with that confident grin.

"*She* brought it?" I stammered with an inquisitive look.

"It's really pretty simple. She gets us a few pounds of pot. She wraps it up real tight and seals it. She packs it in her big handbag and walks aboard—right up the after brow—as a guest. It's not rocket science," he explained.

Wow, that explains a lot, I thought.

"Here, have another hit and let's get these lobster tails cooking," he said.

It wasn't long before the rest of the gang returned from the beach. We all drank beer, ate lobster, and partied the weekend away like kings. Sun, suds, sand, and beach babes in bikinis— just what every sailor dreamed of. It was a summer of fun.

———

On the morning of August 22ʼ it was once again time to set our sea and anchor detail, this time as we departed for a ten-day cruise to conduct flight operations off Northern Japan. From there we proceeded over to the East China Sea to participate in several exercises.

Early on September 1, we arrived in the harbor of Pusan, South Korea for a four-day port visit. We anchored out in the bay and waited for the Korean harbor tugboats to bring a camel

barge out to us. The water was rough that morning and it took a while for the crew to get the camel tied up along the side of the *Midway*.

The camel acted like a floating dock for the liberty boats to tie up to while loading and unloading sailors and marines going ashore and returning. The boatswains lowered the accommodation ladder from the hanger bay level to the camel. From the camel, the challenge then was to successfully board the liberty boat without getting soaked from the choppy water or falling in the bay.

The line for the liberty boats was long and wound through the hanger bay. It took hours for people to get off. The ones that did were lucky. The ones who didn't were stuck on board when the camel broke loose from the rough water and wasn't attached until the next day.

———————

On the last day of liberty, we finally made it off the boat and took a cab to a mountaintop amusement park, reachable by a special tram. We didn't have much of a visit, but we managed to get some shopping in. Korea was a great place to get blankets, coats, and shoes. By the end of the day, most of us were just anxious to get back to Yoko.

The morning of September 5, we pulled anchor and headed for the Tsushima Straits, probably one of our shortest at-sea periods, just three days.

Early on the morning of September 8 we entered Tokyo Bay. With the help of the harbor tugs, as soon as we entered Yokosuka Bay, we were turned around, backed into the pier, and tied up. The forward and after brows were then craned into place and shore power hooked up before the water had stopped churning around the hull. Everyone was anxious to get back and continue enjoying the final fleeting days of summer.

CHAPTER NINE
TAD

THE FIRST SIX OR SO months an enlisted sailor spends on board the *Midway* is a time to get to know your way around the ship. The next phase is a temporary additional duty (TAD) period, usually a three-month stint to the S-2 Department (food service).

Morning muster was over. Chief Kusano turned to me and said, "Mr. Cool, it's time for you to go TAD. You are to report to the S-2 office on the aft mess deck. They will tell you what to do from there."

I checked in to the S-2 office. They gave me my new working uniform, long white pants, a white folding paper hat and a white T-shirt that said *MIDWAY MAGIC* across the front.

"Dorgan, you've got the night shift in the pots and pans scullery. Go get some rest and report back here at 1930," my new supervisor, "Wolfman," said.

The TAD food service shifts were twelve hours on and twelve hours off. General quarters assignments remained the same during TAD. The good thing was there was no standing watch while TAD. I didn't realize it at the time, but later I was glad to have the night shift, there wasn't nearly as much work as day shift.

———

At 1930 sharp that evening I checked back into the S-2 office.

Wolfman, as the first class in charge, said, "Follow me Dorgan, I'll get you started."

We made our way across the mess deck. Since we were at sea, the evening meal was still going strong and almost every table and chair was full. On the port side of the mess deck, we walked through an open hatch leading to a small passageway. To the left was a doorway leading to the *King Kong*.

King Kong is a machine that grinds all the food waste by the trashcan full and spits it out of the side of the ship. It was not used while in port, but huge sharks sure did like to follow in our wake while at sea!

I followed Wolfman through the hatch to the right and into the pots and pans scullery.

"Hey, you guys show the new guy what to do!" he yelled to the two sailors standing over the steaming stainless-steel deep sinks, as he disappeared out the door behind me.

"Aye, aye, skipper," said the one closest to me.

"What's your name buddy?" said the other guy. "My name's Tom, the wise guy here is Ski-bo."

"Bob," I replied.

"Hey, you're from Power Shop, aren't you?" Tom asked.

"Yup."

"We're from E Division too, and almost done with TAD," Tom replied.

Just then a pushcart with a huge stack of greasy sheet pans came through the hatch.

"Okay Bob, there's your first stack," said Ski-bo with a big grin as he handed me a huge pair of thick black rubber gloves and a brush. "Here's your sink. Your job is to scrub these nasty pans clean. No hurry—we're gonna be here all night anyway."

Our job was to clean all the huge pots and pans used in the crew's galley from the previous meal. Third mess was the worst. Burnt, and dried -on food, grease, and sauces, you name it, we saw it. The mess cooks seemed to just keep coming in with more pots and pans. They would even stack them up out in the passageway.

The pots and pans scullery was a cramped, hot, humid, miserable place to work. Big spray nozzles hung down over the stainless-steel deep sinks to spray off the pans after we finished scrubbing. We usually finished up around 0200 or so. Other than a few occasional pots and pans from the forward galley, the rest of the nights were usually quiet until breakfast started up. Sometimes the bakeshops would drop off a load in the middle of the night just to annoy us.

Most nights seemed to go by quickly. The mess cooks kept us busy with load after load of dirty pots and pans and we worked hard. The three of us got along well. You get to know a lot about a person when you work side by side, hour after hour, seven days a week at sea.

We had a lot in common. Tom was from Norristown, Pennsylvania, not far from Valley Forge. Ski-bo was from south Jersey. They had arrived on the *Midway* several months before I did and made the last Indian Ocean Cruise in '77. Ski-bo was tall and muscular with blond hair. Quiet and easygoing, he just told things the way they were. Tom was tall too, with dark hair and a bit heavier, maybe didn't work out as much. Tom was always more of a talker, always had a smile, and could always come up with something to laugh about.

After about four weeks of pots and pans we got replacements. Tom and Ski-bo had completed their TAD and were transferred back to E Division. Tom was assigned to the lighting shop. Ski-bo was assigned to the aviation and ordnance electrical workshop. I was transferred to the main mess deck scullery to wash dinner trays, cups, and silverware. I was out of the frying pan and into the fire, as they say.

During this cruise, the *Midway* participated in several exercises off the coast of Northern Japan, in the Okinawa zone and the Tsushima Straits area.

The scenario for the exercise ReadEx 1-79, held September 24–30, was the opposed transit of a geographical choke point, in this case the Tsushima Straits, by *Midway*, the aircraft carrier USS *Enterprise* (CVN-65) and our task group against air, surface, and submarine forces. Despite one of the worst radar environments in the western Pacific (land drag, maximum merchant traffic, and fishing fleet activity) our task group was graded as outstanding in performance on the graded evaluations.

During these exercises, it seemed as if when we were not

scrubbing pots and pans, we were at our general quarters battle stations.

On October 1, a real-world alert was launched as a VAW-115 squadron (*Midway*) E-2 Hawkeye provided control for F-14 Tomcats from the *Enterprise* to detect and intercept three Russian Bear aircraft that were closing in on both *Midway* and *Enterprise*. The Tomcats swiftly escorted the Bears away from our task force air space without incident.

This cruise had been tiresome. We were all glad to hear liberty call over the 1MC when we arrived on the morning of October 4 in the harbor of Pusan, Korea for a five-day visit.

Pusan was well known by sailors and marines as a good place to do some shopping. Great deals were known to be found around every corner. We made several trips ashore. With winter approaching, I loaded up on blankets, leather jackets, sweaters, and gloves. I bought all I could carry and wear back to the boat. We all had stuff crammed in every locker, workshop, and storage compartment we could use.

One day Lenny, Lite Weight, Brian, and I decided we would take a trip to the mountaintop amusement park we had visited the last time we were in Korea. We all piled into a taxi and explained to the driver where we wanted to go. Luckily, he did speak a little English, so we hit the road north out of the city of Pusan.

We arrived at the park area at the bottom of the mountain and the driver dropped us off. There were not nearly as many people around the area and in the shops. We found the booth where we had purchased tickets for the tram ride to the top of the mountain the last time.

To our disappointment, we learned that with summer vacation over, the tram was closed until spring.

That didn't stop us. One of the workers told us some of the rides, exhibits, and shops at the top were still open. We started hiking up the long walking path. When we reached the park at the top, Lenny and Lite Weight were puzzled as to why suddenly Brian and I seemed to think everything we looked at was laugh-out-loud funny. It didn't take them long to realize we had taken a hit of the purple microdot that had been in circulation on the ship, as we began our trek up the mountain. The stuff had finally kicked in. The remainder of the day was a real "trip."

———————

On the morning of October 9, we got underway for a quick, three-day cruise back to Yokosuka and arrived early on the morning of October 12 to a pier full of people.

Unlike our normal routine, after tying up to the pier and lowering the brows, we did not hook up shore power. We wouldn't be staying long. This time most of the crowd on the pier would be coming aboard. It was time for the 1978 Dependents Day Cruise.

By the time the brow was raised again and our mooring lines cast off, over 3000 dependents and Japanese visitors had boarded the *Midway* for the day to see how the ship operated at sea.

After we left Tokyo Bay and entered open ocean waters, the guests were treated to an airshow by the five squadrons of Carrier Air Wing Five. The pilots performed all sorts of maneuvers in their aircraft, as well as formation flybys.

Halfway through the show, with the flight deck full of crew and spectators, an F-4 Phantom screamed along the port side at flight deck level, breaking the sound barrier. Seeing the Phantom pierce through the sound barrier and the following sonic boom was always a crowd pleaser.

The *Midway* bake shop even baked a cake for the guests. The cake was an eight-foot-long replica of the *Midway*, icing catapults and all. It was a hit with everyone.

By the end of the day, we were back again in Yokosuka Bay, moored alongside the pier, for a well-deserved, four-week in-port period.

———————

Even with a break from being at sea, we were already excitedly talking amongst ourselves about our next cruise destination— Thailand.

By mid-October, Hayama Beach had quieted down from the excitement of the season. The summer vendor shops were closed up and moved away for winter. The crowds were gone, but the Hayama party house was still going strong.

One evening, there were a bunch of us at the house. We were talking about what we could do to have some fun.

Lenny spoke up, "Let's go on a motorcycle run this weekend."

Most of the members of the club were there, and we were all on board with the idea.

That Friday afternoon, all of us who were going, met up at the motorcycle clubhouse.

"Smokey" and his wife arrived first. Smokey was a tall, lean fellow with a long beard. He could have doubled as one of the band members of the Grateful Dead or ZZ Top. He was really laid back and easy going, and he and his wife were good people, still living the 60's. Smokey was riding his bike. His wife was driving their little Japanese minivan. She would be hauling all the camping equipment, food, drinks, and anything else we would need for the trip.

Sweeney rode his Yamaha 650 with his Japanese girlfriend as passenger.

Lenny rode his Yamaha 650. I was his passenger.

Lite Weight rode his Honda.

We saddled up and headed out of the main gate north, past Tokyo, to Nikko National Park. It was a long ride to Nikko. Lenny and Smokey had lived in Japan for over two years now and were able to find their way around well. Highway signs were written in Kanji, Hiragana, and Katakana, or a mixture. Road numbers were the main way we *gaijins* found our way around.

By the time we arrived in the camping area, it was late and it was dark. We made our way down a winding gravel one-lane mountain road to a quiet spot with tall hardwoods that offered a large leafy tree canopy. We could hear a waterfall from a nearby stream. It seemed like a good place to set up camp.

After gathering some wood, we made a little campfire. We pitched our tents, gathered around the campfire for a little while, then called it a night.

Lenny and I shared a little three-man tent. We rolled out our sleeping bags and it wasn't long before I was asleep.

In the middle of the night, I remember waking up briefly to the sound of rain coming down on the tent and all around us. It was autumn. The leaves had changed color and were falling. As the night went on, the rain seemed louder, falling on the leaves over the ground and the ones still left clinging to the trees.

Suddenly, at dawn, I awoke, cold and wet.

"Lenny, wake up! What the hell!" I stammered as I sat up in my soaking wet sleeping bag.

The night's rainfall had apparently been much heavier higher up in the mountains. The rainwater rushing downstream and over the falls had overflowed the banks of the stream. The spot we had pitched our tent was now covered in almost a foot of water.

We crawled out of our soaked sleeping bags and out of the tent. The only others who had escaped the encroaching waters were Smokey and his wife, who had climbed into their van when the rain began.

We broke camp. Squeezed the water out of everything the best we could and headed for the nearest hotel to dry off and warm up.

All day Saturday and Sunday, until we left to return to base, was spent at the hotel. It was a great time. We had come prepared. We had our camping supplies—food and beer. It rained the whole weekend, and most of the trip back.

Apparently, no one had checked the weather forecast.

Early November was passing quickly, and soon it would be time for us to get underway once again. Lenny had spent almost three years stationed aboard *Midway* and his tour of duty would soon be finished. Our last week in port, he was packing up his stuff from the Hayama house to ship back home to New York.

"Hey, Mr. Cool, you want to ride up to Yokohama with me Monday?" Lenny asked.

"I'm going to borrow a pickup, load the bike on, and drive it up to North Pier to ship it to the States," he continued.

"Sure, I'll go," I replied. "I'm always up for an adventure."

I was still TAD, and I knew I would not be working that day.

Monday arrived. We went over to the motorcycle club, loaded up his bike, and drove to Yokohama's overseas shipping terminal.

I could tell he had mixed feelings about some of the upcoming changes. You make a lot of friends in the Navy. You experience much. Some you will miss. But there was also the excitement of going home and the new beginnings.

As we were driving back to Yokosuka, Lenny asked me, "Are you excited about going to Thailand?"

"Yes, I am," I replied. "Have you ever been there?"

"No, I haven't, but I hear they have pretty good Thai sticks there," he said with a grin.

"Twenty-four days and a wakeup and we'll find out," I said.

He replied, "Twenty-four days and a wakeup, shipmate."

CHAPTER TEN
THAILAND

THREE DAYS LATER, we were once again underway. Although headed north to use the USS *Oklahoma City* as a simulated enemy target for our flight operations off the coast of Japan, most of us already had our minds on our next liberty port—Pattaya Beach, Thailand.

Throughout the ship, in workspaces and berthing compartments, you could hear cassette players cranked up high to "Passage to Bangkok" from the most recent album from Rush, *2112*. This was to be the first port visit to Thailand in *Midway's* history.

Recently I had been moved out of the main mess deck scullery to duty on the crew aft mess deck, the largest crew dining area. Still on the night shift, the mess deck was a good place to be. Night shift was fairly simple. When the meal was over at 2000, we removed and refilled all of the condiments, wiped down the tables and moved them all to one side, swabbed the deck, then we set up for breakfast. That left us with several hours till we were working again with the start of breakfast.

Barry was one of my TAD mess deck buddies. Barry was TAD from V-3 Division. His regular job was moving aircraft in the hangar bay. He was known as a *yellow shirt*—a plane handler.

Barry was from a small town in New Mexico. He was a tall fellow with blond hair, was really laid back, and could have passed as a surfer dude from Southern California.

During our early morning break, we would wander around the ship. We would pop in to visit guys we knew who were on watch or working the midnight shift, too. There was always activity going on around the ship while at sea. He introduced me to a lot of guys he knew from the Air Department who performed all sorts of jobs in service to the aircraft.

Sometimes in the early morning hours after the flight deck had secured from flight operations, we would walk all the way to the front edge of the flight deck. At the very front of each of the two steam catapults used to launch aircraft, there were two ramps, which extended even farther out from the flight deck known as the *bridle horns*. We would walk out on the bridle horns, lie down with our backs to the deck, and stare up at the night sky. The sky is so black at sea, it is easy to see many shooting stars in just a short period of time. It's a great opportunity to identify the constellations.

One night we couldn't get Barry to come down off the deck after he did all four sections of a four-way windowpane of the blotter LSD that was going around at the time. Luckily, it was a quiet night, and he wasn't missed on the mess deck.

After destroying the flagship of the Seventh Fleet, the USS *Oklahoma City* (CG-5)—known as the *Okie Boat*—in our simulation, we set a course for the South China Sea.

This next exercise was to be CV/CV EncounterEx. On November 16, aircraft from *Midway*'s VAW-115 squadron provided targeting and vectoring information for a CVW-5 strike group, which successfully located and simulated a missile attack against the USS *Constellation* (CV-64).

The *Connie* had departed San Diego on September 26, 1978. Following our joint exercises, she would soon be heading to the Indian Ocean. No one knew at the time that due to unforeseen upcoming events, she and her crew would not be returning to San Diego until May 17, 1979.

After another week of flight ops, on November 28, we headed toward the Gulf of Siam and our long-awaited destination. The word was, "Whatever it is you are looking for, you can find it in Thailand."

Our first day in the Gulf was political. General Krianysak

Chamanan, members of the Thailand military, and other dignitaries were flown aboard for a tour of the ship. Of course, what tour of an aircraft carrier at sea would be complete without a show of our air superiority, complete with the dropping of a few 500-pound bombs and the sonic boom of an F-4 Phantom speeding past the angle deck.

Finally, the morning of December 1 arrived. We anchored just off the coast of the resort town of Pattaya Beach. As luck would have it, I had duty the first day.

The next morning, after catching a short nap following the night shift, I put on my civilian clothes and was ready for an adventure. I stopped into Power Shop to see if anyone else was heading to shore.

"Hey, Mr. Cool, you ready to hit the beach?" I heard Lenny ask as he stood up from behind the workbench, closing his locker.

"What are you taking?" I asked.

"A pair of swim trunks, a towel, flip flops, and a change of clothes in this flight bag, just in case," he replied.

A flight bag is a fatigue-green nylon bag with a zipper and handles on the top. They are about three feet by two feet by two feet. They are very handy and you can pack a lot of stuff in there on liberty.

My bag was already packed so I replied, "Ready when you are."

We made our way up from our berthing compartment to the hanger bay to get in line for the liberty boats. The Navy had contracted with some of the local boat owners to use their tour boats to shuttle *Midway* sailors to shore and back.

Finally, it was our turn and we made our way down the accomodation ladder and on to the awaiting boat. Our small boat looked like it could accommodate forty passengers or so. We both agreed, maybe having duty the first day wasn't such a bad thing. We avoided the big rush and a long wait in line.

When we arrived ashore, it was really just a beach. There was no pier. The boat pulled right up to the sandy beach. One at a time, we each made our way up to the bow and jumped off the boat onto the sand. Luckily, we timed our jump just right and landed dry. Others were not so lucky and ended up soaked by the crashing waves.

We had finally arrived. Pattaya Beach seemed like a tropical paradise. In either direction, as far as you could see, the beach was lined with palm trees and little thatched palm-roofed shelters. Hobie Cat catamaran sailboats were available to rent. Out in the bay, ski boats pulled skiers and parasailers, who dangled high above the water from bright, colorful parachutes. Girls lined the beach in bikinis.

We walked up from the beach and stepped over a short sea wall to the weathered blacktop of the old beachfront road. There were many scooters and small motorcycles driving up and down the road. A few cars and small delivery trucks passed us by. As we walked along, we passed several scooter rental stands. You could rent by the hour or by the day.

Lenny hailed a cab. We jumped in.

"Where to?" the driver asked.

"That big hotel up there on the top of the hill overlooking the bay," Lenny replied.

After driving a mile or so on the beach road, we began to go up a hill. As we reached the top, we could see the Royal Cliff Beach Hotel at the top of the bluff. As we drove up to the main entrance, we could tell this was a first-class resort.

After paying the driver, we went inside to the check-in counter. Some of our buddies from E Division had checked in the night before. We asked what rooms they were in and took the elevator up.

We arrived to find they had two rooms on the fifth floor overlooking the pool.

Lenny knocked on the door.

The door opened. It was Lite Weight.

"Hey, we heard this is where the party is," Lenny exclaimed.

"Come on in here, you salty dogs!" Lite Weight replied.

We went in. It was a nice place all right, great balcony too, and what a view! I had to take a leak, so I turned to go to the bathroom.

"Don't go in there. He's packing his ass," I heard someone yell from the other side of the room.

Apparently, a couple of shipmates were headed back to the boat. There was word going around that every tenth person returning to the ship would be strip-searched to check for drugs. These guys were not taking any chances.

Thai Sticks were the popular item everyone who smoked pot was looking to find. Highly potent marijuana buds tied around a small stick, they were about the size of a small cigar. Anyone who had ever had Thai Stick in the past had purchased them individually and paid a high price. Here, sailors were buying Thai sticks by the brick of twenty, and cheap!

My shipmates had decided to remove the little wooden stick from the center of their Thai Sticks, grind up the buds, pack it into a condom, then shove it up their ass to evade detection when they returned to the ship. That idea didn't sound like much fun to me.

I grabbed a beer and stepped out on the balcony to sit down, relax, and take in the view.

"Here Bob, have a hit of this," one of my shipmates said as they passed me a little bong filled with ice.

As I did, I could feel the smoke expand in my lungs. Just one hit was enough. It was at least an hour before I got up from that chair overlooking the pool and the bay. What a beautiful paradise we were in.

"Come on, let's go down to the pool," Lenny said after we all had spent enough time out on the balcony enjoying the view. We were on the west side of the hotel. It was afternoon now, and with the sun beating down on us, we were beginning to roast.

Several of us changed into our swim trunks, took the elevator down, and headed out back to the huge swimming pool overlooking the bay. We left our towels on some poolside chairs and jumped in.

"Wow! Now this is living!" Lenny said, as we swam up to the poolside bar.

We sat down on the submerged barstools and ordered a couple of beers.

"Bob, I'd like to get some of that Thai Stick back on the boat too, but I'm not packing it up my ass!" Lenny turned and said to me with a grin. "What about you?"

"No, I'm not packing, either, buddy!" I replied. "Got any ideas?"

"You know, if we could get a bunch of those bricks of sticks aboard, we could both make a boatload of money," he whispered. "You got any money to invest? I mean serious money."

Lenny and I had two main philosophies in common: *take care of business before pleasure*, and *work hard, play hard*.

We sat there for most of the afternoon, relaxing at the tropical poolside bar. After a couple of beers and a sandwich, we had come up with a plan.

The next morning, we headed back to the ship to put our plan in motion.

I had been saving up some money toward buying a motorcycle. It was a bit of a drag, being in the motorcycle club without a motorcycle.

While I got my cash together, Lenny gathered his. We made a few preparations, then boarded the liberty boat back to shore.

By now it was midafternoon. The sun had moved west in the clear blue sky, out over the bay, and was beating down on the beach and the steamy asphalt of the beachfront road. It was hot and we were hungry and thirsty. It was a good time to grab a bite to eat before we got started.

We crossed the street and found a small casual beachfront restaurant. After a meal and a cold drink, we were revived.

"Hey Bob, let's get started," Lenny said after we paid the waitress. "You head south and I'll head north. We'll meet back in the middle in an hour or less if we've had any luck."

So, we set out. All along the beach road were vendors selling and renting anything tourists might need in a tropical vacation hot spot. You could rent catamarans to sail, motor scooters to drive around on, motorboat drivers with boats to take you waterskiing or parasailing. As far as we were concerned, they were all prospects who might be able to point us in the right direction to achieve our goal.

We did not speak any Thai, but the locals had enough exposure to international tourists to carry on enough English to get our point across.

"Thai Stick? Thai Stick? Do you know where we can get Thai Stick?" was our only question.

After about fifteen minutes of discreetly asking and having already received my fair share of noes, I saw Lenny coming my way.

"I found a guy," Lenny said excitedly. "He rents scooters up the road and can take us to a buddy of his who can score us some quantity."

"Cool!" I exclaimed. "Let's go."

After walking about three city blocks, we came up to a long row of motor scooters and small motorcycles parked just off the road under some palm trees along the beach. Lenny introduced me to his new friends. They were two short, skinny Thai men, their skin dark and weathered from the sun. They looked to be in their early thirties. One of them, Joe, appeared to be the owner of the rental stand. The other, Somsak, was helping. They had a friendly, casual way about them, which put me at ease.

"Come on. I take you to my friend's house. You talk to him," said Joe.

They each backed a motorcycle out of the row and kickstarted them.

"Let's go," said Somsak.

Lenny climbed onto the back of the first bike behind Joe and I climbed on the back of Somsak's bike. With a twist of the throttle, we were off down the road, weaving in and out of traffic. It wasn't hard to keep track of Lenny. The bike he was on was smoking like an old diesel. After getting a couple of lungs full of that, I was glad my driver decided to hang back a little and keep his distance.

We headed east from the beach, out of the main tourist area. Soon the buildings we passed became smaller and farther apart. As the roads narrowed, we passed open fields, elaborate Buddhist temples, and rural scenes. We turned left onto a dusty, dry dirt road and through a grove of tall shade trees, finally coming to a stop in front of a traditional, two-story Thai home.

"Wow! That was a wild ride!" I said, getting off the bike.

"I'm used to being the driver, not the passenger," replied Lenny.

Joe motioned to us, "Let's go in. You meet my friend."

We followed Joe and Somsak into the house, up a stairway to the left of the front door to the second level, and into a small modest room with one window covered by a curtain. There was no furniture in the room except for a small, short table. We were to sit on the floor around the table.

"You wait here. I get my friend," said Joe as he turned and left the room.

After about half an hour had passed, I turned to Lenny and said, "What do you think?"

"Be patient," he replied, "This kind of stuff can take a little while."

Just then Joe returned to the room with another man. He looked much like Somsak.

"My friend have Thai stick," Joe said, motioning to the other man. "You smoke."

With that, the other guy opened a cardboard cigar box. Inside the box was a small pipe, a lighter, and three bricks of Thai sticks. He handed us both a brick, looked at us and said, "Thai stick."

I had never seen a brick of Thai sticks before. After looking it over, I put it up to my noise for a sniff. "Mmmm—Thai stick," I said, turning to Lenny with a grin.

Lenny grinned back, "Just what we're looking for."

While Lenny and I were drooling over the merchandise, Somsak had taken a stick from the third brick, broken off a small end of a bud and filled his pipe with it. Handing it to me he said, "Here, you try."

It only took one hit apiece for us to realize this was no dog shit.

With a grin, Lenny said, "Let's talk business."

We wanted as many bricks as we could buy with all the cash we had brought with us. Our host seemed surprised but eager and willing to help us. Our plan was in motion.

The next step was to get back aboard the ship.

I left Lenny with our new friends, wrapping our huge blocks of bricks of Thai sticks, each about the size of a cinder block, in clear, Saran Wrap-like plastic, to insure they stayed dry on the next leg of their journey.

Somsak drove me back to the beach on his motorcycle. By then, the sun was setting. I had to hurry along. There was a full liberty boat on the beach, ready to shove off. Running across the sandy beach, I made it just in time. After climbing on with wet pants and shoes, I took a seat for the choppy ride back to *Midway*.

———————

Back at the house, Lenny found himself haggling with our new "friends."

"I need a ski boat to take me to the ship," Lenny continued.

"I have a jet ski you can use to get out there to your ship," Joe replied.

"The bay will be too choppy for a jet ski, and I don't know the waters," Lenny said. "It has to be a boat with a driver."

"Okay, lets go back to the beach," said Joe.

With that, they packed all the Thai sticks into the trunk of Joe's friend's car and headed back to the beach road, leaving a trail of dust in the setting sun.

After arriving at the edge of the bay, Joe jumped out of the car and motioned Lenny to follow him. "This way!"

A short walk from the car, they arrived at a small wooden picnic table covered by a thatched roof.

The weathered man under the roof turned and greeted Joe with a big smile. They talked awhile and Joe explained the situation.

Joe turned to Lenny and said, "My friend can take you in his ski boat, but it will cost more money."

"I don't have any more money. The deal was to include getting me and the sticks to the ship," replied Lenny, firmly.

Joe turned to his friend and talked a little more.

The man at the table then rose to his feet, turned to Lenny and said, "I like that belt buckle you have there. I have never seen anything like it."

Whenever Lenny was in civilian clothes, you could always count on him wearing his big shiny silver belt buckle he'd had custom made in the Philippines. He was very fond of it.

"I'll take you and your load out to the big ship in the bay in my ski boat if you'll give me that belt buckle," said the man at the table.

At this point, as much as Lenny liked that belt buckle, he really didn't have any options. Lenny unbuckled the belt, unsnapped the big silver buckle from the leather band, and handed it to the weathered man at the table.

With a huge smile across his face, admiring the new treasure in the palm of his hand, the man read the large silver letters spanning the width of the heavy buckle one by one—L-E-N-N-Y. He then looked up at the young sailor who had just given up his prized possession and simply said, "Okay, lets go."

───────────────

Back on board, I made my way to our berthing compartment. It was quiet, not many of our crew were onboard, other than those with the duty. There were no distractions while I changed into my work dungarees. I slipped into Power Shop to pick up my tool belt full of hand tools and fastened it around my waist, as if I were on duty. Grabbing my empty flight bag, I headed up to the hanger bay.

The hanger bay was quiet, too. I walked all the way forward to the port front corner of Bay One. There was a mooring ring about three feet wide by three feet high that mooring lines ran through. Removing the long rope stashed in my flight bag, I attached the rope to a metal pipe on the side of the bulkhead then lowered it out of the oval hole and down to the waterline. Next, I headed through the forward bay hatch, up the ladder to the 02 level and out to the port catwalk, just in front of the angle deck.

The normal security routine for the *Midway* when anchored out in a foreign port was to have Marine guards stationed on and patrolling sections of the flight deck. In addition, it was the responsibility of E Division's flight deck lighting shop to install temporary exterior security lighting. This security lighting was made up of floodlights that hung at the end on long poles, suspended down from the catwalks at intervals all the way around the ship. The floodlights all were directed in toward the hull. Each set had a switch in the catwalk, which could be turned on . . . and off.

I stood there in the black of the night, my eyes straining to see any sign of the speedboat approaching from the distance carrying Lenny with our cargo. The angle deck faced the darkness of the gulf, away from the lights and the activity of the shoreline. I looked back over my shoulder to see an armed Marine guard pass by making his rounds, heading away.

"You said the lights would be off!" the weathered man yelled at Lenny from behind the steering console of the speedboat, bobbing in the heavy swells far out in the deep waters of the bay.

With the running lights off, the man continued to guide the boat closer through the darkness of the night toward the angle deck of the huge flattop.

"Just keep it moving closer," replied Lenny. "When he sees us, he'll shut them off."

"You get just one pass!" grumbled the weathered man.

When I turned back around to focus my eyes on the horizon again, there it was, the small outline of the speedboat, headed slowly in my direction in the black water.

Quietly, I reached down and switched off the floodlight for the area just under the angle deck. This was the sign Lenny and the boat driver, were waiting for. The boat then sped up and heading straight for the long rope dangling down below the angle deck to the waterline.

Next, I ducked in through the hatch from the catwalk and made my way down the ladder, back to the hanger bay. The speedboat was there at the bottom of the rope. Lenny had just tied the rope to the handles of the flight bag. He tugged on the rope twice and I pulled it up and in. As I did, I heard the faint sound of the outboard motor as it sped away, delivery complete.

After stashing the coiled rope along with my flight bag full of our cargo behind some wooden pallets, I went back up to the catwalk and switched the security lighting back on. But I wasn't done yet—next I needed to stash our cargo.

During the past eleven months, I had learned my way around the ship. Working as an electrician had given me access of much of the ship, from top to bottom. There are many places to hide things that you don't want discovered. Electricity is in almost every compartment and used for some reason or another.

For now, we had decided ahead of time we would stash our cargo in a locked storage room until we could move it to a more secure location.

After locking up the flight bag, I headed back to Power Shop to store my tool belt. After all that, I was ready to a shower and hit my rack.

Just after dozing off, I felt a tap on my shoulder.

"Hey Bob, did you get it?" a voice whispered close by.

Turning over, I saw it was Lenny standing there next to my rack.

"Hey man, yeah, I did, and it's locked up safe and sound," I replied.

Next, I got up, put on my dungarees, and we headed to the flight deck to fill each other in on our experiences.

Sea duty in the Navy. It's not just a job, it's an adventure!

———————

The following day, with our mission accomplished, we were ready to hit the beach and have some fun!

Lenny, Lite Weight, Brian, and I decided to go visit the famous city of Bangkok.

Our first stop as we arrived in the big city was a small boat dock, a pickup point for small water taxis, that ferried tourists around the canal city. The guide pointed out places and things of interest along the way.

After we were about twenty minutes into the boat ride, the guide pulled the small motorboat alongside another small dock area to let passengers off and on.

The guide told us, "Fight, fight, you go see fight," and pointed up in the direction others leaving the boat were walking.

So, we followed along with the crowd, making our way up to an open area, paved in large old flat stones. The crowd had formed a circle, with a clear open area in the center, about twenty feet across. In the middle was a short Thai man with a wicker basket by his feet.

All around the circle, people were talking and shouting back and forth amongst themselves. Some were exchanging money. Soon another man made his way through the gathering crowd to the center of the circle.

We were taller than most of the locals and after making our way to the front, had a good viewpoint when the man lifted the lid from the top of the wicker basket.

Everyone's attention immediately focused on the wide head of the snake rising out of the basket.

Next, the other man opened the door of his little wooden box and out ran a mongoose, alert and ready for action.

Immediately the fight was on. Mongoose verses king cobra. The cobra slithered out of his basket and assumed an attack stance, head raised high off the ground, neck flared wide out.

The mongoose quickly circled, looking for an opportunity to pounce. And pounce he did, darting in, lunging at the cobra, again and again. The cobra struck back, lunging forward, mouth wide open, fangs sharp as darts, but just missing their mark as the agile mongoose leaped aside.

The excitement of the crowd grew as the opponents tangled in the courtyard. The spectators shouted at the two as they battled.

After some intense sparing back and forth, the mongoose seized his opportunity with a jump, landing on the back of the cobra's neck. Tearing into the snake with his razor-sharp teeth, the match was soon over.

"Wow, now that's something you don't see every day!" Lenny said, as the crowd began to back away and thin out.

He was right—that's something I had never seen before and have never seen since.

———————

Later that evening, we decided to see what kind of night life, there was in Bangkok. We hailed a cabbie and asked him to take us to "the action."

After a wild ride through the congested, crazy Bangkok streets, he dropped us off in front of a nightclub. There was a brightly lit marque sign on the wall just over the entrance. There were a few people milling around along the street out front and we saw some shipmates we knew, so we decided to go in and check it out.

We made our way in, through a lobby area, and on through a set of double doors to a big room filled with little tables with chairs around them. In the center of the room was a stage about four feet up from floor level.

The room was filling up quickly with people, so we acted fast, grabbing a table in the front row. A waitress, dressed only in a bikini, took our drink order. Soon the lights dimmed, and the show started.

It wasn't long into the show, after several of the performers had completed their acts, that we all realized this would go down as the wildest sex show we would ever see in our lives.

One girl was right up there on center stage naked, shooting ping pong balls out of her vagina into the crowd. Another girl's nude performance included sitting back with her legs spread wide open, somehow working chopsticks with her labia. She broke a doughnut into bite-size pieces and fed them to any willing spectators from the audience.

When the show was over, we gradually made our way to the door and hailed a cab outside. As our driver made his way through the streets and back to our liberty boat at Pattaya Beach, we all laughed and agreed we had accumulated quite a few sea stories from this port visit we could tell when we were old and gray.

On the morning of December 7, we pulled anchor and steamed south from Pattaya Beach. It was back to the daily, at-sea grind. For me, it was more wiping tables and swabbing the mess decks on the night shift.

Thailand was a wild liberty port, there was no doubt. We each left with our own memories and some of us with a lot more than memories. We were sorry to hear that several of our shipmates did not make it back to the ship alive, victims of the big H—heroin. They were gone but not forgotten.

CHAPTER ELEVEN
BAGUIO

THE NEXT FIVE DAYS passed by quickly and with as much normalcy as can be for a forward deployed aircraft carrier conducting flight operations at sea.

The year was soon coming to an end. Most of us were looking ahead to the Christmas holidays back in Yokosuka. Some of our shipmates were short timers and were finishing up their tour of duty aboard *Midway*. Those short timers, like Lenny, would be back home stateside, in time to celebrate Christmas with family and old friends this year. However, before returning to Japan, we had one more stop to make.

We left the Gulf of Siam, transited the South China Sea, and arrived in Subic Bay on the morning of December 12 for five days of liberty.

First stop—Florida Club, Magsaysay Drive, Olongapo City—Lite Weight, Lenny, Brian, and I were ready to party.

As we approached the front entrance of the club, we could feel the pounding of the hard rocking music. It was evening now and beginning to get crowed. The bikini-clad dancing girls were up on their pedestals, looking out over the crowd, grinding away to the rocking beat. Other girls were winding their way through the tables,

"Buy me drink? Buy me drink?" After we grabbed an empty table, it didn't take long for the girls to begin hovering. Our waitress got us started, "Mojo, for everyone!"

Mojo was the specialty alcoholic drink of Olongapo, usually served in a pitcher, but not always cold. The recipe insured it wouldn't take much before you were shit-faced drunk! We all poured cups of it and drank it up, round after round.

Many young girls came to the Subic Bay area from all over the Philippines—especially when carriers were scheduled to be in port—with hopes of meeting a nice, American sailor to marry and take her to the States. It was often joked that they seemed to know our schedule better than we did.

There were plenty of girls here tonight and we were in no hurry. Girls would come by and hang out with us for a while. If we didn't like them, we'd send them on their way. If we liked them, they could stay. It was like a beehive in there and money was the honey. Sometimes we wondered who was really getting taken, us or them?

After a couple of hours, we all had a pretty good buzz on. We agreed to was time to move on.

"All right girls, let's go," said Lenny, standing up to leave.

After exchanging money with the mama-san who ran the operation, we all headed for the door, girls in tow.

Arriving at a nearby hotel, we got a few rooms and continued to party on.

The next morning, we all were asking for the aspirin.

At breakfast we discussed what to do next and decided to take a journey high up into the northern mountains of Luzon to Baguio City.

With an elevation of 5,000 feet, Baguio is much cooler and less humid than the rest of the Philippines, making it a favorite destination for vacationers looking to escape the oppressive heat of this tropical island nation. The Philippine presidential palace, known as *the Mansion*, is in Baguio.

The United States believed this cool mountain-top area would make a good rest and relaxation destination when in 1903 President Theodore Roosevelt signed an executive order to set aside land in Benguet Provence for a United States Military Reservation. The reservation was named after Roosevelt's secretary of state, John

Milton Hay. Camp John Hay was developed into a major R and R station for personnel and dependents of the US armed forces as well as US Department of Defense employees and their dependents. It was currently managed by the US Air Force and was designated a communications station, as well as the broadcasting facility of *The Voice of America*. It seemed like a good place for us to spend a couple of days.

When traveling in the PI, it always helped to have a local guide. Maritess, Lite Weight's girl, volunteered to be ours and we gladly gave her the job.

The Victory Liner bus ride up to Baguio on the winding mountain roads was a little hairy, to say the least. The roads zigzagged back and forth all the way up into the mountains. When the bus approached oncoming traffic, it was a tight squeeze. All we could think of, looking out of the windows and past the edge of the road was that it sure was a long way down to the bottom. When we finally made it into town, we were worn out.

When the bus dropped us off at the terminal in the center of Baguio, it was chaos, with people coming and going in every direction. We walked through a large, open-air street-side shopping area and hailed a cab. Maritess had the driver take us on a tour around town to see a few of the highlights.

We also learned a little of the history of the area during out tour.

Camp John Hay was one of the first places bombed by the Japanese in World War II. At 0819 on December 8, 1941 (December 7 on the Hawaii side of the International Date Line) seventeen Japanese bombers attacked Camp John Hay, killing eleven American and Filipino soldiers.

During the Japanese occupation, General Tomoyuki Yamashita used the base as his headquarters and official residence.

On September 3, 1945, Yamashita surrendered to General Jonathan Wainwright as British General Arthur Percival stood as witness. These two generals were both previously defeated by Yamashita in the early days of the war.

Our driver pulled the cab over to the side of the road, right in front of a huge, gated entrance to what looked like a large, royal estate home and grounds. On the stone entrance column was attached a brass sign which simply read *The Mansion.*

It turned out, this really was a mansion, the home of President Ferdinand Marcos. This huge home with its palatial grounds was built in 1940 by the United States as the summer home for the US ambassador to the Philippines and his family. It was later turned over to the president of the Philippines and was now used by Ferdinand and Imelda Marcos, well known for their lavish spending, as a summer home.

We snapped a few pictures, and peering through the Buckingham Palace-style gates, joked about what it would be like to be that rich.

From there we drove over to our destination: US Air Force Base Camp John Hay.

As we toured the base, it reminded me of a mountain state park. On the base there were roughly 290 fully furnished rooms in different cottages, duplexes, apartments, and lodges spread out in different locations around the grounds. There was an eighteen-hole golf course, complete with clubhouse, restaurants, a bowling alley, ball fields, hiking trails through tall pine trees, and an amphitheater.

The most interesting experience for me during our visit to Camp John Hay was the time we spent touring the Cemetery of Negativism.

Unlike other traditional cemeteries, the dead are not buried here. Nestled in a beautiful pine forest is this burial place of negative thoughts. This is a place where all negative thoughts, pessimistic attitudes, depressing emotions, and all impediments to achieving your ambitions can be buried. It has become known as the resting place of *Negativism that has become mankind's self-imposed restriction, his most limiting factor, his heaviest burden.*

As we walked along the cemetery's path, we read the epitaphs inscribed on each of the tombstones. They were funny, yet inspiring:

KANTOU NUTHIN WRIGHT
Born: Dec. 5, 1905
Died: June 14, 1903

WHY DIDENT I?
Born: ?????
Lived Wondering Why
Died For No Reason

LETZ STUDY IT
Delayed Birth
Step Childhood
Never Reached Maturity.

KANT B. DONE
Born January 2, 1904
Died January 1, 1904
Died Before He Started.

UHAFTO OR ELSE
Born of Intimidation
Lived in Resentment
Died Without Fame

There were many tombstones along the path, and they all had a message. During his time as base commander, Major John Hightower was looking for a way to help his soldiers understand that negative thoughts can be unproductive and limit their potential. He asked them to gather all these thoughts and "bury them on that little hill."

There are about fifteen tombstones, each with a saying and a small figure on top. Many of the figures look like small animals.

After spending the night in the lodge, we returned the next day to Subic Bay and the *Midway*. That was a fun port visit, and we all had an adventure we would never forget. The experience that stayed with me most was the cemetery. After reading each of the stones, I believe I was successful in burying any negativism I may have previously possessed there at Camp John Hay.

The words on the sign at exit of the cemetery remain etched in my memory:

Have a good day!
Treat today like it's your last
Though it's the first of the rest—CJH

———————

On the morning of December 17, we said goodbye to Subic and headed once again for open ocean, which is where the *Midway* was meant to be.

This time we had a "cargo" that was most unusual to me.

A large section of the hanger bay was roped off and stacked high with all sorts of furniture and boxes. Apparently, while we were out sightseeing many of our shipmates were out buying furniture to take back home to Japan. With Christmas Eve just one week away, it wasn't difficult to guess what many wives and girlfriends would be receiving this year on Christmas morning. Handmade furniture made from wicker, bamboo, and inlaid wood, shell lamps, wooden salad bowls, woodcarvings, and all sorts of Philippine specialty items were being brought back, duty free.

Our cruise back to Yoko went quickly. We kept busy with our routine of flight operations, battle station, drills and my nights working on the aft mess deck.

We arrived back in Yokosuka early on the morning of December 23, an anniversary for me. It was now one year to the day since I had arrived in Japan and began my tour of sea duty aboard *Midway*.

This was the beginning of a three-week in-port period for the holidays. Lenny left for his home in the States, to be processed out of active duty and return to civilian life. My other shipmates were busy preparing for Christmas and unpacking their cargo and souvenirs from the PI. Meanwhile, I had a cargo of my own to get busy with. Of course, I had no trouble unloading the sticks. Lenny had the best Christmas ever and continued to receive *mailbox money* from me straight through into the new year.

CHAPTER TWELVE
A&O SHOP

OUR IN-PORT WORK ROUTINE was fairly lax during the Christmas holidays. The ship seemed to have more SRF workers onboard than sailors most of the time. Day and night there were the normal sounds of grinding, welding, hammering, and forklifts running about. There was always repair and upkeep work going on in port. It took a lot of man-hours and materials to keep the old girl in top shape. We all worked seven days a week out at sea and enjoyed turning her over to the *yard birds* while in Yoko.

One evening I got dressed in my *mess crank's uniform* of white pants and white *Midway Magic* T-shirt then proceeded to the aft mess deck to start my shift.

When I arrived to check in with Wolfman, he said, "Dorgan, you're done here. Your time's up. Back to E Division for you."

"Excellent!" I said, as I turned to walk away with a spring in my step.

The following day, I checked in at 0800 to the E Division office for my next workshop assignment.

By now, I knew my way around well and had made many friends.

E Division had six workshops staffed with electricians. I did not want safety shop, repairing power tools and battle lanterns all day. Repairing lights and replacing light bulbs as a lighting shop electrician didn't sound like much fun either. Power shop—I had been there, done that. I definitely did not want distribution shop, crawling around below the water line in the heat of the main propulsion machinery spaces and not seeing daylight for days. No way!

That only left two other shops, flight deck lighting and aviation and ordinance electrical workshop. Flight deck lighting involved changing light bulbs on the mast, catwalks, and flight deck. I would get to move around a lot more and get plenty of fresh air. It wasn't a bad option.

"Dorgan, report to A&O Shop," said Senior Chief Stevens.

"Excellent! Just what I wanted! I thought.

Trying not to smile, I said, "Thank you, Senior Chief," turned, and walked out of the office as quickly as I could before anyone in the E Division office could make an objection to the Senior Chief, influencing him to change his mind.

Now A&O Shop was the farthest electrical workshop from our berthing compartment but that was okay with me. Located on the starboard side 02 level, all the way aft and just below the flight deck, it was well hidden away. Across from our shop door was the V-4 berthing compartment. Those guys, the purple shirts, worked shifts around the clock dealing with aviation fuel, so their berthing was always dark and quiet.

The A&O workshop was divided into two compartments—the front half and the back half. The two compartments were separated by a watertight door. The back compartment had a round watertight emergency escape hatch about two feet across. The hatch led out to the motor whaleboat winch room and through to another passageway. In other words, we had a back door in case of emergency.

The front of the shop housed our personal lockers for our tools and gear, a workbench, and our job assignment board. In the back section was another workbench, a spare parts cabinet, and the shop supervisor's desk.

Our shop supervisor was Chief Lay. Chief had served at quite a few duty stations over the years and was getting to be a short timer on the *Midway*. He was a quiet, no-nonsense sort of fellow with a medium build and a reseeding hairline. He always showed up in his kaki uniform. After handing out the day's work assignments, nobody really saw much of the chief, unless you went down to the Chief's Mess. He seemed to keep a low profile.

EM1 Dunca had been transferred from Power Shop up to A&O. That was fine with me. We always got along well in the past.

EM2 Elmer was our second-class petty officer. A Filipino guy, he was soft-spoken but knew his stuff.

In addition to those three, there were seven of us, ranging from fireman apprentice to third class petty officers, responsible for getting the job done.

A couple of days after checking into the shop, Dunca issued me a new at-sea work uniform so I would be prepared next time we got underway. Four pairs of green fatigue pants and four long-sleeve apple-green turtleneck flight-deck shirts.

We wore blue dungarees in port and green flight-deck uniforms at sea.

I was excited about my new assignment and actually looking forward to getting underway again. Soon I would be on the *roof* where the action was. The aircraft were the reason we were all here.

The days before we went back to sea passed quickly. Once the word was out that I was the man with the Thai stick, I was soon collecting wads of cash. There were several buddies from different departments of the ship who would come see me. I'd give them bundles of sticks. They would give me bundles of cash. I'm sure they were getting a markup, but I didn't care as long as they took them off my hands. It was a risky business, so I only dealt with a select few shipmates I had known for a while, trusted, and who also kept a low profile.

Suddenly there was a new problem: what to do with all the cash? It would be difficult to explain if my locker were ever searched and big envelopes of cash were found packed in there.

As the task of learning the locations of all the equipment under the responsibility of A&O Shop began, I soon realized some great hiding places for those envelopes of cash. There were so many electrical connection boxes mounted on bulkheads in clear sight along passageways that no one paid any attention to and never opened. Perfect!

They say, *"Don't keep all your eggs in one basket.* Well, I didn't.

I'd walk around the ship with my tool belt on, unscrew the cover of a box, slip an envelope of cash in it, close it up, and head on to the next one. Clean and dry, just like money in the bank. My toughest challenge was to keep track of where it all was.

January 11 came along and once again it was time to head to sea. The Japanese winter had so far been cold, damp, and rainy. We were all looking forward to heading south to the Okinawa operational area for warmer weather and our next port of call, Hong Kong.

Along with my new flight-deck work uniform, I was issued an olive drab insulated field jacket. On the back, in big black letters was stenciled *E DIVISION*. Since A&O Shop was now my new sea and anchor detail station, I was glad to have it on when we made it out to the open sea from Tokyo Bay.

This cruise began my hands-on training on the responsibilities of our shop.

As a segment of the ship's Engineering Department, we were responsible for pretty much all of the ship's equipment that serviced the air wing, including; the three deck-edge aircraft elevators and stanchions, weapons elevators and conveyors (which transported bombs from lower decks to flight deck.), hanger bay divisional doors, deck-edge elevator doors, AFFF high-capacity fire fighting stations, JP-5 fueling pump stations (as well as the huge fuel pumps all the way down in the pump rooms that pumped fuel up to the flight deck), motor whale boat winch, forward and aft liquid oxygen and nitrogen production plants, and my least favorite—the aircraft electrical starting stations and aircraft electrical cables (AESS).

The equipment ran smoothly most of the time due to the many hours we spent performing routine preventative maintenance (PMS). However, when the equipment did stop working, it was our responsibility to get it up and running again immediately. Nothing was to stand in the way of flight operations. Nothing!

We electricians of A&O Shop did not operate the equipment, although we knew how. We were the ones called on by the operators to repair the equipment when it broke down. Which brings me back to the AESS Cables.

Our first day at sea after being in port for the Christmas holidays was primarily a *recovery day*. The aircraft of the air wing were returning to *Midway* from Atsugi Naval Air Station.

One after another, each plane lined up in the air at an angle behind the *Midway* for their landing approach, their opportunity to touch down and catch one of the three arresting cables, jerking the plane to a complete stop in three seconds. Or, if their alignment did not look just right, they would be waived off by the landing signal officer (LSO) near the Fresnel lens, and full throttle the aircraft straight off the angle deck and circle around for another attempt.

In A&O Shop, located just below the flight deck at the ramp, we could hear every plane as they passed just above us, descending to the deck. *Screech—bam! Screech—bam! Screech—bam!*

Eventually, all the Carrier Air Wing Five aircraft landed safely back on board. Soon, it would be time to begin what seemed like our never-ending day and night cycle of flight ops.

One of the first A&O Shop repair calls we received back at sea that day was to repair an Aircraft Electrical Service Station (AESS) cable head. All the way around the flight deck, in the catwalks, strategically spaced apart, are AESS cables, coiled up on racks and ready for use. These are like heavy-duty extension cords, about an inch wide and fifty feet or so long. At one end they are attached to an electrical control box mounted in the catwalk. On the other end is a large, rectangular rubber head, which plugs into the aircraft to provide 400-Hertz electrical power to the plane during startup and maintenance.

These cables take a beating daily on the flight deck. Exposed to the weather, saltwater spray, and constant use, it is no wonder they are regularly in need of repair. The most common problem is that the little round metal inserts in the cable head come out. The result is no electricity to the aircraft when plugged in. That's when the A&O Shop is contacted and someone is sent out right away.

Generally, in A&O we always practiced the buddy system. We worked in teams for two reasons: first, because two heads are better than one when solving a problem. Second, for safety.

Sure enough, the next day it was time for my first call to repair duty on the flight deck during flight operations.

I was partnered up with EM3 Sweeney. I knew Sweeney from the motorcycle club and the Hayama house. He was a sharp electrician and seemed to know his stuff.

"Hey, Bob, grab your tools, float coat, and muffs. We've got some cable heads to fix on deck," Sweeney called out to me from the other side of the shop where he was gathering up some inserts.

Whenever we went on deck during flight ops, we wore inflatable green life vests with reflective patches on the front and back. The vest was complete with two small compressed-air cartridges that could be activated to fill the vest with air immediately, if the wearer happened to find himself floating in the ocean after surviving a fall from the flight deck.

In addition, we wore a cranial helmet with earmuff hearing protection and goggles.

With hearing protection on, it was especially important to keep a watchful eye for any aircraft activity going on—in *any* direction.

"Let's start at the bow in the port catwalk and work our way back," said Sweeney.

"I'll follow you," I replied.

We left the shop and headed down to the hanger bay level. Weaving our way through the aircraft in the now-full bay, we soon found ourselves all the way forward. We took the stairs on the port side up to the 02-level.

I opened the door to the catwalk, stepped out and stood up. WOOSH!

The shadow of the F-4 Phantom's wing blocked out the sunlight as it passed just above my head, the roar of its jet engines deafening. I choked as I inhaled the hot jet exhaust rolling off from the flight deck above to me. Looking back toward the bow, I could see the F-4, by now soaring up in the air, steam rolling back toward me in a cloud from the track of the just-fired catapult.

Wow! I thought, *Now, that was exciting!*

Turning around, I saw Sweeney had come out to the catwalk and was standing behind me.

"You've got to keep your head down out here!" he yelled.

We first looked around to see there were no more aircraft approaching the catapults, then walked forward along the catwalk to the first AESS station on our list for repair.

After completing repair to the cable head, we climbed the short stairway to the flight deck from the catwalk and walked aft toward the angle deck. All kinds of activity was going on. Flight deck crew, all with different jobs, were coming and going in every direction. Yellow shirts, blue shirts, brown shirts, purple shirts, red shirts—everyone with a job to do between launch and recovery cycles.

My main focus was following Sweeney to the next AESS station, keeping my eyes open in every direction and making sure I didn't have any more surprises.

Just as we completed our last cable head, the voice of the air boss barked out over the loudspeaker, "Clear the flight deck!"

Walking toward the aft starboard catwalk, we could see in the sky just behind the destroyer escort following us, two aircraft turning in to the landing approach pattern. We scurried through the catwalk doorway just before the first plane hooked a cable.

One of the benefits of working in A&O, along with the added excitement, was an addition to our paycheck—flight deck pay. Fifty-five dollars per month. It was not a lot of money, and it was in no way proportional to the additional danger a sailor is exposed while on the job on the flight deck, but I sure wasn't going to turn it down.

In addition to my assignment to the A&O Shop working all hours of the day and night, I was back again on four and eights switchboard watch. Apparently, my performance was satisfactory under supervision at Two Board. I was now assigned to Three Board to stand switchboard watch alone.

Three Board was a quiet, out of the way board to stand watch. It was a long narrow room with circuit breakers on each side of the aisle that led through the center of the room. There was an entrance door on the aft side of the room and a door on the forward side of the room across from the switchboard that led down to the generator room. There was a constant hum in the space from the electricity passing through the circuit breakers, just like Two Board.

Not many people ever popped into Three Board unexpectedly, except the machinist mates who worked in the generator room directly below. Generally, nobody noticed if I caught a few z's on the mid-watch on Three Board.

Occasionally, there were visitors stopping by for a while to shoot the shit. Sometimes they would surprise me with a joint to smoke and then they would be on their way, leaving me there to contemplate the universe.

On January 16, while en route to Hong Kong, Master Chief Carney, *Midway*'s senior command career counselor, was presented the Golden Anchor Award by Vice Admiral Coogan. This award is given to the ship with the highest sustained retention rate in the Pacific Fleet. At the same time, thousands of miles away, militant followers of the Ayatollah Khomeini were in the process of overthrowing the Iranian government and Shah Mohammad Reza Pahlavi. Khomeini, who was exiled from Iran in 1963, was fanning the flames of anti-Americanism, beginning with the youth of Iran.

The shah of Iran had fled to Egypt and relations with the United States were becoming tense. The political climate was changing in the Middle East but most of us had no idea of how it would affect our future. We were more concerned with the good times we were planning for our upcoming liberty.

I was finding out that, while most of us bitched about being onboard *Midway* and the working conditions, many sailors requested to extend their tour when their time came up to transfer. So far, I was happy with the way things were going and how far I had come from the same time the year before. Shit, I was planning to buy a brand-new motorcycle when we returned to Japan!

CHAPTER THIRTEEN
HONG KONG

EARLY ON THE MORNING of January 18, we made our way northwest through Lamma Channel and into Victoria Harbor, which separates Hong Kong Island from Kowloon.

After coming to a stop in the bay, we dropped anchor and the members of the special sea and anchor detail prepared for our five-day visit. Since we were not steaming and conducting flight ops, we could shut down several boilers and generators, allowing us to operate on a smaller four-section duty crew.

The previous day, representatives from Hong Kong were flown aboard to bring us some information in preparation for our visit.

We were all presented with little card that read: *H is for HEROIN.* This warning was that heroin was strong in Hong Kong and we were told to stay away from it. It reminded me of the 1969 Woodstock warning: *Stay away from the brown acid.*

This time, I was not disappointed to have duty the first day. Since we were anchored out, once again, the only way to get to the beach was by liberty boat. Yes, the line to go ashore was long and everyone seemed anxious to get there.

At lunch on the aft mess deck, I ran into one of my "delivery buddies," Pic. Pic was a radioman from Communications Division. He spent most of his hours working in the cool, air-conditioned communications rooms on the 02 level, clean work. Those guys went through a lot of my Thai sticks, too.

We set our trays down at a table and pulled up a couple of chairs.

"Hey Pic, are you going out tomorrow?" I asked.

"Yeah, you?" he replied.

"Yeah, you got any ideas on what to see?" I continued.

"Well, there are some sightseeing spots in Hong Kong, but they say the best bars and hot spots are in Kowloon," Pic replied.

We finished lunch and agreed we would meet up in the hanger bay in the morning to take the boat in to the pier at Hong Kong.

———————

At 0800 the next day we were off duty and ready for an adventure. The liberty line in the hanger bay was not too bad that morning. We waited about forty-five minutes for our turn to climb down to board the little boat. Soon we were on our way through the dampness of the morning fog and the light chop of Victoria Bay.

As we approached Hong Kong Island, we could see the base of the island, down to the waterline, was covered with thousands of buildings, large and small, short and tall. Behind the buildings, the island's green mountains stretched high up into the clouds.

Looking around the bay, there were many boats of various sizes moving in every direction. It was easy to tell this was one of the world's largest trading ports.

After arriving at the pier, we walked up the ramp and out into the hustle and bustle of the city.

Numerous cabs waited nearby, knowing there would be plenty of American sailors looking for a ride and paying with American dollars.

We jumped into a cab.

"Can you take us to Tiger Balm Gardens?" Pic asked the driver.

"Sure. I take you," replied the cabby.

The cabby jockeyed through the traffic east along the bay and up the mountain a ways before stopping to let us off at our destination. We paid the man, thanked him, and sent him on his way.

Located in the Wan Chai District and surrounded by tall buildings, Tiger Balm Gardens was a most unusual tourist destination.

The park was created in 1935 by brothers Aw Boon Haw and

Aw Boon Par, who made their fortune from the sale of the popular curative balm. At a cost of sixteen million Hong Kong dollars, the almost seven-acre site is a grotesque and surrealistic conglomeration of colorful concrete animals, pagodas, religious figures, and numerous other garish objects. The gardens are a gaudy version of what some have called a Chinese Disneyland.

We paid our entrance fee and entered through the gates to the hillside fantasyland. There were all sorts of bizarre statues and dioramas depicting scenes from Chinese folklore, legends, history, and illustrations of various aspects of Confucianism.

At the age of nineteen, not knowing much about Chinese folklore or legend, most of the strange scenes did not mean much to us, except that the goriness of it all was something we would never forget.

Towering high above the park was a seven-story Tiger Pagoda, the only one of its kind in the huge city.

After snapping a few photos and getting our fill of decapitated and gored bodies, we exited the park, hailing a cab to take us to our next destination.

Hunger was on our minds now, so we stopped into a small restaurant near the waterfront. When in Hong Kong, why not try the sweet and sour pork on white rice? Yes, it was excellent!

"Hey Bob, have you seen the James Bond movie, *The Man with the Golden Gun*? Asked Pic.

"No," I replied curiously.

"Let's go across the bay to Kowloon and see if we can find the night club where they filmed some of the movie. It's called the Bottoms Up Club," Pic continued.

"Sounds good to me," I said.

We walked to the waterfront terminal of the Star Ferry service, which shuttled thousands of people across Victoria Harbor daily.

By now it was late in the afternoon and hundreds of other people were also entering the terminal for their trip across the bay. The boarding process was an unforgettable experience.

After purchasing our tickets, we filed into the terminal ramp holding area. Passengers were being assembled in groups of about a hundred or so. There was a waist-high rope stretched from wall to wall across the forty-foot waiting area. There was another group in front of us with about the same number of people and another group in front of them.

Each time the group in front of us moved forward, our rope would be dropped and we all shuffled forward until we came to the next barrier, then we all stopped again and waited.

"Looks like the Pavlov's dog experiment to me," commented Pic.

This stopping and starting went on and on until we finally turned a corner, narrowed down, and boarded the iconic green and white double-decker ferry boat.

The ferry ride across the bay went quickly and we were glad. Between the cramped space we shared with all the other Chinese commuters and the strong smell of diesel fumes coming from the engine, we were anxious for this ride to come to an end.

Back on dry land, we asked a cabby to take us to the Bottoms Up Club. He dropped us off right in front. The sign over the door made it easy to identify the club, as it was one of the only signs in English.

We walked down a short set of steps to the lower-level nightclub. Inside were five separate round bars. In the center of each bar, on a bar level cushioned pedestal, there sat a half-naked woman. We ordered a couple of beers and took in the scenery.

A couple of beers later, after becoming mesmerized watching our hostess serving drinks around and on the other side of the bar, we realized she did have a face. She was a full-busted English redhead. She didn't seem shy at all as she leaned over on her knees to serve her patrons.

"Hey, Pic," I heard a voice call out above the music and the noise of the bar as two of Pic's radioman buddies walked up.

"We're going up the street to a tattoo parlor to get a couple of tats. You coming?" said one.

Next thing I knew, we were outside walking down the street, looking for a tattoo parlor in the middle of the night in Kowloon, China.

We found a sign pointing to a stairway leading to a second-story tattoo parlor. When we got upstairs, the artist was more than happy to let us in. He offered us a seat in a little lobby area with a couch and a couple of chairs. Our host returned shortly with a cold beer for each of us.

Pic and his buddies seemed much more excited than I was as

they paged through the three-ring binders of pictures of tattoos to choose from—samples of the artist's work.

The first guy got in the chair and pointed to a photo in the binder. "Can you do this one for me, right here?" as he pointed to his left arm.

With a huge grin the little Chinese man nodded as he replied, "Can do, can do."

A moment later, another short Chinese man entered the room from a back door, ready to go to work on the next victim.

"What kind of tat are you getting, Bob?" Pic turned to me and asked.

"I don't think I need one," I replied.

"Look, they have plenty here to choose from. They'll custom make one for you, if you don't see anything you like," Pic pleaded.

"No. I think I'll head back to the boat." And just like that I found myself walking down the dimly lit little stairway and out into the street, hailing a cab to take me to the Star Ferry terminal.

Back in my rack in E Division berthing, as I closed my eyes to sleep long after midnight, I thought, *Which tattoo would I have picked?*

———————

On the morning of January 23, we raised anchor and steamed south out of Victoria Harbor for our next destination, the Philippines.

This cruise was probably the shortest cruise of my naval career. Within forty-eight hours of departing Hong Kong, we had sailed all the way across the South China Sea and arrived in Subic Bay. By 0900 on the morning of the twenty-fifth, *Midway* was tied up to the pier and ready for liberty call, the beginning of our nine-day visit.

We were standing four-section duty, which meant this visit really would be a good R and R break in the tropics. Besides the nightclubs and duty-free shopping in Olongapo, the base really did have many activities available.

My favorite hangout became Dungaree Beach also known as Ski Beach.

Across the bay from the main naval base was Cubi Point, an airfield where carrier air wing squadrons would often land while aircraft carriers were tied up to the pier. At the far end of the airfield, the south side, was a nice, wide sandy beach on a small inlet from the bay. The beach had an area with covered picnic table areas and charcoal grills for anyone to use. Hidden from the winds of the open bay, the waters were not as choppy and made for good waterskiing.

At the water recreation pier on Cubi Point, waterskiing boats were available for rent, complete with a driver. The center provided all the equipment too: skis, lifejackets, and anything else you needed.

Dungaree Beach was a great cookout and party destination. Groups of us would head over there for the day and stay till late. We all had our assignments. Some would bring coolers with beer. Some would bring coolers with meats and stuff to grill and other food. You name it, we brought it, and of course, there was never any shortage of girls willing to be our guests on base for a fun time.

Having worked at a YMCA summer camp on the Chesapeake Bay teaching waterskiing as a teenager, of course I choose the job of going to get the ski boat and equipment. I made it a point to time it so when I showed up at the beach in the boat, everyone else had already arrived with the supplies. The beer was cold, and the grill and the girls were hot!

This was our "spring break" party time, and it was only January of 1979. It was looking to be a very good year!

––––––––––––––

On the morning of February 3, we heaved a heavy sigh as we waived goodbye to Subic Bay once again. After steaming north to the Okinawa Operational Area, we then spent the next seventeen days participating in Multiplex 2-79. This multi-threat exercise was designed to test the *Midway* Battle Group's ability to defend itself against coordinated surface, sub-surface, and air attacks.

During one exercise, WasEx 2-79, the USS *Oklahoma City* was successfully located, identified, and targeted by an E-2B for a thirteen-plane strike on the carrier group flagship.

In DamEx, a massive air combat maneuvering exercise pitted *Midway* F-4J's against Navy and Marine Corps aircraft from Okinawa.

During the exercises in the Okinawa area, a large percentage of the aircraft recoveries were at night, with the largest emergency-condition recovery totaling twenty-two aircraft. In other words, the flight deck was hopping during this cruise and we in A&O had plenty to do twenty-four seven. At least the weather was comfortable.

Arriving back in Yokosuka on the morning of February 20, many of us still sported our dark suntan from nine days in Subic, even though it was the middle of the cold, damp Japanese winter.

CHAPTER FOURTEEN
ZUSHI

With Lenny gone and no longer in control of things, the Hayama house was getting to be too crowded. Seems like everyone had found out it was a hot spot. Too many people were stopping by to party then crashing for the night. There was also too much bickering about who was paying for what.

Pic and I decided we would go in together on a rental, but we did not want to stay in Hayama. We ended up renting a house in the beachfront town of Zushi, just a few miles away.

Zushi turned out to be a great choice. Located on the Sagami Bay, between Hayama and Kamikura (the home of the Great Buddha), Zushi had a much larger beach than Hayama. In addition, there was a large, shopping district downtown, near the train station.

Since neither one of us had a car or motorcycle at the time, the train station, just a short walk from our doorstep, was a big plus. Taxicabs and busses were available at the train station too. We could board the commuter train at Zushi in the morning and arrive at the Yokosuka train station in just minutes, then take a cab to the main gate and arrive on time for 0800 morning muster aboard *Midway*.

Our new pad was modest. There was a small kitchen, dining room, toilet room, tub and shower room and two main rooms that doubled as bedrooms at night. I took the bigger room. Pic got the smaller room. You had to walk through Pic's room to get from the kitchen to the tub room.

Outside was a fenced patio area, with a gated entrance at each end.

We did not have any furniture, so suddenly shopping was on our minds. "Time to spend some of that sea pay we've been saving up!" I said to Pic. And shop we did!

The first thing I did was go to the Navy Exchange and buy a brand new 1979 black and chrome Yamaha 750 Special with shaft drive.

Next, we borrowed a pickup truck and loaded it up with furniture, area rugs, dishware, linens, and a shitload of stereo equipment. We filled that place up, added some groceries and beer and settled in right nice.

Driving a motorcycle in Japan can be much more challenging than one might expect. To receive a license to drive my new bike off base, the first requirement is to drive on *base only* for one month. Seeing the logic in this policy, there was no disagreement from me when issued my learner's permit. (In early '78 I had received a regular driver's license to drive in Japan, on or off base.)

During this training period, I kept my bike at the motorcycle club and drove it on base daily. For the meantime, Pic and I continued to ride the train back and forth to Zushi.

Being late February, there was not much exciting relating to beach life in Zushi, but we knew we would be ready when summer arrived.

———————

February 26, we departed Yokosuka once again and spent three days en route to the East China Sea. From there, we spent the next seventeen days participating in Team Spirit 1979. This was to be the largest coordinated US forces annual combat exercise in the Pacific Theatre. USN, USA, and USAF units combined with South Korean forces to defend South Korea against a multi-threat scenario.

During this cruise, real world Soviet, Chinese, and Vietnamese tensions were mounting and Soviet surveillance flights in the area increased. Our *Midway* aircraft logged in multiple intercepts on eight Bears and fifteen Badgers during this exercise while operating in the East China Sea and the Sea of Japan.

After leaving the bitter cold of the Sea of Japan, we arrived back in Yoko on the morning of March 18. There were just four days of winter left. We were all anxiously looking forward to spring.

———————

The next three weeks passed quickly with a mix of work and play. On March 21 the USO entertained us.

March 22 Rear Admiral Holcomb presented Captain Brown the Commander, Naval Air Forces Pacific Battle "E" Award. This highly coveted award cited *Midway's* excellence as the top performing aircraft carrier of the Seventh Fleet for the eighteen-month period ending December 31, 1978.

March was a busy time for receiving guests aboard *Midway*. On the 31st, Girl Scouts from local American and Japanese troops toured the ship. They even brought cookies.

During March, I received my official motorcycle driver's license. That's right. I was now street legal to drive anywhere in Japan. Let the fun begin!

I had all the gear needed for any weather: two helmets, rain gear, leather boots, leather jackets from Korea, and gloves. Each day, leaving the main gate, I explored different roads and discovered many scenic ways to get across Miura Peninsula, home, and back. What a great a new sense of freedom!

It was the first week of April, the famous cherry blossom season in Japan. Spring had sprung, as they say.

After almost three weeks in port, we had all settled into a comfortable routine.

There is an old saying, *When things are going well, get ready, they are going to change.*

———————

On the morning of April 6, I rode my bike from home and parked it over by the SRF shed on the pier, across from the *Midway*. Usually, I just locked my helmets to the side lock of the bike and today was no different.

As I approached the after brow leading up from the pier to the hanger bay level, I noticed there seemed to be an unusually increased amount of activity going on around me for a Friday morning. Usually, by Friday the tempo was slacking off. Not today.

Turning to the left after stepping aboard and into the hanger bay, I headed up the long stairway to A&O Shop. I figured I'd change to my work dungarees in the back of the shop and be ready for 0800 muster.

When I stepped into the shop I was met by the solemn, unhappy faces of my workshop buddies.

"Hey Dorgan, have you heard the word?" Sweeney asked.

"What word?" I replied, puzzled.

"We're headed to the IO, shipmates, and I'm getting my shillelagh ready for all you slimy wogs!" blurted out EM3 Rat, "You pollywogs are gonna wog-way for me, arrr!"

Just then Chief Lay stepped in through the shop doorway. The room got so quiet you could hear the clock on the wall tick.

"Well fellas, I guess you've heard the news by now," the chief started out. "Yesterday the *Ranger,* on her way to the Indian Ocean, collided with an oil tanker in the Straits of Malacca. She sustained substantial bow damage and is headed to Subic for a temporary fix before steaming up here to use our dry dock for repairs and we're going to take her place in the IO, relieving the *Connie.*"

The shop seemed to fill with a mixture of excitement, depression, and confusion.

"When are we leaving, Chief?" was the next question.

Tomorrow morning, 0900," Chief replied.

A hush came over the room. Nobody was ready for that.

"Get your gear in order and be sure you're back on board, ready to get underway in the morning," the chief said. "No missing ship's movement or you'll be in the brig."

We were all stunned.

I had just paid my rent. Now I would have to go home and pay my landlord at least another two months rent in advance. The least of my concerns was the money. I just wasn't ready to go out to sea again. My routine was just getting comfortable: go aboard in the morning, muster, work a little, go eat lunch with my buddies on base, skate the afternoon away, then leave early. It was good duty. We weren't at sea.

Fall of 1976 Valley Forge Military Academy.

Boot Camp RTC Great Lakes Circa 1977 USN.

Underway Replenishment. USN

"Wog Washdown" Elevator One. Circa 1979.

"Approach" USS Midway CV-41 Courtesy of Curley Culp, Pilot VF-161.

Bob Dorgan forward catwalk USS Midway. Circa 1979.

"Shit River Bridge" Olongapo, Philippines circa 1978.

"Been there—Done that, got the T shirt." IO Circe 1979.

GONZO STATION. USS Kitty Hawk CV-63, USS Midway CV-41,
USS Nimitz CVN-68 , 1980.

"Rogue Wave." Bill Purcell.

Aviation & Ordnance Shop Electricians circa 1980. IO.

Number one electrical switchboard. "JoJo" circa 1980.

Aftermath of collision with Freighter Cactus circa 1980 USN.

Aftermath of collision with Freighter Cactus circa 1980 USN.

Crew formation on the flight deck in Subic Bay,
following Cactus collision USN.

Cubi Point Airfield, US naval Station Subic Bay, Philippines circa 1980.

CHAPTER FIFTEEN
RANGER

THE SUN WAS NOT YET UP, when I called a cab to come pick me up at the motorcycle club. It was a dreary, cool, and damp morning. The fog from Tokyo Bay had drifted in thick around the two club buildings by the water. After my early morning ride in from Zushi, I had locked my bike in the garage next door, where it would await my return—whenever that would be.

We were headed to warm waters. Any ports we might have the opportunity to visit would certainly be tropical. I packed lightly. With my flight bag at my side, I was ready when the taxi arrived.

Saying goodbye to the clubhouse with one last glance, I climbed into the back seat of the taxi.

"*Midway* dozo," I told the old man behind the wheel.

"Ah so, *Midway* go to sea today," he said.

"Hai, *Midway* go to sea today, long time," I replied dishearteningly.

"Time fly," he said, smiling back at me.

With that, I also grinned and nodded. "Time fly."

By the time he dropped me off at the pier, the sky had turned a lighter shade of gray. Dawn was breaking.

It wasn't long before the rat guards had been removed, mooring lines cast off, and we were steaming out of Yokosuka Bay.

Heading south into the open ocean water, *Midway* left a wide white wake behind her, making a beeline for our next stop, Subic Bay, to take on supplies.

———

The report was, that at 0544 on April 5, 1979, in a dim, hazy predawn, the USS *Ranger* CV-61 (a 78,000-ton Forestal-class aircraft carrier) had collided with the Liberian flagged (Taiwanese owned) tanker *Fortune* near the eastern approach of the Straits of Malacca en route to Singapore. The *Ranger's* bow hit amidships of the tanker, opening the carrier's bow from the main deck down to the water line. The huge gash in the hull of the *Fortune* allowed 10,000 tons of crude oil to spill into the South China Sea. There were no injuries aboard the *Ranger*. (However, the commanding officer, Captain Thomas Moore, was later relieved of duty.)

On the morning we were scheduled to arrive in Subic Bay, the plan was to take on supplies at the pier and leave for the IO four hours later. No liberty. No one would be allowed off the ship. This stop would be strictly business.

Nobody seemed to be very happy about the emergency cruise to relieve the *Constellation*, but we quickly fell back into our normal, at-sea routine.

———

That first afternoon out, I had the watch down at Three Board. After a couple of hours, the hatch popped open and in came Ski-bo.

"Wake up! No sleeping on watch!" he yelled.

"No sleeping here—that's for the mid-watch," I replied with a laugh.

Leaning up against the switchboard he said, "You know, this trip to the IO is going to be a long one, good time to make some serious money while at sea."

That fact wasn't news to me. When sailors are at sea, getting paid regularly and bored, it is amazing how much money someone will spend for a simple pleasure. In the past, I had been known to bring cases of instant cup ramen soup and boxes of freezer pops to sell while at sea. Even those simple pleasures bring a huge markup.

"What's on your mind Ski-bo?" I replied, with a grin.

He pulled up the box I had been using as a foot stool, sat down, and presented me with a plan. It was ballsy.

On the morning we pulled into Subic Bay for our four-hour replenishment stop, the sky was gray and overcast. We tied up to the carrier pier at Cubi Point. This became the first wrench in our plan. NAS Cubi Point was a long taxi ride to the main gate and would certainly eat up much of our precious time.

The pier crane set the forward brow to the hanger bay level and then the evolution of loading pallet after pallet of supplies began.

Ski-bo and I, dressed in our blue work dungarees with our cash strapped underneath, walked up to the officer on duty at the quarterdeck. We each had a large bag of trash slung over our shoulders.

"Permission to go ashore?" I asked the officer. "Trash duty."

"Permission granted," he replied.

Ski-bo, right behind me, did the same thing.

Walking down the brow, we spotted a dumpster about five hundred feet out to the right. After tossing out trash, we ducked behind a building and found a taxi on the other side, just off the main road.

"Can you take us over to the main Exchange?" Ski-bo asked the driver.

"Sure, let's go," The young Filipino driver replied with a smile.

We climbed in and off we went. The wind blowing through the open cab windows helped cool us from the heat of the humid day.

The blacktop road from Cubi to the main base is a smooth, flat drive as it follows along the bay. It is only a few miles but today, on our time schedule, it seemed to take forever.

Arriving at the main Exchange, we got out, paid the driver, and went inside.

The Subic Base Navy Exchange was a huge store. They carried everything from food to household goods. Our interest today was the men's clothing department.

We each bought a complete change of civilian clothes—shirt, pants, belt, and tennis shoes.

Next, we grabbed another cab outside to take us to the bowling alley. There we changed clothes and stored our uniforms in a locker of the men's locker room. Then it was off to the main gate.

As we walked up to the guard, we could see the Shit River Bridge and Olongapo on the other side. The smell of the river was particularly strong that day.

In our brand-new civilian clothes, we walked up to the Marine on duty at the gate. We showed him our military ID cards, as is customary when leaving or entering base.

The Marine looked at us both with a stern face and said, "No *Midway* sailors allowed off base today, no exceptions."

With that, we looked at each other dumbfounded then turned and walked back in the direction we had come from.

After we were out of earshot from the guard shack, we said to each other, "*Midway* sticker."

All the sailors assigned to the *Midway* had a small sticker on our ID cards next to our photo. Easy solution there, we peeled off the stickers and put them on the back of our ID cards.

We couldn't go back to the main gate and take a chance of being recognized, so we grabbed another cab and directed the driver to take us to the west gate. This gate area seemed to be less traveled by most sailors.

It worked. We held our ID cards up in front of the guard and he waived us ahead, no questions asked.

After walking over the bridge, Ski-bo stopped a trike driver and asked him to take us to Magsaysay Drive. We got in and held on. Those trike drivers are crazy!

About halfway down Magsaysay Drive he had the driver stop and let us off. We knew where we were going and how to get there. We just didn't know the street names, which was probably better anyway.

After taking a few wrong turns, we arrived at the front door of our PI connection, Edna. We knocked at the door. Ski-bo was a regular. She smiled at us both and welcomed us in.

Edna was a short middle-aged Filipina who had been around the block a time or two. She had a modest two-story house, not far from the main strip. She always had some working girls around who seemed to live with her.

After some small talk, she asked us, "What are you sailors looking for today?"

"Hash," we replied.

Smiling, she said, "How many slabs you want?"

"As many as we can carry under our clothes," Ski-bo replied. "And we need them fast, we don't have much time."

"Okay. I'll be back. You wait here with the girls. They'll take care of you." And with a nod of her head, she was gone.

We waited for what seemed like forever for Edna to return. Meanwhile, the girls served us a couple of beers and kept us entertained.

Finally, entering through a back room of the house, Edna returned carrying a full big brown heavy-duty paper shopping bag. Sitting down on the couch next to us, she reached into the bag and pulled out an eight-inch square by half-inch thick, dark brown slab of Pakistani hashish.

She handed us each a slab and said, "Now this is the good stuff!"

Then she cut off a small corner of one slab, put it in a pipe and handed it to us with a lighter. "Give it a try," she smiled.

We each took a hit and smiled back.

After paying Edna, we packed our slabs under our clothes and in our pants. We thanked her and headed out the door.

"Man, we've got to hurry," I said as we were huffing it along Magsaysay Drive toward the bridge over Shit River to the main gate.

We didn't have time now to go back the same way we came, so we had to chance it that the same guard who turned us away the first try, either wouldn't be there or wouldn't remember us.

As we approached the guard shack, we both looked for that guard. We didn't see him, so we kept right on moving. We presented our IDs to the guard on duty and he waived us in.

We were both stoned from the hash and the beers, but we kept focused on the plan and just keep moving forward.

The walk from the main gate to the bowling alley was about a block and a half and we were truckin'. Dashing into the locker room, we changed back into our dungarees, repacked our slabs, dumped our civilian clothes in the trash can and went back out front to grab another cab.

"Cubi Point as fast as you can and there's a big tip in it for you," I told the driver and he punched it.

As we rounded the bay, seeing *Midway* still pier-side, we both let out a sigh of relief.

Of course, the cabbie pulled right up in front of the ship. To our shock, there was now a full marching band on the pier playing away, loud and proud. People from the base were standing around waiving. There were two shipyard workers on the brow, bolting on the steel cable from the pier crane boom, preparing to lift it away.

We paid the driver, rolled out of the cab, and ran across the pier and straight up the forward officers' brow, almost knocking over the yard workers. My heart was beating so hard I could hear the blood pounding in my ears.

Today really was our lucky day. We had remembered on our return cab ride to put our *Midway* stickers back on the front of our ID cards. As we reached the top of the brow, we held up our ID cards to the officer on deck. He just smiled, shook his head, and waived us on.

We made our way to the nearest ladder and down to the second deck. Turning in to the first head we came to, Ski-bo said to me, "Here you take these. I'm supposed to be on watch."

Pulling out slabs of hash from under his clothes, he loaded me up then split. Next, I headed aft, down the starboard passageway to number two deck-edge elevator machinery room—one of my favorite and quiet hiding spots—to unload and store our goods.

By the time I returned up to the hanger bay, from my viewpoint looking out of the open elevator doors, there was open water on each side. Walking over to stand by the stanchions at the open doorway of elevator two, I noticed my heart was no longer racing. *Wow, we made it.* I thought. *The toughest part is out of the way. We'll have plenty of time during this cruise to divide and sell all the hash. We should wait a week or so before we get started, though.*

From the vibration of the ship, and the speed at which we were passing through the water, I was sure all four screws were turning, and fast. We were now sailing off into the sunset, destination: Indian Ocean.

CHAPTER SIXTEEN
INDIAN OCEAN

IT HAD BEEN ALMOST A WEEK since we departed Subic Bay. By now it was the normal day-to-day, twenty-four-seven routine of life at sea, but it was hot. Hot and humid. It was an inescapable heat throughout the day and night that I had never experienced before. Even the air-conditioned spaces did not seem to be cool anymore.

We all had to use more caution everywhere we walked. When decks and passageways were swabbed, they seemed to take forever to dry. There was so much humidity in the air, it was oppressive. It seemed to suck the energy out of everyone.

Salt tablets were issued during meals to help us keep from getting too dehydrated.

After transiting the Straits of Malacca without incident, we passed through the Bay of Bengal and entered the Indian Ocean.

———————

The morning of April 16 was another hot one, just like all the rest since we entered the Indian Ocean. It was a hazy gray day, without a hint of a breeze in the air. The sea was as smooth as glass when we approached the *Connie*.

The aircraft carrier USS *Constellation* (CV-64) had departed San Diego September 28, 1978. She and her battle group had been directed to the vicinity of the South China Sea in response to the internal crisis in Iran and because of vital US interests in the Arabian Gulf.

On January 16, 1979, the Shah of Iran departed his country for exile.

Due to the tension in Iran, all US Government dependents and nonessential American citizens were ordered to evacuate the country on January 30.

In response to the conflict between North and South Yemen, President Carter ordered the *Constellation* and her battle group to the Gulf of Aden on March 7.

Their relief delayed due to the *Ranger*'s collision; the *Connie*'s crew was happy to see us arriving on the horizon with the sunrise. Our last joint exercise was back in November '78. We would soon take over her duty station.

We cruised along side her at just a few knots while helicopters flew back and forth between the two massive flattops. Looking across the placid water, we could see daylight straight through the Connie's hanger bay doors, and the silhouettes of sailors walking forward and aft, even waiving to us. They were no doubt anxious to get back home to San Diego, with of course, a liberty stop in PI first.

After the helos completed their shuttle trips, the two carriers broke from their parallel course, *Connie* happily to the east and *Midway* to the west, onward in our mission toward the Gulf of Aden.

However, before we arrived on station in the Gulf of Aden, we did have one more evolution to complete.

Bang! Bang! Bang! "Get out of your racks you slimy pollywogs! Rise and shine, it's your special day!"

This is how our day began the morning of April 18. Today we would cross the equator. All of us first timers had a date to appear before King Neptune and his royal court—a day none of us would ever forget.

Lying in my rack, I could hear commotion and activity all around. Then the overhead florescent lights of our berthing compartment came on.

Again. Bang! Bang! Bang! "All you wogs get up and dressed. It's chow time!"

I checked my wristwatch it was only 0530. Someone was banging a trashcan lid with a broomstick, making the announcement all of us pollywogs had anticipated since we left Yoko back on April 7. This was the beginning of our shellback initiation.

Before I could even get out of my rack, there was Lite Weight, standing next to me.

"Let's go, wog! You're mine today, Dorgan!" he barked.

All around the compartment, there were shellbacks grabbing up pollywogs like it was a feeding frenzy.

"Come on, get dressed, it's time for breakfast, wog!" Lite Weight continued.

I opened my locker and got out the oldest pair of boot camp dungarees I could find and a white T shirt.

"Give me that shirt," Lite Weight barked.

After laying it down, flat on the deck, he spraypainted a big black P across the front, then flipped it over and did the same on the back. Just like that, I was branded for the day. . . *pollywog*.

After getting dressed in my uniform of the day, he then tied a rope around my waist with enough left over for him to hold on to as a leash. Then off we went, through the berthing compartment and up the port ladder toward the aft galley line, me on my hands and knees, and Lite Weight leading me like a dog.

Passing across the aft mess deck was wild. Shellbacks were dressed in all sorts of pirate-style garb—cutoff shorts, cut up shirts with skull and cross bones logos, striped shirts, head bandanas, eye-patches, you name it. It was chaotic!

Some shellbacks had sections of fire hoses cut in three-foot sections, *shillelaghs*, to smack the wogs on the ass with if we were not moving fast enough or not following orders.

Making our way to the galley was a challenge. The whole crew was swept up in the excitement of the day. There was food and slop all over the deck. Everywhere you looked there were wogs on their knees, licking their special breakfast off their round, disposable plates.

After waiting in line at the aft galley, it was my turn to stand up and be served my breakfast. I stuck my plate out in front of me for the mess cooks, standing on the other side, to load me up.

Splat: A scoop full of green spaghetti noodles.

Splat: A scoop full of stinky chitlins (cooked pig intestines).

Splat: A scoop full of green scrambled eggs.

That was enough for me. Following Lite Weight through the passageway toward the mess deck, I held my plate out straight in front of me thinking, *How am I going to get out of eating all this crap?*

When we arrived at the aft mess deck, Lite Weight noticed Elmo and Spencer with wogs of their own. They had just tied the leashes of their wogs to a pole, so we joined them. There we were, us three wogs on our knees, hands behind our backs, licking the breakfast off our plates, with the added harassment of a shillelagh across the ass from any shellback who happened by. Food was all over the place and a lot of it was a result of it being dumped on a wog, or worse, from being puked up.

Next stop: hangar bay.

We wogs were led to the forward section of the hangar bay near aircraft elevator one. The E Division pollywogs assembled in a square to await our transport to the flight deck. There King Neptune would oversee our initiation. Ordered to lay flat on our stomachs with our arms stretched straight out in front of us, we simulated swimming in the ocean. Our trusty shellback overseers monitored our performance. Those not performing got a whack across the ass with a shillelagh.

Before long, it was our turn to go up.

"On your feet, you slimy wogs!" a voice shouted out.

Just then, the huge aircraft elevator lowered from the flight deck to the hanger bay. The stanchions dropped, and we were given the order to board the elevator.

There were several divisions of us boarding at the same time. By the time we were all on the elevator and sitting down, our number seemed to be around 275.

Then the elevator began to rise toward the flight deck. As it did, we began to feel water showering down from above, salt water. As we got closer to the top, the streams of water became stronger and stronger. We were receiving the fire hose wash down, to ensure all pollywogs were clean prior to stepping foot on King Neptune's royal flight deck.

As our elevator reached the roof, looking around we could see we were about to be surrounded by shellbacks with shillelaghs. Their job was to herd us off the elevator and onto the deck, then we would await our turn to go through the initiation gauntlet.

After being lined up on the flight deck, I heard a voice from behind me, "Come on you slimy wog, I'm gonna make sure you don't miss out on any of the fun!" It was Lite Weight. He had walked up the ladder from the hanger bay to meet up with us, take me through the line, and snap a few pictures.

"You need your teeth cleaned from that delicious breakfast," said Lite Weight. "Next stop, the royal dentist."

Well, if my teeth were not dirty before, they sure were after my visit to the royal dentist, and his assistant. After sitting me down in their "exam chair," they injected a concoction in my mouth that tasted like a mix of hot sauce, vegetable oil, and lard and then brushed my teeth with it using a nasty old toothbrush, "Yuck!"

After that, it was to the stockade. My head and both hands at the wrists were locked into a wooden, medieval device I stood behind. As I stood there, Lite Weight and Elmo broke eggs on my head, smeared them into my hair and let the yolks run down my greasy face.

"Ha, ha, ha, just what you need, wog, an egg shampoo!" laughed Elmo.

"It's time for you to kiss the baby's belly, wog!" Lite Weight continued as he lifted the wooden top off the stockade, releasing me from my shame.

There were actually three "babies." These were big, fat, trusty shellbacks, sitting in chairs with no shirts, their big bellies all greased up with lard.

"On your knees, wog!"

"Kiss the baby's belly!" was the command, and I did. As I did, the "baby" grabbed my head with both of his hands and pushed my face into his nasty, greasy belly, rubbing his belly in a circular motion with my face. I tried to pull away, but he wouldn't let me until he was done with me. "Yuck!" That, too, was nasty!

"All right wog, next it's the poop shoot for you!" said Lite Weight, as I gladly got to my feet, eager to get away from my last ordeal.

A long line of wogs had assembled to wait their turn at the poop shoot, so it took a while to complete.

There were several set up. Each was about forty feet long, about three feet wide and made of canvas. There was a round support at the beginning and the end, with several along the way to help keep its round shape. The shoot was filled with old, rotting food waste saved up from the mess decks and galleys over the past few days. As I crawled through during my turn, I realized there was also lots of fresh vomit from previous wogs who blew their cookies along their way inside the shoot.

After the shoot, it was on to the *coffin*.

The coffin was a wooden box big enough for two men to fit in.

When it was my turn, JT and I climbed in together.

"On your stomachs, wogs!" we were commanded.

Next old food slop was dumped on top of us, and the lid was placed over the top. As soon as the lid was closed, JT blew out breakfast, all over me. At the same time, were told to roll around in it. As we did, the box shook from being beaten on by the shellbacks outside. When the lid was finally removed, we climbed out. We were a mess.

We made our way to our final "test."

All day long, whenever a pollywog was asked by a shellback, "What are you?" the only acceptable answer was, "I'm a slimy pollywog!" Once we completed this final part of our initiation, we would no longer be pollywogs.

After waiting in a long line, it was time to dive into an open tank of dirty water, and swim underwater the length of the tank, about twenty-five feet. At the other end of the tank was a shellback waiting to ask the question as you stood up: "What are you?"

If you answered the question, "I am a slimy pollywog," you were sent back to the beginning of the gauntlet to do it all over again.

When I came up out of the filthy water on the other side after swimming the length and the question was asked of me, I replied, "I'm a trusty shellback!"

With that, the questioning shellback reached out a hand of congratulations and helped me out of the tank. With a grin he pointed to the line of new shellbacks along the edge of the flight deck where a fire hose was hooked up to a temporary open shower. I waited there in line and as my turn to shower came, I did like everyone else, stripped off all my clothes, threw them over the side of the ship to the ocean below then showered off the filth.

After walking all the way down to our berthing compartment butt naked, I got my soap and towel, then took another shower. It was days before I got all the grease and grime off.

The daily grind was beginning to get to everyone. After thirty-one days at sea, we were all in need of a break. There were many smiling faces when we first caught sight of land on the morning of May 8.

At dawn, we approached the eastern coast of Africa. Soon we would be anchored off the coast of Kenya. Our next liberty port: Mombasa.

Mombasa is a big port city with two large bays, created by two rivers flowing out to the sea. The point at which they flow into the Indian Ocean is one of the few inlets in the area safe for shipping. Much of the coastline is buffered from the ocean by huge coral reefs, running parallel to the coast. The coastline is dotted by rusting skeletons of old ships that misjudged their locations and ran aground to die a long, agonizing death on the reef.

Too large to enter to inlet, we dropped anchor just outside the reef.

In preparation for the cruise, we had loaded on a couple of landing craft that could be used as liberty boats, in addition to our regular liberty boats.

Once again, I had duty on the first day in port. Fortunately, I was not alone. Ski-bo was on the boat too. Anchored out without the luxury of shore power, the Engineering Department kept steaming as usual. We stood our watches. Got a little rest. By morning of the second day, we were ready to hit the beach.

Before leaving the ship, we found out some of our buddies were staying at a beachfront resort north of Mombasa, the Reef Beach Hotel.

The liberty boat ride was rough. Luckily, we had the wind at our backs and rode the waves in.

After arriving on dry land, we asked a cabbie for a ride to the Reef Beach Hotel.

Driving north, through the dusty streets of Mombasa it seemed as if we were looking through the pages of a National Geographic magazine. It was a busy city, with people coming and going in every direction. There were many shops and street vendors.

Driving north on the coast road, we passed several luxurious beachfront hotels. Our cab driver was a heavy-set black woman who spoke perfect Queen's English and did a lot of talking as she drove. She explained that many Europeans come to the beaches of Kenya on holiday, especially the British.

It was a hot, dry, and dusty drive to the hotel, and we were happy to arrive. She dropped us off in front then went on her way with a bright, happy smile.

Entering the lobby, we looked around and found the check-in clerk. We knew Pic had checked in, but we didn't know what room. The clerk told us, pointing in the direction of his bungalow.

As we left the main lobby and began looking around on our walk to our destination, we began to realize what a huge resort this was. There were restaurants, hotel buildings, pools, beachfront area and many palm trees everywhere. It was all first class.

Pic had a bungalow attached to another private bungalow. Both had back patios facing the beach. It wasn't hard to tell which bungalow was theirs with all the of noise and the music coming from inside.

We knocked on the door. Brian opened the door with a cigarette in hand, as usual.

"Gin fizz!" he yelled out holding up a glass in his hand.

I could tell he was shitfaced already.

"Bring these sailors gin fizz!" he yelled out.

Over my shoulder, I noticed a short Black waiter in black pants with a white shirt and tie standing behind me with a tray. On the tray were drink glasses filled with a bubbling white beverage, on ice. Gin fizz would become the drink we remembered this liberty port for.

We went inside. Lite Weight and Pic were there too. They too had had their share of gin fizz.

"Hey Bob, bring any of that Pakistani with you?" Pic asked with a big grin.

"You bet," I replied.

"Here you can have my gin fizz if you'll fire up some of that shit, shipmate," Pic said.

Soon the waiter returned with another tray full of glasses of gin fizz, and another tray, and another tray, and another tray. By midafternoon we were hammered. We had the same waiter all day. We had him bringing cartloads of food to us: sandwiches, hors d'oeuvres, and pitchers of gin fizz. Between the food and the drinks we took in, he must have made a fortune on the tips we forked over to him. He was a good sport; we even had him drinking a couple and laughing along with us.

Our three days of liberty in Kenya went fast. On the morning of the twelfth, we left Mombasa in our wake as we steamed away, heading north to the waters off Yemen.

Midway and our battle group would continue a significant naval presence in this oil-producing region of the Arabian Sea. North and South Yemen had just agreed on a peace treaty ending their war against one another. Much of Afghanistan was in open rebellion against their government. Tensions were high in Iran. The Middle East was a powder keg, and we were just miles off the coast.

"They found our stash!"

During my 1200 to 1600 switchboard watch, those were the first words out of Ski-bo's mouth as he opened the door to my switchboard room and ran in.

"What?" I replied, stunned.

"The master at arms raided the A&O storeroom and found our stash," Ski-bo replied, white-faced and sweating.

"Well, it wasn't in our possession," I replied calmly.

"Yeah, but our fingerprints are probably all over the place. They're sure to check," Ski-bo said anxiously.

"Anyway, it's a good thing it wasn't all in there," I continued, trying to ease his mind.

"Shit. I knew we should have worn plastic gloves," he whined.

"Has anyone asked you anything about it yet?" I asked.

"No, I just overheard it in the berthing compartment," he answered.

"Well, we'll just keep our mouths shut and be surprised like everyone else, because we don't know anything. Right?" I did my best to reassure him.

As the days went on, the bust was all the buzz around E Division.

Everyone had their ideas of whose it was, but most everyone was pretty cool about it. Smoking a little pot at sea was fairly commonplace. Everybody knew it went on, and more people did it than I had even realized. It helped break up the monotony. Just don't do it under dangerous circumstances and don't get caught. A shaved head, reduction in pay grade, and some time in the Marine Corps brig was no fun.

One Sunday, we were given holiday routine schedule, which include a no-fly day. Even though we still had to stand our four and eight watches, the lights were left off in the berthing compartment all day long, so we could get a little extra rest. In E Division, the only required work was anything of an emergency nature.

One of my cook buddies in the bakeshop was working the previous night shift. When I stopped in to visit him, I gave him a plastic baggie of chopped up Pakistani hash. In the morning when I returned, he had a stainless-steel cooling cart stacked full of sheet pans of chocolate brownies, which was on the lunch menu for the day.

"Hey Bob, the bottom tray is yours," he said with a smile. It looked to me like he must have already tried a couple, for quality control of course.

After cutting my tray into squares, he boxed them up into two separate boxes and I headed out the back door of the bakeshop. On that no-fly day I felt like Santa Claus, spreading joy to my nearest and dearest friends throughout the ship.

While the *Midway* was involved in several training exercises involving various escort ships; USS *Downes*, USS *England*, USS *LaSalle* and a French naval ship *DuQuesne*, during this IO cruise, most of our time was spent reacting to real-world situations.

During this deployment, forty-five intercepts were logged with F-4Js and A-7Es with a plethora of Soviet May and Cub aircraft being detected. On the average, these enemy aircraft were detected 185 nautical miles out from the task group with our fighter join ups averaging 105 nautical miles out.

In addition, *Midway*'s VAW 115 Liberty Bells squadron was tasked with the responsibility of maintaining the daily plot and location of the USSR *Minsk* (Russian aircraft carrier) task group as it transited the Indian Ocean from April 25 to June 2. *Midway* aircraft conducted extremely long-range reconnaissance of the *Minsk*, exceeding 700 nautical miles, using A-7Es, A-6Es, and the E-B Hawkeye.

On June 7 we departed our operational station in the Arabian Sea and sailed for the South China Sea, back the same way we had come, through the Straits of Malacca.

En route to the Philippines, we passed through four time zones in four days, which was great for me. I had the mid-watch every night from midnight to 0400. Since we set the clocks ahead each night by one hour, my four-hour mid-watches turned in to three-hour mid-watches. Lucky me!

By 0900 Monday June 11, we were tied up to the pier in Subic Bay, ready to get off the ship after thirty days at sea.

This visit was to be a short one, only three days, and there was much to do in preparation for our return to Japan. We were all looking forward to summer vacation. Our upcoming schedule had us in port for nine full weeks to complete our extended incremental ship's restricted availability (EISRA) period. In other words, the entire air wing would fly off to Atsugi and the ship's company crew would be in Yoko for a ship's overhaul period with lots of time off.

I was scheduled to have all three days off in Subic. No duty for me this trip!

The first afternoon, Ski-bo, Tom, Ralph, and I headed out the main gate to get a little of the Olongapo nightlife. Ralph, a fellow A&O Shop electrician, always seemed to have the latest rock and roll albums for me to borrow and record onto cassettes. After having our share of the town, we made our way to Edna's house, back down one of the side streets off Magsaysay Drive.

She was home and invited us in. Who in Olongapo would turn away a sailor or marine at their door with pockets full of US dollars, even at the hour we had come knocking?

"Edna, we need a few pounds. Can you take care of us?" Ski-bo asked.

"Sure, we can take care of you boys, but you'll have to spend the night," replied Edna. "My guy can drive you back on base in the morning."

Now there was not much about Olongapo that seemed normal to me, and Edna's house was no different. This city was a sort of an adult Disneyland. Any vice you were looking for, you could find here.

"Come in, make yourselves comfortable. Want a beer?" Edna asked as she led us into her living room.

She had two long couches, several cushioned chairs, a coffee table, and a couple of end tables. It wasn't luxurious, but it was comfortable. On one side of the room was an entertainment system with a TV in the middle surrounded by a stereo system and speakers, pounding out a familiar rock and roll beat . . . Aerosmith. The room was dimly lit with a three-tier shell lamp hanging from the ceiling in two of the corners.

"Make these sailors feel at home," she said to the girls, who were looking to see who had come to visit.

We turned to each other with a grin and the realization we would certainly be entertained for the night.

In the morning we got up early to prepare for the task at hand—getting our pot from point A to point B.

When I walked downstairs, I looked around to see Ski-bo and Ralph in the living room.

"Hey, where's Tom?" I asked.

"Haven't seen him yet," replied Ski-bo. "He's probably still in bed bumpin' Bumpy."

There was one girl often at Edna's who had a strange affliction. She was slim, well rounded, and had beautiful long dark hair, but she had rounded bumps all over her body. We all noticed Tom had taken a liking to her the night before.

Just then I turned around to see Tom coming down the stairs buttoning his shirt.

"Tom," Ralph yelled out. "Spend the night with Bumpy?"

"Hey, man," Tom replied with a shit-eating grin. "In the dark, all cats are gray."

As always, Edna had come through again. She had our pounds in the kitchen waiting for us when we got up. The clock was ticking, so we got right to the job of packing.

The key is to compress the pot into as small a package as possible. Wrap it all in plastic to seal it. Pack it into cardboard boxes then double wrap the box with plain brown paper. Tie a shipping string around it and you're good to go.

We completed our packing job just before our driver arrived.

After thanking Edna, we said goodbye and piled into the car.

Just before arriving at the Shit River bridge, our driver stopped to let us out. It was much safer for us to walk across the bridge to the base and enter on our own than to attract attention to a Filipino base worker with four sailors in his car, a sure recipe for being searched by the guards at the main gate.

After successfully entering, we caught up with our driver a couple of blocks ahead. We all piled in again and he dropped us off close to the pier.

Shortly after, our storekeeper buddy came by with a truck, added our "supplies" to his and continued his journey to the *Midway* where he and his crew loaded the contents of the truck on board—simple as that.

Next, we grabbed a taxi and headed for breakfast on base, stage one completed.

———————

After breakfast, we returned to the *Midway* for a shower, a change of clothes, and to pick up some more cash, after safely stashing away our stash on board.

Today was to be a shopping day. Furniture was on my mind.

This time Pic came along to help.

Once again, we walked out the main gate and across the bridge, looking over the railing at the kids in boats and in the water calling out for pesos.

"Peso. Peso. Give me peso!" was the familiar cry.

We continued about halfway down Magsaysay Drive before we began searching seriously for some deals. Usually, the closer to the main gate, the higher the prices.

After a lot of haggling, I ended up with a big wicker oval papasan chair, a princess chair, glass-topped wicker end tables and coffee tables, shell lamps, woodcarvings, and a few other items. I had to have a delivery truck load it all up and deliver it to the *Midway*, to be stored in a roped off section of the hanger bay with all the rest of the PI furniture for the four-day trip back to Japan.

―――――――

The third and last day of our liberty was Ski Beach day! A bunch of us loaded up with supplies for the day and met out at Cubi Point. I, of course, arrived with the ski boat. Good Times!

―――――――

The following morning, June 14, we steamed out of Subic Bay, heading north to the Okinawa Operational Zone for Cope Cherry 1-79.

This exercise with the Japanese Air Self Defense Force on Okinawa had *Midway* CVW-5 aircraft flying over a dozen different inbound raid profiles toward the island.

Early Monday morning, June 18, we tied up to the pier once again in Yokosuka. During this cruise, all members of the crew and air wing were awarded the Navy Unit Commendation Ribbon and the Navy Expeditionary Medal for service under short notice in the Indian Ocean, Gulf of Aden operational area.

After the high tempo of endless days and nights at sea, the only thing we all had on our minds was a light in-port work routine, four-section duty, and some well-deserved time off.

I was headed to the motorcycle club to fire up my bike and then get home to Zushi!

CHAPTER SEVENTEEN
SUMMER FUN

AFTER UNPACKING MY NEW FURNITURE and souvenirs from the Philippines and Mombasa at home in Zushi, I began to contemplate this *summer of fun* in Japan for our EIRSA.

Life was looking good. I was living just minutes from the beach with a brand-new motorcycle, time off, and money to spend. *What's next? How about a summer girlfriend? Hmmm, something to consider.*

Our daily work routine fell into a very simple pattern: 0800 muster in A&O Shop, hear the plan of the day, do a preventative maintenance job for the morning, then meet up with a couple of buddies at the *Windjammer* Petty Officers' Club on base for lunch and a couple of beers, then sometimes report back to the ship for the afternoon—or sometimes not (especially if the weather was good).

The lunch crew was always a different mix. Generally, we could always count on Ski-bo, Tom, Ralph, Brian, Lite Weight, Kenny, Elmo, and Pic most days. There were always other shipmates who knew us who would join our table. We usually seemed to attract a crowd.

Some days we met up at the motorcycle club and grilled out in the late afternoon. We partied on. There was plenty of daylight on those long summer days. Some of our shipmates crashed in the clubhouse for the night. Some staggered back to their racks on the ship. Me, I had the luxury of jumping on my bike and driving home to Zushi, maybe with a stop at the beach.

One day while heading out to lunch, I ran into Greg, a fellow electrician.

"Hey Greg, are you still seeing the same girl from last summer?" I asked.

"No, I haven't seen her in awhile," he replied. "Didn't work out."

The previous summer, Greg and I were at Hayama Beach one weekend and met two beautiful Japanese girls who had taken the train down from Kawasaki for a day at the beach. I don't think they planned to meet two young American sailors, but they did. We flipped a coin.

Greg ended up with Kiyomi, and Chieko cozied up to me. At the time, I had wished it was the other way around, but that one was on the coin.

"Do you mind if I give her a call?" I asked Greg.

After fumbling through his wallet for a minute, he handed me a small piece of paper with her name and number on it.

"Here you go, good luck. Tell her I said hi," replied Greg as he climbed into a taxi and disappeared into the traffic.

After a couple of unsuccessful attempts, I did reach Kiyomi by phone. We agreed to meet up at the same place we had first met, Hayama Beach on Saturday.

Saturday came and I was there on time, waiting by the beach with my bike and extra helmet.

She had not changed much from the previous year and was easy to spot. When she saw me, she came jogging over with a spring in her step, her long straight dark hair swinging from side to side. It was easy to tell she had already been working on a summer tan from the bronze tint of her skin. Her tiny bikini was like a bow around a tightly wrapped gift. *Wow,* I thought. *I'd like to unwrap that package!*

We hit it off well and it wasn't long before she was a regular guest at the Zushi house. I spent the weekdays doing our normal in-port routine and found myself looking forward to the weekends more and more.

One Friday, Kiyomi and I left for a weekend motorcycle run to

Shimoda, a beach resort town on the southern tip of the Shizuoka Peninsula. We stayed at the Prince Shizuoka beachfront hotel, perched high on the cliffs overlooking the white sandy beach. Everything was first class. When I received the bill upon checking out, I was in sticker-shock. Fortunately, I had brought along plenty of cash.

After seeing all the freedom and fun a motorcycle was enabling me to have, it wasn't long before Pic bought himself a bike.

During an evening cookout at the motorcycle club, we decided it was time to take another run to Nikko National Park.

Friday afternoon we packed up, saddled up, and hit the road. It is great fun riding as a pack of bikers through the little streets of Japan. We turned a lot of heads, American bikers with our biker chicks riding on the backs of our big motorcycles. The largest size motorcycles sold at the time for domestic use were 650cc bikes. Everywhere we stopped, we attracted a crowd of curious onlookers, with smiles and questions. People were always curious about our *colors*, the Yokosuka Roadmasters Motorcycle Club embroidered patch, sewn on the back of our denim jackets.

We arrived at Nikko that evening and yup, you guessed it. It started raining again! This time, we didn't mind. We all stayed in a hotel, and yes, partied like wild sailors on liberty.

The next week, during 0800 muster in the shop, I was jolted back to reality. Chief told me to report to the Navy Investigative Service (NIS) office on base at 1000.

After the master at arms (MAA) found the hash in the A&O storeroom during the IO cruise, we expected there to be an investigation, but so much time had passed, we'd almost forgotten about it.

Arriving at the base NIS office early, I took a seat in the waiting room.

"Petty Officer Dorgan," I heard a voice call out.

"Yes, sir," I replied.

"This way, please," said a first-class petty officer dressed in summer whites, as he motioned me over toward the doorway where he was standing.

I entered an office full of old metal desks and assorted tall four-drawer metal file cabinets. It appeared to be an office shared by seven or eight people.

He sat down at a desk and pointed to a chair. "Please have a seat, Petty Officer." He asked, "Do you know why you are here today?"

"No, I don't," I replied, with a confused look on my face.

"We have some questions for you about the hashish that was found in the A&O storeroom during the last IO cruise. What can you tell me about that?"

"I don't know anything about it," I replied, "except for the rumor that some hash was found."

"Well, Petty Officer Dorgan, we have reason to believe that you may know a lot about it and that in fact, you may have been involved in bringing it aboard," the first class said, staring at me with a piercing glare.

At this point in my military career, I really did not know very much about the Uniform Code of Military Justice but, my experience so far in the Navy and from Valley Forge, had taught me to keep my mouth shut. Let the burden of proof be on the one asking the questions. I certainly wasn't going to help him hang me.

"I really don't know anything about it," I stated again.

By this time, he was beginning to look frustrated. Apparently, he didn't like my answers. But hey, I wasn't there to make friends with him.

"Petty Officer Dorgan, would you be willing to take a polygraph test to verify that?" he asked.

"Sure," I answered.

"Okay then, you are free to go for now, we will contact you to schedule a time for the test," he said as he rose from his chair, pointing in the direction of the door for me to leave.

I left the building and walked to my bike. As I put on my helmet, I thought, *This may get complicated.*

I rode over to the Windjammer Club for lunch. Ski-bo and Tom were there. I sat down with them and told them what had happened.

The next day, Ski-bo had the same thing happen, and repeated my performance. In the often-repeated words of Sergeant Schultz of Stalag 13 in *Hogan's Heroes*: "I know nothing."

We did our best to put the thoughts of the NIS investigation out of our minds. We had big upcoming plans. Japan Jam was on our calendar for this weekend.

The Beach Boys, Heart, Firefall, TKO, and Southern All Stars were scheduled to play two all-day concerts August 4 and 5 on Enoshima Island. We had tickets for the Saturday show. It was predicted to be a sellout and it was.

By now, several of us had girlfriends. Ski-bo was dating Tokuko. Ralph was dating Masako. Kiyomi was hanging out with me when we were in Yokosuka. Of course, we would all be going to Japan Jam together. But, since we sailors stationed aboard the *Midway* deployed for months at a time, she and I were not exclusive. Kiyomi had her own life and I was considered a temporary guest visiting her country.

On Saturday, we all met up on Enoshima Island for the show. Kiyomi and I rode my bike, so parking right up front was easy for us. Ski-bo had a Mitsubishi station wagon. He and Tokuko packed up plenty of party supplies and people in their car but parking for them was a little tougher.

We arrived early and staked out a spot with blankets on the field in front of the elevated stage. As we looked around, we noticed a few more of our E Division shipmates had also staked out spots in the field for the show. There was even a good showing from A Gang. The crowd filled in around us and by the time the show started, it was a zoo. Summer was in full force. We all partied the day away into the night.

I took a few days off and returned to the *Midway* on August 10. I learned there was a fire onboard the day before, caused by a broken acetylene line. Tragically, one SRF workers was killed, and seventeen sailors were injured while putting out the fire. Fire was our number one shipboard enemy. There was the lingering smell of smoke throughout the ship and a lot of cleanup going on that day.

Coincidently, oceans away, Iran had just canceled a nine-billion-dollar arms deal with the United States made during the Shah's reign. If we all had been following the international news closer, we might have looked at that event as an omen of things to come.

Early the following week during morning muster, once again Chief told me to report to the NIS office on base at 1000. Again, arriving early, I sat in the waiting room.

This time I was called into a different office. It was a small room with one desk upon which a small machine on top that looked like an electric typewriter, only with some small wires coming out of it.

A man in civilian clothes greeted me. "Petty Officer Dorgan, we have you scheduled for a polygraph test today," he said. "We will get started in just a few minutes."

As he turned and left the room, I looked cautiously at the machine in front of me and thought, *Time to switch things up.*

The agent soon returned to the room, sat down across the desk from me, and began to explain how the test would be conducted.

Just at the moment he was ready to start the test I looked at him and said, "I have changed my mind. I am not going to take this test. I have heard they are not always accurate."

He looked across the desk at me with wide-eyed disbelief, as if I had just knocked the wind out of him. Stammering for the right words, he blurted out, "These tests are very accurate, I assure you!"

"Well, it's my future at stake here and I don't want to take any chances on a machine," I replied.

With that, I got up from the desk, excused myself and headed out the door. That was the last I saw of the NIS agent.

Ski-bo didn't have the same experience. He didn't agree to the lie detector test in the first place.

Early Monday morning the following week, August 20, we once again headed out to sea. This time it was for a short *Shakedown Cruise* to ensure the ship was in good working order following our EISRA. In eleven days, we would be anchored in the Victoria Bay for liberty.

Our cruise en route to Hong Kong was intense with extensive refresher operations and drills testing the ship, the aircraft, and the crew, both day and night.

At the end of the fourth day out of Yoko, steadily making way in our southern route, we could feel the air changing as we approached a tropical storm heading our way.

Flight ops had concluded for the day. The "birds" were all chained down and, despite the rolling and pitching of the ship as the sea became heavy, there was a relaxed feeling of calm across the flight deck as the sun set. Squadron plane crews performed maintenance, V-2 did their routine gear checks on the cats, and V-1 plane handlers took a well-deserved break to take in the balmy breeze of the humid night air.

All the way forward at the edge of the flight deck, near the bridle horns, Lyons, Ryles, Pimental, and "Pinky" took their break. The handlers believed the best air was always at the bow. It was easy to see from their vantage point how our aircraft could seemingly just lift off as they reached the end of the deck from every cat shot. Standing along the edge, looking forward into the blackness of the night, with arms stretched out at their sides, they felt as if they too could take flight as the planes did.

As the ship increased its rocking motion with the pounding of the growing waves against the bow, Pinky decided to take a seat at the edge of the deck for a rest, just right of the starboard bridle horn.

Suddenly, the bow of the flight deck seemed to drop into the darkness. Then with a huge shudder, a wall of seawater came bursting over the bow, on to the flight deck. When the water drained away, Pinky was gone without a trace.

"Man overboard! Man overboard!" yelled out Lyons, Ryles and Pimental in disbelief as they searched the darkness for our shipmate.

GMG3 Sullivan of Weapons Department heard the shouts of the three men and immediately called the bridge. Just moments later, six blasts from the ships horn and word over the 1MC announced: *"Man overboard. Man overboard."*

Fighting to swim to the surface in the churning waters of the receding rogue wave, Pinky's head bobbed above the surface of the frothy ocean water just in time to see the huge dark hull of the *Midway* passing by in the darkness.

"HELP! HELP!" yelled Pinky as he treaded water to stay afloat.

Standing watch on the starboard sponson, Prayne and Harrer of S-6 Division and McGowan of VA-93 heard Pinky's screams for help from the darkness as he floated by in the rough sea.

Without hesitation, Prayne threw a life ring to Pinky.

"He's got it!" exclaimed Harrer.

The three stood there helpless as *Midway* continued to slide forward through the water, Pinky disappearing into the blackness behind us, grasping his life ring.

Back up on the flight deck there was a flurry of activity around HC-1's rescue helicopter, "Angel," as the crew prepared for lift-off from its perch on the angle. Lt. Hill, Lt. Ivy, AMS1 Piper, and ATAN Gatchell were well experienced in this maneuver.

All throughout the ship, our crew, officers, and air wing jumped to the alarm of *man overboard*. We all hurried to our man overboard stations so a complete muster could be taken of all hands. Luckily for me, Ski-bo and I were already in the A&O Shop. All we had to do was wait to be counted.

Meanwhile, the storm was really taking hold and it was feared Pinky would not be found in the darkness of the black night.

Many were involved in the rescue. Samuelson was on watch in Combat Information Center (CIC). He rang up Main Engineering Control to get the water intake temps to determine the probability of shark attack. It was high, especially knowing the ship regularly pumped out food waste from the scullery, pots and pans scullery, and the King Kong after meals.

Just minutes after the alarm was sounded, Angel was in the air. Lifting off the flight deck the helo then circled back behind the *Midway* to commence the search. The USS *Parsons* (DDG-33) soon came into view. The destroyer had maneuvered in behind *Midway*, her searchlights scanning the heavy swells, to assist in the rescue.

Miraculously, it did not take long to spot Pinky. There he was, bobbing in the swells, kept afloat by the life ring fitting securely around him.

As the rescue helo hovered above, rescue swimmer ATAN Gatchell prepared to pull Pinky from the angry sea.

It didn't take long to get a relieved Pinky into Angel's cabin. The pilot then reported the sailor's name as Fox as they headed back to the flight deck. This was HC-1's 1,600th rescue.

The mustering of our entire crew took only forty minutes, and the muster was accurate. ABHAN Curtis "Pinky" Fox was the only man missing.

Back on board, following a brief medical examination, Fox was deemed to be in excellent condition following his experience, suffering only a minor scrape on his left knee.

His Pink Panther tattoo had not faded a bit from his exposure to all that salt water.

Upon our arrival in Victoria Bay on August 31, our first course of business was a visit from Vice President Walter Mondale. He toured the ship and was briefed by the brass. For the enlisted men, our focus was getting on dry land for some fun!

After a three-day visit, we pulled anchor for another quick two-day transit cruise to the PI. Arriving early on the morning of September fifth, we tied up to the pier for four days of R and R.

Many of us were anxious to get back to Japan and continue with our *summer of fun*, when we steamed out of Subic Bay on the morning of September 9. We talked a lot about what we would be doing once we arrived back in Yoko.

Our liberty schedule had been great since returning from the IO. We had been getting a lot of time off. Duty was light. Most of us did not know our upcoming schedule very far in advance. We just did our jobs, worked hard, had fun whenever we could, and tried to make the best of each day. However, we all had that underlying thought that one day again soon, we would be headed back again to the IO, possibly for a long time. Good thing for us we didn't know just how long the next cruise would be.

CHAPTER EIGHTEEN
PLAN AHEAD

"PRIOR PLANNING PREVENTS piss poor performance," was a saying learned early on, back during my days at the Forge.

We were now back in Yokosuka for a sixteen-day stay and the word was out. On September 30 at 0900, *Midway* was scheduled to depart once again for our second IO cruise of the year, with a planned return to Japan just in time for Christmas.

The clock was ticking. Some were excited in anticipation of our upcoming visit to Australia and other ports. Others were not. As for me, many of my thoughts revolved around, *How can I make the most out of this IO cruise?* The voice that kept echoing in my head said, *Prepare.*

The days before we departed Yokosuka, I made every trip to the ship count, bringing aboard supplies for the cruise—boxes of freeze pops, cases of instant ramen soup cups and other luxury items that would be coveted after weeks at sea. I had stuff packed away everywhere. Supply and demand was the formula, and I knew the demand would certainly be there.

September 30 arrived much too quickly. Pic and I set our alarm clocks to ring early. Having packed one last carry bag the night before, there wasn't much left to do. I said goodbye to Kiyomi, who was still half asleep. We stumbled outside and through the early morning darkness to our motorcycles parked in the driveway of the Zushi house.

"Are you ready, bud?" Pic turned to me and asked as he kicked up the kickstand on his black Yamaha.

"I was born ready," I replied, firing up the engine of my bike, followed by a couple of revs.

Usually, I tried not to over do it. I was certain the engine noise of our bikes had to carry through the thin walls of the houses and apartments of our cramped neighborhood. We already had enough of a reputation of being rowdy, noisy Americans.

"Let's enjoy this ride into the clubhouse. It's going to be awhile till we're on them again," I said to Pic as we started out into the street.

It was still dark outside but as we drove along through the narrow streets, the darkness gave way to early morning light—the fresh, magical time of the new day. Lights were on, though not many people were stirring yet. Traffic was unusually light, making the ride that much more enjoyable.

We drove through the brightly lit tunnels with our horns blaring. Over the winding hills and finally slowing down to approach the main gate of the United States Naval Base Yokosuka.

Stopping at the entrance, the guards checked our base passes and waived us through the gate. There was a steady stream of people and vehicles, all heading in one direction—the *Midway*.

We joined the procession but continued straight through the tunnels when we reached *Midway*'s Pier. Next stop, Yokosuka Road Masters Motorcycle Club Garage.

There was daylight all around us when we arrived at the club to store our bikes.

"Hey Pic, can you call a cab while I open up the garage?" I said over the noise of the engines.

"Sure, as long as you tuck her in for me," Pic replied, motioning to his bike.

"Yeah, you want me to give her a big sloppy kiss for you too?" I said with a laugh.

I unlocked the garage door and rode the bikes in one at a time, putting a cover over mine. Looking around, it seemed most of the other bikes of *Midway* club members were there, except Lite Weight's.

One more glance, then I closed the door. After locking up, we jumped into our awaiting cab and headed for the pier.

––––––––––

As the harbor tugs revved up and the mooring lines were cast away, releasing the *Midway* from the pier, I made my way out to the catwalk on the starboard side of the flight deck near the A&O Shop. Looking down at the pier, there he was, waiving and smiling like the cat that just ate the canary.

Lite Weight had received his orders. He was not shipping out this time. He was to spend a month on base before flying out to Naval Station Treasure Island near San Francisco. Lucky dog! That short timer's tour of duty was over and was headed stateside.

As for the rest of us, it was time to change into the at-sea uniform and get back to sailoring.

As we lost sight of land, it was once again time for the foreign object debris (FOD) walk-down, and the beginning of the fly aboard so we could head south for operations in the South China Sea.

For a week we performed flight operations, battle station drills, man overboard drills and worked our asses off. Many of us were a little rusty on getting back into the routine. Little did we know, this level of pace was nothing compared to the pace we would see in the months ahead.

Around the globe, tensions were rising. Oil prices were heading up and up. Other than embassy personnel in Tehran, all Americans had been evacuated from Iran. The Soviet Union was intervening in Afghanistan, and Iraq and Iran were preparing for war.

On this cruise, we all would certainly be earning our sea pay. My goal was just to make a little more.

––––––––––

When we arrived in Subic Bay on the morning of October 8, Ski-bo and I knew we did not have much time to mess around. After two days of loading up supplies for the IO, *Midway* was scheduled to get underway at 0900 on the tenth.

After bowling a couple of games on base, Ski-bo, Tom, and I headed out of the main gate, across the Shit River bridge and down Magsaysay Drive. We settled in for a few drinks and some rock and roll at the Florida Club. Around 2300 we decided it was time to make our way over to Edna's house to place our order.

Arriving at Edna's house, she let us in as usual.

"Business good, Edna?" Tom asked.

"Business very good," she replied. "*Kitty Hawk, Coral Sea, Connie, Ranger*, you sailors buy lots of pot. Good for us!"

As we all talked that evening in her living room, the realization sunk in that there were a lot of other sailors from lots of other ships buying pot in PI and bringing it back on board.

For us on *Midway*, smoking a little pot once in a while was a break from the high pressure and constant intensity of the never-ending routine of work, drills, and standing watches, seven days a week. Apparently, there were many others in the fleet who felt the same way. Hell, we knew our jobs so well we could practically do them with our eyes closed and one arm tied behind our backs.

The next morning we followed our normal routine, tightly packing our pounds of pot into brown cardboard boxes for the journey to the boat. Our driver loaded them into the trunk of his car, and we all headed to the main gate. Of course, we bailed out just before reaching Shit River to let our driver enter on his own.

There we were, sitting on a park bench when he drove up, right on schedule.

After unloading our plain, brown cardboard boxes, tied at the top with brown twine, he closed the trunk lid of the car, turned to us, and said, "Thank you for your business. See you again at Christmas. Stay safe."

"Thank you. See you at Christmas," we replied with a wave as he climbed back into his front seat and drove off.

Before we even had a chance to sit down again, our guy from supply came driving up in his truck.

"Chuck your boxes in the back. Gotta hurry, I'm running late today. I have to unload this and make another trip," he said. "Pressure from the top on down."

"You got it," I replied. "We'll catch up with you later today on board."

Later that day, Ski-bo and I met up with our supply buddy to recover our boxes. After hiding them away in storage for safekeeping. I said to Ski-bo, "This is going to be a busy cruise. While everyone else is out on liberty tonight and the boat is quiet, let's bag as much of this up as we can."

"Let's do it," he replied. "What time do you want to get started?"

"How about 2200?" I asked.

"Sounds good," he said. "I'm going to get a nap in between now and then."

"Me too," I replied.

———

The time to meet Ski-bo arrived quickly. We took our boxes up to the A&O Shop. Before settling in for a long night of work in the back room of the shop, I went out the front and closed the door, replacing the combination lock with an identical lock, which only I had the combination for. Then, walking out of the passageway and into the motor whaleboat winch room, I went into the back room of the shop through the round escape hatch from the winch room. Locking the hatch behind me, we were sealed in, so we would be uninterrupted for the night. We had a lot of work to get done in a short period of time.

We had all our supplies with us: pot, boxes of baggies, and plastic gloves. In an effort to add something of value to my bags, we had purchased boxes of Zigzag and Top rolling papers to add to each of my two-finger bags. We worked nonstop until 0500, but it seemed like only minutes. We were in such a hurry and, of course, we did not finish, but we did make a big dent in the job. This was time well spent and would serve us well when we hit the IO.

Once, in the early morning hours, there was an uneasy moment. From the back room of the shop, we noticed voices at the door, rattling the hasp, trying to get in. After a couple of unsuccessful attempts at the lock, they left. That got our hearts racing! The thought of someone barging into the compartment with us sitting there with pounds of reefer spread across the workbench was not pleasant.

———

Later that morning, we got underway, heading south out of Subic Bay. After transiting the Sulu Sea, we entered the Celebes Sea. There, as the *Midway* Task Group continued south, we conducted exercise PassEx 2/79, an EmCon Strike on the HMS *Norfolk*.

The temperature increased as we sailed closer to the equator, as did our anticipation of the upcoming ceremony for crossing the line. There was a summons from King Neptune to all *Midway* pollywogs that was inescapable. On the morning we crossed the equator, Navy tradition continued as usual. This time though, I got to help dish out the fun as a trusty shellback.

––––––––––

After transiting the Bali Sea Basin, we passed the island of Bali on our starboard side and entered the Indian Ocean. We soon lost sight of the island and there was nothing but wide-open ocean in every direction. Next stop, Fremantle, Australia.

––––––––––

When we arrived on the morning of October 20, liberty call meant liberty boats again. Fremantle Harbor could not accommodate a ship of our huge size. Liberty boats meant a long wait in line if you wanted to get off the boat on the first day. For that reason, I wasn't disappointed to have duty on day one, again. Ski-bo and I used that time to our benefit and packed some more bags.

––––––––––

On day two, we hit the beach.

Fremantle is a shipping port at the mouth of the Swan River, on the southwest coast of Australia. The largest modern city in the area is Perth, a thirty-minute drive inland. We quickly decided that was where we wanted to go. After arriving on the pier, Ski-bo, Tom, and I rented a car and off we went on another adventure. After driving around and doing some sightseeing, we stopped into a bar to play a little pool.

Some Aussie chaps challenged us to a couple of games. We soon found their standard beers were much larger than our standard-sized beers. We were soon shitfaced, and they were winning at pool. We were all good sports about it, and they had a good laugh at our expense.

The next morning, we left our hotel and headed for the downtown shopping district of Perth. Tom insisted on having a couple of suits tailor-made.

We sat there in the store patiently while the tailor measured Tom for his suits.

"Sir, please relax while I take your measurements," the tailor said as he attempted to measure his waist. Tom had sucked in his gut in anticipation of the measurement.

"I am planning to lose some weight on this cruise," Tom replied to us all.

The next day we returned to the tailor's shop and Tom proudly picked up his elegant, custom-made suits. Of course, Tom never lost the weight, and he never wore those suits.

Later that day we went to the beach. It reminded me of the beaches in Southern California, with long expanses of wide open, sandy beaches gently sloping down to the ocean.

The women of Australia were especially nice to us young sailors. The ratio of women at the time (we had heard) was ten to one. The day we pulled out of Fremantle, the news quickly spread that several sailors who had too much fun, including my old buddy Greg, had missed ship's movement and were AWOL.

Greg had met a young girl while surfing at the beach, went home with her and had such a good time that he decided to stay in Australia. We all knew later there would be a *rest of the story*.

After hoisting anchor, we sailed west into the great expanse of water known as the Indian Ocean.

Meanwhile, on October 22, while enjoying our time off in Perth, the exiled shah of Iran left Mexico for Cornell Medical Center in New York for emergency cancer care. This hospitality shown by President Jimmy Carter toward the former shah enraged a group of radical Iranian students.

We had no way of knowing that, as the United States' only contingency carrier and task group in the Indian Ocean, the *Midway* was steaming straight toward a new era of history.

The next two weeks were made up of routine at-sea operations. We passed through time zone after time zone, adding an hour of sleep for those lucky enough to have the luxury of sleeping at night. To many of us, it meant our mid-watch was now five hours long, instead of the normal four hours. Ugh!

We all performed our jobs, stood our watches, and enjoyed what little free time we could steal away for ourselves. In the Navy, I truly learned the meaning of the saying, *Moments of freedom will never be given to you . . . You must take them.*

I made it a point to make my way to the weight room up at the bow as often as I could, pretty much daily. Ski-bo and I had become serious about our weightlifting and fitness routines. We ordered all kinds of supplements and vitamins from Joe Wielder Company. Every time we heard the announcement of "COD on the ball with mail," we made sure to time it just right, so we would be in our berthing compartment close to the E Division office to pick up our packages. We spent a small fortune on the stuff.

Some guys watched TV. Others caught a nap anywhere they could. Often, there was an evening movie on the forward crew's mess deck. The officers and the chiefs had evening movies in their own ward rooms. My old buddy Brian was in charge of the movie booth.

The movie booth was a small E Division office just forward of the hangar bay on the starboard side. Reels of current feature-length films were kept there and could be checked out and shown at locations around the ship. That was Brian's job. He also had to keep the projectors operational. Talk about easy duty. That was it!

The movie booth was a good hideout. Nobody looked for anyone there. Sometimes a few of us would get together with Brian up there and check out the most recent flick that was flown aboard before it was issued to the crew. We kept our own little stash of homemade applejack brandy and grape wine fermenting up there. With a couple of doobies and some snacks, we were in good shape!

Back at the stern, some of the marines passed time by lining up on the ramp of the flight deck for target practice, shooting at the sharks that followed in our wake scavenging our garbage.

One of our A&O Shop responsibilities was the forward and aft O2N2 plants, which produced liquid oxygen for aircraft pilots and crewmen and nitrogen used in aircraft tires, struts, and canopy release systems. We electricians were responsible for maintaining the electrical equipment used in the production of oxygen and nitrogen. The machinist mates of A Gang maintained the mechanical equipment and manned the O2N2 plants twenty-four seven, standing rotating watches. At least two MMs were always on watch in each plant.

One morning during quarters, I was assigned a work order for the forward O2N2 plant. A dryer element in the LOX plant had gone out and needed to be replaced as soon as possible.

Strapping on my tool belt, I headed out the shop door, to the right and down the stairs to the hangar bay. The aft O2N2 plant was conveniently located close to our shop, all the way aft off Bay Two on the starboard side.

On the other hand, to reach the forward O2N2 plant, I had to negotiate the maze of aircraft that filled Bay Two, all in some stage of maintenance or repair, with parts and tools strewn about the deck. After ducking under wings and dodging the tie-down chains securing aircraft to the deck, I made it to my destination, about halfway forward in Bay One on the port side.

MM1 Orlando was leaning over the watch stand writing something in a logbook when I stepped through the hatch of the forward O2N2 plant.

"Hey Dorgan, are you here to fix the dryer?" he turned and asked.

"Yup, don't mind if I take a nap in here when I get done, do you?" I replied. I had been standing four and eights, midwatch, and that was the first thought that came to my mind.

"Yeah, that sounds about right; if you need an electrician, just check all the good nap spots!" he responded with a laugh. "If you need any help, Belgum's back there somewhere."

I proceeded on my way, straight past Orlando, all the way to the port bulkhead. When I reached the bulkhead, I turned left. On my right was a row of about twenty, four-foot-tall red CO2 cylinders strapped to the bulkhead. On the other side of the bulkhead was the outside of the ship.

To my left was the LOX plant, a huge piece of equipment resembling a cube, about ten feet high by about fifteen feet square. The small aisle between the plant and the cylinders was barely three feet wide—but it was wide enough to fit a chair, and there sat Chris Belgum.

Chris looked up at me from his seat with his casual smile and said, "Finally, an electrician on the job."

The youngest of five, it wasn't difficult to figure where he picked up his easygoing manner. Chris's father was a highly regarded pastor and professor of theology at California Lutheran University. His mother also worked at CLU as executive secretary to the president. Growing up in Southern California probably helped contribute to his laid-back attitude.

Like me, Chris was very interested in history and stories about World War II. After graduating from Thousand Oaks High School, he, like many of us, decided to join the Navy and see the world. He was a hard worker and always willing to lend a hand.

"You got anything I can stand on to get to this dryer?" I asked

"Yeah, I think so, I'll be right back," he replied.

Now, the air dryer isn't a difficult component to change. It is kind of like a heating element in a residential water heater. You just make sure the power is secured, disconnect a couple of wires, pull the old unit out, and slide a new one in. Reconnect it and you're done.

I grabbed the chair Chris had been sitting in, wedged it in front of the LOX plant, stood on the top of the chair, and had the job completed before he returned.

When he returned with a tall stool, he found me sitting in the chair, kicking back under the vent where I had found him when I arrived.

"Are you done already?" he asked.

"Yup," I replied, "Got any sodas?"

"I think so, but I'll have to cool them off," Chris said as he set the stool down and disappeared around the corner.

If the LOX plant crew wanted anything cooled off, they had the liquid nitrogen to do it.

I'm sure it took some trial and error to get it just right, but they had figured out that if they placed a couple of cans of soda in a metal bucket and place it under the drain faucet of the liquid nitrogen storage tank and open the valve for a moment, they would instantly have perfectly chilled, refreshing sodas.

It wasn't long before Chris came around the corner again with two chilled sodas.

"Here you go, Bob," he said, handing me a cold can. As he sat down on the stool, we popped the tops and took a swig.

"Ahh, perfect!" I exclaimed.

He smiled.

"This is pretty cramped back here, between these cylinders and the plant," I said, pointing to the port bulkhead.

"Yeah, but it's the coolest place to sit while on watch," he replied as he pointed to the vents overhead.

We shot the shit for a while, finished our drinks then, I headed back to the A&O Shop. Next, my mind was on lunch.

Time seemed to pass quickly and before we knew it, it was early morning, November 9, 1979, and the special sea and anchor detail had been set in preparation for our port visit to Mombasa.

Once again, we dropped anchor just outside of the Great Barrier Reef and unloaded our liberty boats.

Later in the day, after the liberty line had shortened, a few of us decided to venture out. After a rough ride to shore, we grabbed a cab to make our way north up the coastline to an upscale seaside luxury resort.

We enjoyed a nice lobster dinner in the main dining building and decided to call a cab and check out the night life. The cab arrived and picked us up directly out in front of our hotel. We asked the cabby if she knew of any exciting bars in the area. She was a heavy-set Black woman with a thick British accent. She gave us a big smile and said, "Yes, the Bush Bar."

We all laughed out loud and said, "That sounds good! We like bush," figuring there would be a lot of girls there.

It had become very dark out as she drove on through the night across the barren countryside. After a while we began to wonder, "Where in the hell is this woman taking us? Are we about to be kidnapped or what?"

We ended up on some far-out dirt road, with no sign of civilization anywhere around. Finally, we could see some lights in the distance. She pulled her cab right up to the front door, stopped and said to us, "This is the Bush Bar."

As we got out of the cab, I pulled out a fifty-dollar bill, tore it in two, gave her one piece and said, "Wait here for us."

There we were: at night, out in the middle of nowhere, in front of this run-down single-story concrete-block building with a thatched roof that looked to be no bigger than a four-car garage.

We all looked at each other doubtfully but agreed, "We're here; let's go in and check it out."

Inside the lights were turned down low and the speakers were pounding out a tribal rhythm. The floor was dirt and there was dust in the air from the couples dancing. We sat down at an empty table and a young Black waitress quickly took our order.

Waiting for her to return with our drinks, we looked around, noticing we were the only white people in the room. Ski-bo turned to me with a smile and said, "I guess this is how a Black man feels in a room full of White people."

With the first sip of our warm Tusker beer, we realized we would not be staying long. A couple of people came to our table, greeted us with a friendly, "Jambo," and asked us where we were from. They were very curious about the United States.

After enough time had passed by to be polite, we got up and made our way to the front door. Our cabby was right there, waiting for us. We piled in and said, "Take us back to the hotel. We've had enough entertainment for one night."

———————

The next day Ski-bo and I got in a cab, destination: downtown Mombasa. We asked our driver to take us to the shopping district so we could buy some clothes. Just like the night before, we had her wait for us while we did our shopping. It was never a good idea to be stranded in a foreign country.

After making our way through several shops and sipping on some fresh coconut juice right out of the shell, we found ourselves in the right store. After a little haggling and fitting, Ski-bo and I walked out of the store wearing our brand-new Khaki safari suits, complete with outback hat pinned up on one side. Now, we really did feel like we were in a National Geographic episode.

Upon returning to the ship, we learned of the news: On November 4 a group of about 400 militant followers of the Ayatollah Khomeini (calling themselves Imam's Disciples), who had come to power following the overthrow of the Shah, had seized the US Embassy in Tehran. Sixty-six Americans were being held hostage. All liberty was hereby cancelled. All *Midway* sailors and marines were to return to the ship immediately. No Exceptions. The *Midway* Task Force had been called to action.

November 11, the day we learned of this news, was also the day President Carter embargoed Iranian Oil. The presence of the US Navy in the Arabian Sea would quickly be expanding. The *Midway* and her support ships were the only carrier task force in the Indian Ocean and we were to be the first on station.

CHAPTER NINETEEN
THE ORIGINAL GONZO STATION

AS WE STEAMED NORTH, a visit to the *Midway* by the commander of the Seventh Fleet, Vice Admiral Sylvester R. Foley, on November 15' was an indication to us all the high level of attention this area of the world would soon be receiving.

On November 19 the *Midway* Task Force arrived in the northern Arabian Sea, off the coast of Oman. Gulf of Oman Naval Zone of Operations or Gulf of Oman Northern Zone was soon referred to simply as GONZO Station. In an effort to make light of a stressful situation, a cartoon character, similar to a gooney bird, soon evolved, making appearances in the *Midway Multiplex* (our onboard newspaper), creating light humor of our situation —stranded indefinitely at sea. He was known simply as *Gonzo*, and he did give us a laugh or two.

Just two days later, November 21, the aircraft carrier USS *Kitty Hawk* and her battle group joined us on station. The *Kitty* had departed San Diego for a West Pac cruise in October. Her schedule was also changed due to the crisis. This was the first time since World War II the United States had two carrier task forces in the Indian Ocean at one time in response to a crisis.

After being at sea for a couple of weeks in a continuous high state of readiness, with no end in sight, I figured it was time to put the word out to my buddies around the boat that the "store" was open.

There is an old saying, "You don't shit where you eat." I never felt it was a good idea to sell pot to the guys in my division. There were others onboard doing what I was doing. At least they wouldn't be getting it from me. It would have increased the risk tenfold. I could just imagine someone waking me up in my rack in the middle the night, "Hey Dorgan, can you sell me a bag of reefer?" *Busted*!

And no, that never happened.

By now, I had made key friends all over the ship, but my main connections were in Engineering. BTs, MMs, HTs, and A Gang. These were the guys who worked in and crawled out of every rat hole and Godforsaken space below the water line; the places everyone else in their right minds avoided like the plague. They were hot, dirty, noisy, and dangerous (and they could be a little scary).

There was a tight bond among shipmates. The average age of a *Midway* sailor was nineteen, but you wouldn't guess it after you got to know us. The responsibilities of operating and keeping up the equipment we were assigned to matured us all beyond our years. Whether it was making steam in the boilers, running the turbines that turned our propellers and generators, controlling the evaporators that made our fresh water, or hundreds of other jobs, "Engineers get the job done!"

Now that's not to say anyone else worked less or their jobs were not as important, Engineering was just my first home. Supply Division, V-3, and V-4 shipmates were always happy to see me, too.

It never really took long to make my rounds around the boat. However, to me, the one with the electrician's tool belt around my waist, carrying the yellow metal toolbox or large brown paper bag full of baggies of reefer, complete with rolling papers, it seemed like hours. Hell, if I had ever been stopped and searched, the master at arms would have had a field day with me. Getting busted for pot in the Navy was not known to have good aftereffects. It usually meant a trip to captain's mast, and if found guilty; a reduction in rank and pay grade, confinement to the ship's brig, and extended confinement to the ship and extra work details, as well as a shaved head. The worst-case scenario could be a general court martial and a dishonorable discharge, if found guilty.

During the past two years, the Navy had added additional

deterrents to try and stem the so-called marijuana problem. During the previous couple of visits to PI, there was a drug sniffing dog at the after brow, ready to search sailors and marines as we returned to the boat. Guests in the PI were not allowed aboard as easily as before either. The days of having your PI girlfriend smuggle your pot aboard in her purse were pretty much over. There was even the scare of a urine analysis, which, luckily, I was never faced with.

We didn't realize it at the time, but this was the beginning of changing times in the Navy. None of us had any idea of what would be coming down the line. There were no women stationed onboard the *Midway* and the thought of that possibility never even crossed our minds. Shit, when we had our crossing the line ceremonies, we had men who dressed up as women to complete King Neptune's court. Some of them did a pretty good job at it too. You'd do a double take, especially during the judging for the queen of Neptune's court.

Scurrying through the passageways, up and down the ladders, my main focus was to get the goods to them. From there, they would spread it out however they wanted. I had no doubt those two-finger bags were divided time and time again.

It turned into a fairly simple exercise: deliver the goods and receive a big wad of cash.

I didn't really smoke pot much. Usually, when I wasn't troubleshooting electrical equipment: (weapons and aircraft Elevators, AESS systems, fuel pumping systems), or standing electrical switchboard watch, I was in the weight room or catching some z's. I was just interested in the result . . . cash in my pocket: the real "sea pay."

Another four weeks passed and the news didn't get any better.

December 23 was my two-year anniversary of arriving on the *Midway*. Before we arrived in Mombasa, I had submitted a request chit to extend my tour, which was, of course, granted. At that time, we all thought we would be back in Japan by Christmas.

On December 24 the Soviets air-lifted 5,000 Russian airborne troops and equipment into Afghanistan's capital of Kabul.

December 25 came and went. We did our best to make the most of a bad situation, but it wasn't a very merry Christmas.

Then, on December 27, a Soviet-backed coup installed a new president in Afghanistan. Our two-carrier battle group was then ordered farther north in the Arabian Sea—as close as we had ever been to the coasts of Iran and Afghanistan.

And still, the American hostages in Iran had not been released.

———————

That evening after we lifted weights, Ski-bo and I began our walk back through the hanger bay toward E Division berthing. As we passed a roped-off aircraft surrounded by several heavily armed Marine guards, we realized they were practicing loading a nuclear bomb on to the aircraft. Through the open aircraft elevator door, we could see the golden hue of sand blowing in the air on the horizon from the desert out to the sea. The rays of the setting sun shining through the dust storm into the hanger bay gave everything an eerie red glow.

I turned to Ski-bo and said, "Is this how it's going to start?"

"Is this how what's gonna start?" he replied.

"Nuclear war," I said.

He stopped, turned to me with his normal sarcastic grin and said, "Lets go to the booth, smoke a joint, and watch a movie."

We turned around right there in the hanger bay and did just that. Brian was there when we arrived, glad to see us. He even had some cold apple jack to quench our thirst.

———————

After spending over eight weeks at sea, the routine gets very boring. Everyone seems to operate in auto-pilot mode. More accurately, zombie-mode. The only break in the unceasing monotony was the excitement of an UNREP.

When we were all just about as burned out as could be, we heard the news: a steel beach picnic was scheduled for January 18.

Hallelujah! A holiday routine day!

After sixty-six days at sea, the thought of a no-fly day sounded pretty damn good!

S-2 Division was primarily responsible for the picnic. There were huge grills to set up on the flight deck, back toward the ramp, downwind of the rest of the deck due to all the smoke created during the grilling of all those hot dogs, hamburgers, and steaks. There were, of course, cans and cans of baked beans. Pallets of cases of soda. In addition, enough hot dog and hamburger buns to feed, well, yes, the entire crew of an aircraft carrier. Just imagine, if every sailor on board ate just one hot dog that would be over 4,500 hot dog buns!

Anyway, you get the picture. Those boys would be packing a lot of cases of food and supplies from the lower-level storage compartments up to the flight deck. That was one working party I did not want to have any part of!

The eighteenth finally arrived. Holiday routine at sea is *great*. It is basically a non-workday, except for those sailors with the responsibility of keeping the ship sailing. From the radar rooms of the 02-level to the boiler rooms, even on a holiday, many of us still had our seven-day-a-week responsibilities. Mine was standing four and eights on Four Board (my favorite board—the largest, cleanest, and with the best air-conditioning). I had the 0800 to 1200 watch that day, so my afternoon was free.

I was getting hungry by the time my relief came, so I headed up to the flight deck to get into the long line that snaked its way along the flight deck.

The deck was busy with activity: football, frisbee, joggers. There were guys with folding beach chairs, and guitar players strumming away. Most of the crew had their shirts off, soaking up some rays. Those of us who made it a point to get out in the sun as often as possible with our shirts off had that dark Indian Ocean tan. However, most of the crew looked pasty white from the lack of sunlight and long hours in closed steel spaces.

There were many sunburns that day! Even those who didn't make it up to the picnic were just glad to have a couple of hours of extra rest. Lights were turned off all day in our berthing compartment—an unusual treat.

Additional exciting news was that we were soon to be joined by a third carrier battle group, the USS *Nimitz* (CVN-68), home ported out of Norfolk, Virginia, which had been operating in the Mediterranean. In early January, she was given the order to sail for the Indian Ocean around the southern tip of Africa to join us on GONZO Station.

This nuclear-powered battle group joined us on station January 22 after sailing at speeds in advance of twenty-five knots in their route around the Cape of Good Hope and into the Indian Ocean.

On the next day, January 23, Task Force Seventy lined up all three aircraft carriers (*Kitty Hawk*, *Midway* and *Nimitz*) side by side, surrounded by escort ships, for a historic photo. Coincidently, this was also the same day as President Jimmy Carter's State of the Union Address.

This huge saber-rattling display of US naval power was the largest group of ships assembled in the Indian Ocean since World War II, yet there still had been no change in the hostage crisis in Iran and the Russians were doing as they pleased in Afghanistan. Nothing seemed to be getting accomplished on our side.

Two weeks later, on February 5, we were relieved by the aircraft carrier *Coral Sea* (CV-43) and her battle group.

There are sometimes astounding sights while at sea. As we departed the IO, I was working on a JP-5 fueling station in the forward starboard catwalk. It was the early afternoon of a beautiful sunny day. We were approaching the western entrance to the Malacca Straight, just north of the northernmost tip of Sumatra. As I looked out over the horizon ahead of us, there was a long white line that looked like a whitecap wave coming toward us, as far as you could see, from right to left. As we sailed closer, the wave continued in our direction.

The water we were sailing through was almost as smooth as glass. I stood there, mesmerized by what seemed like a wall of water coming toward us. As it flowed closer, I could see it was rough and swirling.

Hypnotized by this strange occurrence, I continued to watch as our bow sliced into the wave. It seemed to be only about a foot or two in height, but you could see the power of the current it contained. Just as we had passed about forty feet into the churning waters, a hammerhead shark jumped out of the water and over the crest of the ocean wave. He swam along parallel to our ship a little farther, and then disappeared.

I thought, *Now that's something you don't see every day.* And I never have again.

We were finally leaving the Indian Ocean. Next stop: the Philippine islands.

––––––

By the time we arrived in Subic Bay, we had set the longest at-sea record for any US warship since World War II by staying at sea for ninety-one consecutive days.

The continuous state of alert and the constant high tempo of operations drained everyone. *Midway* was regularly subjected to over-flight surveillance attempts by Soviet and third world aircraft. During November and December alone, airborne intercepts totaled over one hundred against Soviet Mays and Cubs, Omani Canberras and Jaguars, Pakistani Atlantiques, and Iranian P-3s. Initial detection of these inbound aircraft averaged 200 nautical miles out from the carrier battle group, with our fighter aircraft intercepting these enemy aircraft within 110 nautical miles.

These approaching enemy aircraft and ships often led to the call: "General quarters. General quarters. All hands, man your battle stations. Set condition Zebra throughout the ship. With the exception of watertight doors, hatches, and main passageways, all watertight doors, hatches, and main passageways will be sealed in four minutes." The bonging of the bell would then resound throughout the ship.

Yes, if you were not at your battle station within exactly four minutes, you were stuck in whatever compartment you happened to be in when the doors and hatches were closed and dogged down.

Whenever we did not have aircraft in the air, we had the Alert Five aircraft prepared to launch at a moment's notice. Two F-4 Phantoms sat ready on our two steam-powered catapults, with pilots in the cockpits ready to go.

In recognition for our performance of sustained operations in this high-tension zone during this cruise, crew members and air wing were awarded the Meritorious Unit Commendation Ribbon and the Navy Expeditionary Medal.

When we tied up to the pier at Subic naval base February 11, as you can imagine, it was a mad dash to get off the boat. There were sailors stopping to kiss the ground immediately upon stepping off the brow. Anyone who did not have duty was not sticking around for long, that's for certain. You could be sure the streets of Olongopo would be hopping tonight!

Lost in the excitement of the sea-weary sailors getting off the boat were sailors who had been waiting to get on to the *Midway* to begin their tour of duty. One of those "Boot Camps" was assigned to our shop the next morning and introduced to us by our supervisor, EM1 Baski.

"This new addition is Fordyce," said Baski.

Fordyce had just completed EM A School at Great Lakes NTC and endured the brutal Lake Michigan winter before receiving his orders to the *Midway*.

"Enjoy your stay in the PI, did ya?" asked Hurst sarcastically.

"Yeah, went from ice, snow, and three-point-two beer to humid weather, Mojo, and loose women. I knew life was getting better," replied Fordyce.

"Well, vacation's over now, bud. Your ass is ours now!" continued Hurst, and with that everyone else echoed a laugh in agreement.

"Hey Fordyce, I didn't see you in our berthing compartment, you staying at the Holiday Inn?" asked Fogarty.

"There weren't any open bunks, so they have me in aft A Division berthing for now," Fordyce replied.

"Why don't you bunk with Hurst, he's always looking for company," laughed Kelly.

"Fuck you. I've got your mama bunking with me," snapped Hurst.

After a wild five days in PI, we departed on the morning of February 16 for a fast cruise to Yokosuka, just long enough to get within range to launch all the aircraft of Carrier Air Wing Five off to Atsugi, have a traditional steak and lobster tail dinner, and get a night's rest before arriving pierside at Yokosuka.

On the morning of February 20, we were greeted with a hero's welcome. As the harbor tugboats maneuvered the *Midway* in parallel to the pier, the huge crowd assembled, screamed, and waived homemade signs. Wives, children, girlfriends, family, and friends were all looking toward the ship in anticipation to catch sight of their sailor or marine. Even the SRF workers were happy to see the return of the "Mighty *Midway*." The scene was electrifying.

My first stop after stepping off the boat was the motorcycle club. My lucky day, there was ice-cold beer in the fridge, and I helped myself. I popped the top as I sat down on the couch in the clubhouse. *Ahh, that beer tastes good*! After dialing up Kiyomi's number, I waited for her to pick up on the other end of the line. It didn't take long. It seemed like everyone in Japan knew the *Midway* returned today. She said she would be on the next train to Zushi and meet me at the house.

After hanging up the phone, I headed next door to the garage. Inside, there she was, all covered up with her green custom cover, just the way I had left her almost five months earlier. I pulled off the cover to find my bike was as clean as could be, not even a bit of dust. It had been a long time since I had put her up in the garage September 30. The motorcycle club seemed like a time capsule. We had a few club members who were not stationed on the *Midway*, but everyone stuck to the policy of not messing with anyone else's stuff.

I swung my leg over the seat and with both of my feet on the ground, rocked the bike forward off its stand. Next, I stuck the key in the ignition and turned it to the on position. As I pressed the start switch, I gave it a little throttle. It fired up right away with a growl, as if it had been anxiously awaiting my return and ready to get back out on the road.

It didn't take much to coax it out of the garage and over to the front door of the clubhouse. There, I put it on its kick stand to let it idle while I helped myself to another beer, closed both buildings, and tied my bag onto the rack.

Pulling my helmet over my head, I knew the ride to Zushi would be a brisk one. My leather jacket was snapped up tight and my leather gloves were snug at my wrists. I was ready.

After raising the bike upright, lifting the kickstand, turning the throttle, and speeding away from the clubhouse, I felt that familiar rush of excitement. As I cruised along the base road toward the main gate, that exhilarating feeling of the freedom of riding a motorcycle grew stronger. Struggling not to exceed the on-base speed limit of twenty-five miles per hour, I thought, *I can't wait to get out of the main gate and give this girl a workout.*

A short time later, after I arrived at home in Zushi, I gave my other girl a workout.

CHAPTER TWENTY
SASEBO

THE NEXT FEW WEEKS consisted of light duty. After our extended period away from Japan, everyone needed some down time. There was good news, which excited us all: beginning in late March, *Midway* was scheduled for two months in the Yokosuka dry dock. Just what we wanted to hear!

After that announcement, Chief turned to me at morning muster and said, "Dorgan, you are to report to the NIS office on base at 1000 this morning."

Well, that threw me. After all the time that had passed since my last visit to the NIS office, I had thought that issue had been put aside. Apparently not.

———————

Arriving on time at the base Naval Investigative Service office, I still ended up waiting over half an hour. I think they do that just to try to make you nervous.

Finally, I was directed to a room and told to wait for the attorney who would be assisting me. A few minutes later, an officer in dress blues entered and I stood up as per naval protocol. He smiled, shook my hand, and introduced himself.

"Petty Officer Dorgan, you have been charged with several violations of the Uniform Code of Military Justice involving marijuana," he said. "These charges include: smuggling, possession and distribution of marijuana in connection with the hashish which was found in the aviation and ordnance storage room early last year. I have been assigned to you as defense council for your upcoming general court martial."

Well, with that news, I had to take a seat.

The officer continued, "Petty Officer Dorgan, you do have the option of hiring your own private council, a civilian attorney, at your own expense, if you are not comfortable with me representing you."

Hmmm, I thought, *The Navy is providing an attorney to defend me against charges brought against me by the Navy. Will I truly receive a legitimate defense?*

I pondered further. *On the other hand, it would cost a small fortune to hire an English-speaking attorney in Japan to defend me in a military court of law. Either way, I'm in a world of shit.*

"This is a lot to take in. Do you need an answer right now regarding representation?" I asked.

"No," he replied. "But I do need an answer as soon as possible. Next week at the latest. And, if you do choose to have me represent you, I am going to need as much time as possible to prepare your defense," he continued. "The clock is ticking."

The next day I caught up with Ski-bo to find out that he, too, had been summoned to the NIS office and had the same experience, but with a different attorney.

"What are you going to do, Ski-bo?" I asked.

"Well, I'll tell you what I'm not going to do, I'm not going to let a Navy-assigned defense attorney send me off to the brig!" he replied. "I'm going to hire my own attorney to represent me."

All that weekend, those thoughts danced around in my head. *Which way should I go? If I do spend a fortune on a private attorney, the court will think I am guilty. Everyone knows an E-4 doesn't make enough money to hire an attorney.*

That was settled. Monday morning, I went into the base judge advocate general's office and requested to see my attorney. I had decided to put my fate in his hands.

He smiled with excitement as if he had just been presented with a great award. "Excellent. We'll need to get started soon, and I will need your help to build our defense," he said. "I will contact you soon to arrange a time to meet for a strategy session."

As I headed over to the Petty Officers Club for lunch, I thought, *Well, the court martial won't be until early July, so I'm going to make the best of the next three and a half months! Let's have some fun!*

At home that evening after dinner, I told Kiyomi, "You're going to need to go apply for a passport tomorrow."

"A passport?" She looked at me puzzled. "Why do I need a passport?"

"When I get back from the cruise to Sasebo, we are going on vacation," I replied with a smile.

"Vacation? But why do I need a passport?" she asked.

"Because we're going to vacation a week in Okinawa and a week at Pattaya Beach, Thailand," I replied.

"Baka!" she said. "You're crazy!"

"That's right, I'm crazy. So, let's go!"

After a few minutes had passed and the shock had begun to wear off, she began to get excited about the idea.

"You know, my brother Hiroshi lives in Okinawa. I have not seen him in years," Kiyomi said, "Can we visit him?"

"You bet! We are going to stay in the best beachfront resorts both weeks and all you need to do is to decide which clothes to take," I replied with a grin.

The next week, *Midway* departed Yokosuka once again, this time for a short cruise to the southern tip of Japan. Our destination was the US naval base in the port city of Sasebo.

In 1883 while surveying the coast of northwestern Kyushu for the site of a navy base, Imperial Japanese Navy Lieutenant Commander Togo Heihachiro selected his location based on its protected deep-water harbor, the existence of nearby coalfields, and its proximity to Korea and China. Founded in 1886, Sasebo Naval District remained a major Japanese naval base until the end of World War II. In addition to the base facilities, the Japanese Navy had also constructed the Sasebo Naval Arsenal, which included major shipyards and repair facilities.

Due to its strategic importance, Sasebo was one of the original seventeen targets selected for the dropping of the atomic bomb. In September 1945, the U.S. Marine Corps Fifth Division landed at Sasebo. In June of 1946, US Fleet Activities was established.

When the Korean War broke out three years later, Sasebo became the main launching point for United Nations and US Forces. Millions of tons of ammunition and supplies flowed through Sasebo. Some one hundred warships and freighters per day swelled the port.

Our destination was the US Naval Ordnance Facility Sasebo to offload thousands of tons of bombs and ordnance stored in our magazines deep within the ship, in preparation for the upcoming dry dock period.

As we sailed toward Sasebo, hanger bays one and two began to fill with pallet after pallet of bombs as they were brought up out of the lower levels of the ship on ordnance elevators. The *Red Shirts*, (ordnance guys), worked nonstop. They had a huge job on their hands. We electricians of A&O Shop were kept active too. There were seven lower stage (magazines to second deck) elevators, three upper stage (second deck to hanger bay) elevators and an assortment of conveyors. It was our responsibility to keep all that equipment running. We were hopping, day and night.

By the time we docked pierside, everyone was ready for liberty call and a little sight seeing.

A few of us decided to take the tour bus to Nagasaki.

After exiting the main gate of Sasebo naval station, we arrived in Nagasaki about an hour and a half later. Our bus driver stopped the bus and let us off at the Urakami District, the location of ground zero of the explosion from the second atomic bomb dropped on Japan near the end of World War II.

The weather that day was beautiful, but it was not long before we realized we were in a solemn and very respected memorial park. Many Japanese from all over the country were visiting the park as well as numerous groups of school children, obviously on organized class trips. The more time we spent at the park, the more we felt we were being watched and even pointed at by children with the comment, "Gaijins."

Our first stop was the hypocenter.

Ironically, the funding for the Manhattan Project, the development of a new wartime weapon, was granted on December 6, 1941. We all know what happened the next day, December 7.

The second atomic bomb dropped on Japan was intended to demonstrate that the United States had a large arsenal. At 11:02 a.m. on August 9, 1945, the bomb, reportedly nicknamed Fat Man after Winston Churchill, exploded in the Urakami District of Nagasaki. The twenty neighborhoods within a one-kilometer radius were destroyed from the heat flash and blast winds from the explosion. They were then turned to ashes by the fires that followed.

Just 1640 feet from ground zero, mass was being held in the Urakami Cathedral on that day in 1945. When completed in 1925, it was the largest Catholic Church in East Asia. At the moment the bomb exploded that day, the church was full of people, as the Feast of the Assumption of Mary (August 15) was near. We noticed remnants of the church were on display in different locations around the park as a reminder of the devastation of the day.

The site for the detonation of the second nuclear bomb had been chosen due to the large number of munitions factories located in the area, and the good weather that day. Over 70,000 people died instantly. Nearly 150,000 total killed and injured from the bomb that leveled about three square miles and destroyed one-third of the city.

After leaving the Hypocenter Park, we crossed the street and climbed up the long stairway to the top of the hill of the Nagasaki Peace Park. This too was a solemn experience.

We rounded a large water fountain, the *Fountain of Peace* and continued down the pathway that widened out to a huge courtyard in front of a statue, ten meters tall, of a man sitting on top of a large rock.

The statue's right-hand points toward the sky, to the threat of nuclear weapons, while the extended left hand symbolizes eternal peace. The mild face symbolizes divine grace, and the gently closed eyes offer a prayer for the repose of the bomb victims' souls. The folded right leg and extended left leg signify both meditation and the initiative to stand up and rescue the people of the world.

In front of the statue is a black marble vault containing the names of the atomic bomb victims and survivors who died in later years.

After returning to the *Midway* that evening, we all seemed to be in a quiet mood. The off-loading of our bombs and munitions was still in progress. I think our trip to Nagasaki gave us all a lot to think about. Sasebo did not turn out to be much of a party port.

On the morning of our departure from Sasebo Bay we were all anxious to get back to Yoko and get started with our two months of dry dock.

CHAPTER TWENTY-ONE
DRY DOCK

IT WAS LATE MARCH and the Yokosuka harbor tugs had a big job on their hands: they had to turn this giant aircraft carrier around in the bay and gently back it into the narrow concrete dry dock slip, positioning it just right so that when the steel gate was closed and the seawater was pumped out, the 69,000 ton Goliath would rest gently on the huge support blocks, which had been positioned at just the right locations at the bottom of the dry dock while *Midway* was in Sasebo.

There was a feeling of excitement in the air all throughout the ship. It was a long time since *Midway* had been in dry dock for repairs and updating. Most of us were new to this event. The SRF workers were out in force too. There was much work to do. Once the ship settled into place and the brows were lowered and secured, they swarmed over the ship like ants, with tools, equipment, and materials. They wanted on and we wanted off.

———

Later that evening at home in Zushi, Kiyomi and I had just finished dinner when she reached into her purse and said, "Look what I have."

She turned and handed me a little red passport with gold lettering on the cover. "I just got it yesterday," she said, grinning with excitement.

"Wow, that was fast. Now all we need are plane tickets and visas," I replied. "Let's get started tomorrow."

Making travel plans went smoothly and our schedule had us departing three weeks later from Narita International Airport for Naha, Okinawa for the first week of our two-week vacation. However, before that, I had another meeting scheduled with my JAG defense attorney to review our strategy for getting me out of the legal mess I was in.

The morning of the appointment with my attorney, I approached the chief as he entered the doorway of A&O Shop. He had the plan of the day with him and some PMS assignments.

"Chief, I have a meeting this morning at 1000 with my attorney on base," I told him.

"Dorgan, am I going to get any work out of you while we're in dry dock?" he replied.

"Probably not," I said with a grin.

"Go ahead, get out of here!" he barked.

After settling in at my attorney's office with a cup of coffee, he began to share his plan for my defense.

"We need to be able to call witnesses into court on the day of the trial who can attest to your good character," he said. "The prosecutor assigned to this case is a Marine Corp attorney. Dorgan, we need to work together on this. I don't like to lose—especially to the Marines," he continued, with a smile.

"We need to present at least three witnesses to the court who will be willing to testify for three different time frames of your life: one prior to your joining the Navy, one from your early Navy days and one from your current Navy time frame," he went on. "Who do you know, from back at home in the States, that would be a good character reference and would be willing to come to Yokosuka to testify?"

I looked at him with surprise and said, "That is going to cost a lot of money, isn't it?"

"Don't worry about that. I will take care of all of the arrangements for making sure our witnesses show up for court," he said with a smile. "That will be on the government's dime."

I thought, *Wow, I sure didn't expect that. It's sounding pretty good so far. I'm glad I went with this guy.*

"Jimmy Woodward is our neighbor back at home," I began. "I worked for him on his farm part-time, on and off, for six years while I was growing up."

"He sounds like he would be a good choice—neighbor and employer," my attorney replied, "How old is he?"

"I don't know exactly, probably about sixty-five or so," I said.

"Excellent!" he replied, as he slapped his knee and stood up, gazing out the window.

"Next, we need someone who you worked under during your early days on the *Midway*," he said. "Who comes to mind?"

Hmmm, who would verify my conscientious work ethic but would not accuse me of being a doper? I thought. *Well, that would have to be another doper.*

"My first few months on board, I worked in Power Shop, under Petty Officer Steve," I replied. "He is stationed on the *White Plains* now."

"Good, Steve should be easy to get ahold of and we should have plenty of time to review his testimony before the trial," he said.

"How about your current shop supervisor, would he speak highly of you?" my attorney asked.

"Petty Officer First Class Chandler, yes, we get along well. There has never been any trouble between us," I replied.

"We are off to a good start, Dorgan. Your general court martial is scheduled for July, so we have about three months to get prepared," he said. "We have plenty of work to do between now and then, let me know if you think of anything that can help, or hurt, our case. I don't like to be surprised."

With that, he showed me to the door and I headed over to the Petty Officers' Club for lunch and a couple of cold ones with Tom and Ski-bo.

———————

"Kiyomi, let's go!"

I had just loaded our two huge suitcases into the taxicab waiting in our driveway to take us to the train station.

"Just one more thing," she yelled back.

"We've got enough clothes to last us six months, and we're only going for two weeks!" I replied. "Come on, we have a train to catch!"

We were traveling to a tropical climate. I would have thought all that we needed were swimsuits and flip flops but I had made the mistake of buying two big suitcases, so of course she figured she needed to fill them up.

"I'm ready," she said, climbing into the cab. Then we were off for the train. Zushi Station was not far, but with our bags, I wasn't about to hoof it.

After changing trains in Tokyo, we arrived at Narita International Airport northeast of Tokyo.

Surprisingly, for being one of the busiest airports in the world, we made it through the boarding process quickly and with no problems. Soon our Thai Airways plane was taxiing down the runway for takeoff. Kiyomi had never flown before. She seemed a little nervous, but she soon relaxed once we leveled off at cruising altitude, and drinks were served.

The flight to Okinawa took only about three hours, just long enough to settle into a good nap after a couple of cold drinks.

"Attention all passengers, the captain has asked that you place your tray table in the upright position and bring your seat all of the way forward in preparation for our landing," the stewardess announced over the public address system. "We have begun our descent and will be landing at Naha International Airport in approximately ten minutes."

Being an international flight in the Far East, the same message was repeated in at least three other languages. That was enough to insure we were all awake.

Sitting on the right side of the plane, all I could see at this point was a big ocean and a lot of water. We dropped lower, lower, and lower in the sky toward the water. When it looked as if our wheels were about to touch the tops of the white caps of the waves, the asphalt runway appeared beneath the aircraft.

Moments after the wheels touched down the voice of the stewardess came across the PA system again: "Welcome to Okinawa.

Please remain seated until the aircraft comes to a complete stop at the terminal. We would like to take this opportunity to thank you for flying Thai Airways and invite you to join us again in the future."

After passing through customs, we grabbed a cab and headed out to find the restaurant where Kiyomi's older brother, Hiroshi, worked as a cook.

———————————

A short time later, our driver dropped us off, with our bags, in front of Morning Sea Restaurant. On the front wall of the building was a life-size mural of two Sumo Wrestlers locked in combat. The specialty of Morning Sea was a dish Sumo Wrestlers were known to eat to bulk up on, *Chanko Nabe.*

After the three of us enjoyed an excellent dinner together and Kiyomi and Hiroshi did a little catching up, we said goodbye and climbed into another cab to head north to our luxury resort destination: the Moon Beach Palace Hotel.

By the end of our week in Okinawa, looking out at the sapphire blue ocean water with beautiful views of the western sunset, we both agreed the Palace Hotel lived up to all the claims in the travel brochures and more.

Next, we were off on the second leg of our vacation adventure, destination: Pattaya Beach, Thailand.

———————————

We arrived in Thailand late in the evening, well after dark.

Located just a short distance northeast of downtown Bangkok, Don Mueang International Airport, at the time, was considered one of the world's oldest international airports and Asia's oldest operating airport. It was officially opened as the Royal Thai Air Force Base in March of 1914 and was now the hub of Thai Airways.

The terminal was still a buzz of activity with people coming and going in all directions. After locating our suitcases in the baggage claim area, we headed out the main door and into an awaiting taxicab.

"Where to, sir?" the driver asked.

"Pattaya Beach," I replied.

"No, not tonight," the driver said as he motioned us to get out of his cab. Apparently Pattaya was a two-hour drive and at this late hour, the driver did not want to spend the next four hours on the road. I guess he had to get home to his wife and kids.

We continued down the line of cabs parked by the curb asking the same question, "Pattaya Beach?" Finally, after five or six rejections a driver agreed to take us.

He was an energetic young Thai man. Jumping out of the cab, he quickly crammed our suitcases in the trunk.

"It's a long drive," he said as he drove the cab away from the curb, passing the other drivers who did not want to make the trip.

"Those guys are old; they only take short fares," our driver continued. "I have plenty of time."

We had not made a hotel reservation ahead of time, so we asked our driver along the way if he had a recommendation.

"I know a very nice hotel near the beach. You will like it. They have a beautiful pool too," our driver replied.

Kiyomi and I looked at each other and smiled. "Excellent, please take us there," I said.

By now it was after midnight and the trip from Naha was beginning to wear on us. Any hotel sounded good at this point.

We arrived in Pattaya a short time later. We could tell the driver knew his way around the city by the way he navigated the narrow maze of streets leading to the hotel. He stopped in front of a dimly lit, narrow two-story hotel with a small entrance. This was not what either one of were picturing as our tropical resort destination.

As we got out of the cab our driver grabbed our bags from the trunk and motioned us to follow him in through the front door. The lobby was a tiny room with only two wooden chairs. He went to the check-in desk and spoke quickly to the girl on the other side. He then turned to us, smiled, and said, "You're in luck. She has a room for you."

He then thanked us, and with a wave, he was out the door.

Kiyomi and I looked at each other, a little disappointed with our surroundings. "It will do for the night," I said.

We checked in and found our way to our room on the second floor.

"What, no air conditioning?" I said when we arrived in our room.

During my time so far in the Navy, I had spent time in some nasty hotels. This wasn't the worst, but it ranked in the same category.

The walls were stained from years and years of cigarette smoke. The linens were old and a mess. There were bugs on the floor. I didn't want to even brush my teeth for fear of drinking the water. Needless to say, we didn't get much sleep that first night.

The first thing in the morning we decided the thing to do was to put on our swimsuits and take a dip in the hotel pool to wash off the layer of sweat and dirt from the journey and the hotel room.

When we went outside, to our shock, the pool water was emerald green from algae.

We did sit at the edge of the pool, with our feet in the water for a photo to prove the water really was green. So much for our opportunity to clean up.

Next, we retrieved our suitcases from the room, checked out at the front desk, and grabbed a cab out in the street.

Our new cab driver took us to the Basaya Beach Hotel and Resort. It was a clean, modern three-story u-shaped hotel building with a beautiful crystal blue swimming pool as its centerpiece. In addition, the private grounds of the resort featured a five-star restaurant and botanical gardens. Located on the beach road overlooking the Gulf of Thailand, it was just a few steps to the sandy beach.

It wasn't difficult to relax in our new accommodations. We enjoyed the sun, water, and the warm weather of the daytime. During the evenings we dined at a different seafood restaurant each night enjoying fresh lobster prepared every way possible.

Before we knew it, a week had passed, and it was time to head to the airport for our return flight to Japan.

We arrived back in Japan to find we had not missed much on base while we were vacationing. However, on April 25, while we were enjoying our Thai beachfront accommodations, a complicated rescue mission had been launched from the flight deck of the USS *Nimitz* operating at GONZO Station in an attempt to rescue the fifty-two Americans held in Tehran.

Under cover of darkness, the USS *Coral Sea* (CV-43) decoyed Soviet trawlers away from the *Nimitz* while eight RH-53D Sea Stallion helicopters were launched from the flight deck to rendezvous with Delta Force soldiers in the Iranian desert.

The operation encountered many obstacles, beginning with numerous equipment failures, and was soon aborted. Eight servicemen were killed when a helicopter crashed into a transport aircraft in the desert. This was one of Delta Force's first missions.

The last three weeks of dry dock went by almost like holiday routine. The workload was light in our shop. We were in a four-section duty rotation, but I didn't spend any weekends on the boat. There was always someone willing to stand duty—for a fee.

There had been many changes over the past few months: Ski-bo had married his Japanese girlfriend and they had an apartment together off base, Tom had bought himself a new black Yamaha 1100 Special, and many of my E Division short-timer buddies (including Brian) had completed their tour of duty and had left the boat. In addition, there were many new faces on board, "Boot camps" who had never been out to sea. Our shop also had its share of new faces fresh out of A School. To me this meant training the new guys the next time we got underway and getting underway was something I was beginning to dread more and more.

During our last week of dry dock, we received the announcement at the 0800 muster in the shop that we would get underway early the next week, destination: Cheju-do Island area off the coast of South Korea. Tensions were rising in the area.

CHAPTER TWENTY-TWO
TIP OF THE SWORD

A US NAVY AIRCRAFT CARRIER battle group can steam anywhere in international waters. Our political decision makers use aircraft carriers as a powerful instrument of diplomacy, strengthening alliances or answering the call of an emergency. When the news of a crisis anywhere in the world breaks out, our leaders in Washington ask: "Where is the nearest aircraft carrier?"

In March of 1980, South Korea's democratization movement was beginning to be revived. With the start of the new semester, professors and students expelled for pro-democracy activities throughout South Korea returned to their universities, and student unions were formed. These unions led nationwide demonstrations for reforms including an end to martial law, democratization, minimum wage demands, and freedom of the press. These activities culminated in the anti-martial law demonstration at Seoul Station on May 15, 1980, in which about 100,000 students and citizens participated.

In response, South Korean Army General Chun Doo-Hwan, who had taken control of the government through a coup d'état December 12, 1979, took several suppressive measures. On May 17 he extended martial law to the whole nation, which closed universities, banned political activities, and further curtailed the press. Troops were dispatched to various parts of the country to enforce martial law. On the same day, troops raided a national conference of student union leaders from fifty-five universities who were gathered to discuss their next moves in the wake of the May 15 demonstration. Twenty-six politicians were also arrested on charges of instigating demonstrations.

On May 18 in the city of Gwangju, South Korea, citizens took up arms when local Jeonnam University students, who were demonstrating against the Chun Doo-Hwan government, were fired upon, killed, and beaten in an unprecedented attack by government troops. As citizens were infuriated by the violence, the number of protestors rapidly increased and exceeded 10,000 by May 20. As the conflict escalated, the army began firing on citizens, killing many near Gwangju Station. In response, protestors raided armories and police stations in local towns and armed themselves.

As this crisis was unfolding, the nearest aircraft carrier was up on blocks in the Yokosuka dry dock. The second closest aircraft carrier was in Subic Bay after spending 102 consecutive days at sea in the Indian Ocean, her crew enjoying well-deserved liberty. The *Coral Sea*'s schedule had her departing Subic to return to her homeport of Alameda, California after completing a long WestPac deployment. Instead, she and her battle group were ordered from Subic to the Cheju-do Island area off the southern tip of South Korea (about 120 miles from Gwangju) and to stand-by there until the *Midway* and her battle group arrived.

"Secure from sea and anchor detail. All hands now shift to the at-sea uniform. Hats are no longer required." Once again that old familiar announcement came over the 1MC as we headed south in the Tokyo Bay, confirming we were once again underway.

It had been nine weeks since we were last steaming. With aircraft recovery operations soon commencing on the flight deck, all our equipment that had been sitting idle would soon be put to the test. To me, that meant lots of equipment repair orders to complete.

Over night, the A&O Shop changed from a shop that was full of experienced third-class petty officers, (the backbone of the Navy) who knew how to fix all the equipment under our responsibility, to new E-3s who couldn't navigate their way through the 02 level. In addition, we had a new chief in the shop and he and I just didn't seem to hit it off very well.

It was noon by now and several of us were back in the shop after lunch. We could once again hear the familiar *screech . . . bam*! above our heads through the steel overhead as the wheels and tail-hook of the returning aircraft hit the flight deck upon landing.

One of the new guys, Fogarty, said, "Man, that's loud."

"You'll get used to it, mon," replied Kelly with a smile, in his characteristic Jamaican accent.

On May 30 we arrived on station off Cheju-do to relieve the *Coral Sea* battle group. They then headed northwest for a few days of liberty in Pusan, just 190 miles away. Their visit to Pusan kept two US Navy carrier battle groups in the area while the crisis calmed down. A little saber rattling can have a big effect.

After three weeks at sea carrying on flight operations day and night, it was our turn for a few days of liberty in Pusan. The situation in South Korea had simmered down, and we could move on. On the morning of June 18 we arrived in Pusan Harbor and this time tied up to a pier on the north side of the inner bay.

The first day in we hit the beach. Tom, Ski-bo, Ralph, and I decided to see what we could get into. As soon as we were on the pier, we jumped into the first available taxi.

The driver turned to us and said, "Where to?"

Tom replied with a big smile and a laugh, "Green Street."

The driver responded with a nod and a knowing grin, "Green Street."

Texas Street and Green Street were well known for being two of the biggest red-light districts in Korea. Many salty sailors had a sea story or two about their experiences while on liberty in Korea. The four of us were salty, but we had not yet crossed Green Street off our list.

We all had read the June 14 story in the *Midway Multiplex*, "General Liberty Hints." The three-page article outlined the general dos and don'ts while on liberty in South Korea.

The Green Street area had over 1,500 registered entertainers. However, during Seventh Fleet visits many more girls would arrive from Seoul, Taegu, and Inchon. The waitresses and entertainers were subject to spot checks by the Korean National Police. All of them had to carry VD cards and were required to be checked by public health officials at least weekly. It was recommended that you always ask to see the VD card. A red P stamped on the card represented a positive VD finding. Black stamps with Korean characters indicated the girl did not have VD on her last check. If a girl refused to show you her VD card or said she lost it, the best thing to do was stay away from her.

The four of us also knew that while on liberty there was safety in numbers. We were confident nobody would want to fuck with us.

After a fast drive through the winding streets of Pusan, the driver stopped, turned to us, and said, "Green Street. Good luck." We piled out, paid him, and sent him on his way.

As we started down the street the cat calls began: "Pssst, hey sailor! Come over here. Hey sailor! Come in here. I show you good time. Hey handsome. I got what you want."

It was midafternoon, so the girls were just getting started. As we expected, the main crowd would not be in until the evening and nighttime. As early birds we had our pick.

After looking in a couple of "store fronts" and not liking what we had seen so far, we went inside the next place and said we'd like to take a look at their girls.

"You sailors just want to look?" the mama-san replied with a laugh.

Tom laughed, "No, he and I want your best girl," pointing to Ski-bo.

"One girl, you take turns?" she stuttered with a puzzled look.

"No. Us two with one girl, same time. Good time," Tom said.

"Ah, you want good-time girl. You want this girl," the mama-san said as she motioned to one of the girls standing on the other side of the room.

The girl waltzed over and smiled at Tom and Ski-bo.

"You like what you see, sailors?" The mama-san smiled.

"She'll do just fine," said Tom as Ski-bo gave her a nod, heading off upstairs.

Mama-san then turned to me and Ralph said, "What you sailors looking for?"

"All I want is a blowjob," said Ralph, looking around at the rest of the girls.

"That will suit me fine too," I chimed in.

We each picked a girl and headed upstairs to separate rooms.

"Hey, Mr. Cool, you done?" I heard Ralph say from the room next door a few minutes later. "Let's get the fuck out of here."

Next thing I knew, he was there in the hallway in front of my room, banging on the door. "Come on, let's go!"

I jumped up and was out the door.

Tom and Ski-bo were in the room across the hall from us. Ralph and I were standing in the hallway on the second floor with rooms on either side, all the way down the hallway. It reminded me of my old seventh-grade school building. All the doors had transom windows above the doors that opened in for ventilation.

Ralph knocked on the door of the room that Tom and Ski-bo were in with their good-time girl. "Come on! let's go!" he yelled to them.

"Ralph, go jerk off! we're busy in here!" Tom yelled out.

I moved over close to the door and motioned to Ralph. "Give me a lift up."

He clasped his hands together to make a footstep and gave me a boost up, just high enough that I could see in through the transom window above the door.

There they all were, naked. Tom and Ski-bo, on their knees like bookends with their good time girl on her knees between the two of them.

"Woof! Woof!" I yelled in through the open window.

With that we all burst out laughing. Ralph was laughing so hard he let go of my foot. I was still up there hanging on to the window frame with both hands, trying to see in, laughing and barking.

"Get the fuck out of here!" yelled Tom, half laughing, half pissed off.

When I let go of the window frame, I fell, landing on Ralph on the way down. Next, we were rolling on the floor laughing.

We turned to see the mama-san running down the hall toward us with a stick in her hands.

"What's going on up here?" she yelled, swinging big her stick at us. "You get outa here!"

Ralph and I jumped to our feet and ran down the stairs and out the door. It wasn't long before Tom and Ski-bo were along right behind us.

We could now cross Green Street off our lists. Ralph never would tell us why he was so anxious to get out of there. We had our suspicions.

The next day back on the boat, I received orders to report to Kim Hae Air Base just west of Pusan to take a COD back to Yokosuka. It seems my court martial was to be held in about two weeks and my attorney wanted to get in some prep time.

After packing a small flight bag, I put on my uniform: black pants, white shirt, and my cover, then headed down the brow to the pier. A small shuttle bus took about eight of us from the pier to Kim Hae Air Base and dropped us off in front of the terminal. It was a long one-story building painted with green, white, and yellow camouflage. There was a waiting lounge on the first floor and a small second-floor section, which served as the control tower.

Just after we arrived at the terminal we were delayed by a brief thunderstorm, just enough to soak everything down and ratchet the June afternoon humidity a couple notches higher.

After our bags were loaded in through the open back loading ramp, we too climbed in and took our seats, facing backward. At this point we were turning our lives over to the Foo Dogs of VRC-50, the US Navy squadron that operated the CODs for the western Pacific.

The flight crew came around to make sure were buckled in for the ride and prepped us on what to expect. I was glad I had brought a pair of earplugs. It was a noisy, cold, and thankfully uneventful flight.

A few hours after takeoff we touched down at NAS Atsugi, Japan. General Douglas MacArthur had arrived at this same airfield thirty-five years earlier on August 30, 1945, in his C-54 Sky Master "Battan" along with 15,000 men of the Eleventh Airborne Division in preparation to accept the formal surrender of Japan on September 2.

Even though the hour was late, we still had plenty of daylight since it was close to the longest day of the year. The sun finally set about the time our shuttle bus arrived at the Yokosuka naval base.

After the driver dropped the other passengers on base, he was nice enough to deliver me to the motorcycle club.

It had been a long trip. After relaxing in the clubhouse for a few minutes with a cold beer and a doobie, I fired up my bike and hit the road. It seemed a little strange not seeing her there as I drove past the empty pier where *Midway* was usually tied up. It certainly was a lot quieter.

––––––––––––

After spending the weekend at home in Zushi with Kiyomi, I reported to my attorney's office first thing Monday morning. We spent several hours over the next few days going over questions and answers to be anticipated during the trial. By the end of the week, the *Midway* had returned to Yoko, and we were ready to go head-to-head with the prosecuting attorney. My attorney had suggested we plead our case in front of a judge only. He seemed to feel a judge would be more impartial than a jury, giving us a better chance. The trial was scheduled for the next week.

––––––––––––

Just before I left my attorney's office on Friday he said to me, "Dorgan. Jimmy Woodward arrived today and checked into his hotel a little while ago. You should spend some time with him this weekend. Make sure he enjoys his visit here in Japan. I'm sure you can handle that, can't you?"

"I sure can and I will—starting with dinner tonight," I replied enthusiastically.

"Don't keep him out too late. He may be suffering from a little jet lag. We want him fresh and alert for court next week," my attorney cautioned.

"Yes, sir. I, too, have a lot at stake here, sir," I said with a smile.

Next, I called Kiyomi and had her meet me at the Yokosuka train station.

Later in the evening we arrived at the hotel where Jimmy was staying. I was glad to see him. It had been several years, and we had a lot of catching up to do. He had aged a bit but was still spry and sharp as a tack.

After we finished our dinner at a nearby restaurant, we escorted him back to his hotel. I could see the long trip had been draining on him and it would be best to turn in for the night. Besides, we had big sightseeing plans for him for the following day.

The *Midway* had returned to Yoko, but it had not brought good news with her return. The word was that after a brief period in-port of about three weeks, *Midway* would be again departing for the Indian Ocean.

It was a good thing I did not know at the time that there would be many events occurring over the next few weeks, affecting many people in several different ways—some enough to last a lifetime. The wheels had been set in motion.

CHAPTER TWENTY-THREE
GENERAL COURT MARTIAL

SATURDAY MORNING was your typical warm summer day for the end of June in Japan. After parking my bike in front of Ski-bo's apartment, Kiyomi and I headed out of the driveway in his car. Ski-bo let us borrow his gray Mazda station wagon for the weekend so we could chauffer Jimmy around for a little sight seeing. Ski-bo had plans with his attorney already or we would have invited him and Tokuko to come along with us. Instead, we invited Ralph and Masako.

We picked Jimmy up in front of his hotel and headed out for a whirlwind sightseeing tour. We tried to fit in as much as possible. The Great Buddha in Kamakura seemed to be one of the highlights for Jimmy. For being a fairly conservative Quaker from eastern Pennsylvania, he was very opened minded and was excited to see all we could show him during his visit.

The thing I will never forget about the weekend was Ralph's nonstop babbling. I think he must have had taken a couple of yellow jackets before we got started, because he just wouldn't shut up, all day long.

_____

Our trials were scheduled for two separate days that week. Ski-bo was up first.

His attorney seemed like a nice, confident man. He was an older

American fellow who was currently living and practicing law in Japan. Ski-bo was paying him and had confidence in his skills. That was all that mattered.

They had chosen to go the jury-trial route.

It was a long first day, with the court hearing much questioning and cross-examining by both prosecution and defense. At the end of the day after the jury had deliberated, they handed the presiding judge their decision: guilty.

———————

"Those motherfuckers on the jury already had their minds made up before it started," said Ski-bo, with a look of disgust on his face. "Bunch of lifers who just wanted to get it over with, didn't take 'em ten minutes to return with their decision—just enough time to hit the head and come back!"

We had joined up with Tom, Pic, Hurst, Fogarty, and a couple of other buddies over at the Windjammer Club after it was all over to break the news.

"Fuck the Navy, boys. Looks like I'm going home early," Ski-bo said with a smile as he raised his beer for a toast. "I'm the short timer now!"

Next Tom raised his beer, "All the Navy's done today is lose a good sailor. Fuck 'em!"

"Another round all the way around," I told the waitress when she returned to our table.

After a couple more Heinekens I decided it was time for me to hit the road. Tomorrow was my big day under the magnifying glass. Time to head home and get some rest.

All considered, Ski-bo seemed to take it well, on the outside. Hell, he was never one to cry in his beer.

When I got up to leave, he stood up, turned to me, and stuck out his hand, with a smile and said, "Good luck tomorrow, Bob. Don't sweat it. They got one of us—that's all they really need."

I smiled back and said, "We'll see bud. We'll see."

———————

That night at home in Zushi, I didn't get much sleep.

The next day I was up before the sun for my ride into the base.

I arrived early in the courtroom, as directed by my attorney. The walls of the entire room were made of dark wood paneling. In the back of the room there were several rows of chairs for spectator seating. Looking forward toward the front, on the left side, was the jury box, with large windows allowing plenty of daylight to enter the room. In front of the judge's bench were two long wooden tables, each with two wooden armchairs. My attorney directed me toward the table on the right.

"This is where we will be for the next few hours, Petty Officer Dorgan," he said, pointing to the large table.

I sat down in my chair a bit uneasy. My attorney had prepared me well, but I couldn't help but feel a bit nervous. He gave me a yellow note pad and a pencil then told me, "Take notes, and let me know if you think of any additional questions I should ask, or items of concern as we go along."

Then my attorney went over to the prosecutor's table and shook hands with the Marine Corps attorney who had taken his place behind his long wooden table. They exchanged a few words. From where I was sitting it looked as if they were about to begin a boxing match. I just hoped I wasn't the one going down.

The court martial began on time at 0900.

"All rise," the Marine bailiff sounded off.

Next, the door in the front of the room opened and the judge walked in and took his seat behind the bench. He was a very distinguished, high ranking Navy officer—a commander, I believe.

"Be seated," the judge said.

After both attorneys completed their opening statements, witnesses were called in one by one to testify. I sat there at my table observing and taking notes.

The prosecuting attorney said, "I call the defendant's workshop supervisor EM1 Baski to the stand."

After a few questions from the prosecutor to the witness in an attempt to discredit me, the judge turned to my counselor and said, "Do you have any questions for the witness?"

My attorney slowly stood and proceeded in asking the witness a few basic questions. Then he hit him with the zinger. "EM1 Baski, isn't it true that several years ago you were convicted of having two wives, one in Japan and one in the Philippines, and receiving dependent housing allowance from the Navy for both of them at the same time?"

You could have heard a pin drop in the courtroom.

Baski's voice replied in just a whisper. "Yes."

"Excuse me EM1 Baski, I was not able to hear your response, could you please repeat your answer for the court?" continued my attorney.

"Yes, sir," Baski replied.

A muffled gasp spread throughout the courtroom and through the audience who had filled the gallery to view the proceedings.

"I have no more questions for this witness your honor," my attorney stated to the judge.

The judge then looked toward the prosecutor, "Do you have any more questions for this witness?"

With a look of humiliation and embarrassment he replied, "No, sir—your honor" and sat down, fumbling through his papers.

The proceedings then continued with our parade of defense character witnesses beginning with my old neighbor, employer, and friend from Pennsylvania, Jimmy Woodward. He took the stand, was sworn in, and gave a brilliantly positive testimony.

Next to enter the courtroom was my old supervising petty officer and friend from my early *Midway* days in Power Shop, EM2 Steve, who was now stationed on the supply ship USS *White Plains*. His testimony, too, was excellent. Even the prosecutor's line of questioning aimed at discrediting my reputation proved unsuccessful.

Next came EM1 Chandler, my current workshop supervisor (Baski and Chandler were both assigned to the A&O Shop). He was sworn in, took the stand, and continued to testify as to my dedication to duty and the mission of the Navy. "I can always count on Dorgan to get the job done and to positively influence those under his supervision to complete the assignment, no matter how challenging it may seem."

After Chandler was dismissed, the judge made a few remarks and said, "We will continue at 1300 after a short recess for lunch. I expect to get started on time, so don't keep me waiting." He glanced at the two attorneys.

My attorney turned toward me and said, "It will be your turn after lunch. I'll see you back here at 1245 sharp." With that he was up and disappeared out of the courtroom.

I stood up, feeling the need to stretch my legs from sitting all morning and from the effect of the stress of being the one on trial. Outside in the hall I found Steve.

"Hey man, what's with the sling?" I asked.

"I broke my collar bone," he replied.

"Wow, that sucks!" I said.

"Not really. Now I'm on TAD to the base. I don't have to go to sea, and I spend most of my time at home."

Steve had married a Japanese girl, Toshiko. They had a daughter and lived in one of the high-rise apartment towers on base.

"No shit?" I laughed, "That's a pretty good deal!"

"Yeah, it's better than a nine to five job."

Following our lunch break, we all returned to the courtroom on time, ready to get started. Nobody seemed to want to piss off the judge. It seemed like he had somewhere he wanted to be at the end of the day, maybe a golf game.

After completing the formalities and a few more questions and answers, it was my turn to take the stand.

"Raise your right hand, Petty Office Dorgan. Do you swear to tell the truth, the whole truth, and nothing but the truth?" asked the bailiff.

With my right hand raised, I replied, "I do."

Then the prosecuting attorney started in on me. I was a little surprised as to his line of questioning. It was mostly verification information: "How long have you been in the Navy?" and "How long have you been stationed on the *Midway*?" He also asked really simple stuff like: "Do you exercise on a regular basis?"

His tone then sharply changed to a serious nature. "Have you ever been in the A&O workshop's storage room on the 02-level port side?"

"Yes, sir," I replied.

"How often do you go there?"

My attorney had coached me to respond with yes or no answers and to not elaborate unless absolutely necessary.

I replied, "Occasionally."

"How often is *occasionally*?"

"When necessary."

"Okay, Petty Officer Dorgan. When is it necessary for you to visit the A&O storage room?"

"When we need parts."

"What kind of parts?"

"Electrical repair parts."

"Okay, Petty Officer Dorgan. So, you visit the storeroom when you need parts to complete electrical repairs. Is that correct?"

"Yes, sir."

"So, Petty Officer Dorgan, how often would you say you visit the storeroom?"

"When necessary."

I could tell the prosecutor was beginning to get a little annoyed with my short responses.

"Well, Petty Officer Dorgan, from your experience, do you find it necessary to visit the storeroom once a week, twice a week, three times a week?"

"It depends whether we are in port or at sea, sir."

"Let's say, when you are at sea. How often do you find it necessary to visit the storeroom?"

"Maybe four to eight times a week."

After continuing along the same line of questioning and seeming to not be satisfied with the answers he was receiving, he picked up a brown manila envelope and pulled out a small clear plastic sandwich baggie. He walked toward me, his right arm stretched out in front of him, holding the baggie out for all, especially me, to see.

Holding the baggie in front of me, just beyond my reach, he asked, "Petty Officer Dorgan, have you seen this baggie before?"

As I sat there motionless, I could feel my heart rate increasing, staring at the baggie, it all seemed to be in slow motion.

I thought, *Of course I have. That's why we're all here today, you asshole.*

My mind was racing. *How do I answer this? How is he trying to trip me up?*

I looked at my attorney. I looked up at the judge. I looked back at the plastic baggie.

By now I thought the sound of my heart pounding out of my chest could be heard all throughout the courtroom. *It all hinges on this answer* said a voice in my head.

Then I felt my jaw moving and I heard the words blurt out, "Yes, I have. We use those for small electrical parts."

There was a hush over the courtroom while the prosecutor stood there speechless in front of me holding that little, now insignificant, plastic baggie.

As I heard the ticking from the second hand of the clock on the wall, I realized his whole case rested on me answering "No." He would have then replied with: "Well, Petty Officer Dorgan, how do you explain your fingerprints on this baggie?"

He then turned around, put the baggie back in the envelope, sat down behind his table, and said, "I have no more questions, your honor."

I was in a daze. My attorney stood up and asked me a few simple confirming questions to shake me out of the state of bewilderment before addressing the judge, "I have no more questions, your honor."

The judge then looked down at me from his seat on the bench and said, "Petty Officer Dorgan, thank you for your testimony. You may now return to your seat," as he pointed toward the table where my attorney was standing.

Both attorneys made a brief closing statement.

The judge did not waste anytime in making his decision.

"Will the defendant please rise."

With that command, I quickly rose to my feet, as did my attorney and the prosecutor.

"Based on the lack of evidence presented by the prosecution today, this court hereby finds the defendant not guilty," stated the judge.

Bam! went his gavel. It was over.

I turned to my attorney and shook his hand.

"Thank you! You did a great job!" I exclaimed with a sigh of relief.

He nodded to me with a smile and said, "I hope I never see you in this court room again, Petty Officer Dorgan."

"Me too! But if you do, I hope we're on the same side, sir," I replied with a smile.

Just then, the prosecuting attorney came over and congratulated my attorney on his victory. For them it seemed to be like just another baseball game; they were certainly keeping score of wins and losses.

As I left the courtroom, I turned to find Jimmy Woodward sitting there on a bench in the corridor. He looked over toward me as I approached his bench.

Rising to his feet he smiled and said, "Congratulations Bob, I am glad to hear you have been cleared."

"Thank you for coming all this distance. I really appreciate your help and support, Jimmy," I replied.

"Bob, I have done a lot of traveling throughout my life, but I had never visited Japan. Thank you for giving me that opportunity. I was glad to help," he continued. "They have me booked on a flight for home leaving this evening, so my bag is packed and ready to go."

"Please say hello to Ruth and my parents for me when you get back home."

With that, he was on his way to the airport with his Navy escort.

When I walked out through the front doorway of the building, I felt as if a great weight had been lifted off my shoulders.

"You're one lucky motherfucker!" I heard a voice echo out.

Turning to the side, I saw Tom coming around the corner of the building.

"We're going to call you the "Teflon Man" because nothing seems to stick!" he said with a smile.

Right behind him was Ski-bo. "Congratulations Bob, what did I tell you?"

"Just my lucky day, I guess," I said with a big smile.

"Come on. Let's go have a couple of beers and celebrate," said Tom.

I replied, "That sounds good to me, I'm buying!"

CHAPTER TWENTY-FOUR
NOT ANOTHER IO CRUISE!

THE MORALE IN THE SHOP during morning musters was at an all-time low. Most of us had become accustomed to life in Japan and were enjoying our summer. We were definitely not looking forward to the upcoming four-and-a-half-month cruise. The next time we would be in Yoko would be Thanksgiving. *Thanksgiving*!

Over the next few days, we went through the motions of working. Most of us just put in a few hours on the boat and then took off as soon as we could. Our days of freedom would soon be over.

Ski-bo was busy packing up all his stuff from his apartment to be shipped to his hometown in South Jersey. He was scheduled to leave the boat in PI and take a flight back home to be discharged at the Philly Naval Yard.

"Hey Tom, Windjammer for lunch today?" I asked as I was closing my coffin locker in our berthing compartment

Tom had the middle rack across from mine. Ski-bo had the rack below me.

"Hell yeah! I'll tell Ski-bo to meet us there," Tom replied.

We met up at the Windjammer Club at noon and ordered a round of ice-cold Heinekens followed by one of our lunch favorites, the Shrimp Boat.

"Shit, I'm sure not looking forward to going to sea next week!" I said as the waitress brought another round.

"Well, I'm not either," said Tom, "But what can you do about it? You signed your life away."

"Three weeks from now, I'll be home. I'm short, boys," said Ski-bo with a laugh.

"How about Steve, he's enjoying his TAD on base," I said.

"Yeah, with a broken collar bone and a sling," laughed Tom.

"I'd take that, if it meant not having to do this IO," I said.

"Ha, ha, ha! I believe you would," laughed Ski-bo.

"No, seriously, I would, after a couple more beers," I replied.

"You're fucking kidding. You'd break your collar bone to get out of an IO cruise?" laughed Tom.

"I believe he would," said "Ski-bo, "I think he could do about anything he set his mind to."

"No, Tom, I want *you* to break my collar bone, with a crowbar, after a few more beers."

"Fuck you. I'm not going to break your damn collar bone, drunk or not. Are you fucking crazy?"

Our lunch arrived and we finished it off with a couple more beers. By now we were feeling pretty shit-faced.

I turned to Tom, "Seriously, will you break my collar bone for me?"

"You gotta say please," said Ski-bo with a sarcastic grin.

"I'm going to go pay the tab for lunch, then head over to the motorcycle club," I said to Tom. "When you get done, meet me over there and break my collar bone, *please."*

"You're crazy. Get the fuck out of here!" he replied.

"No, seriously Tom. I'm counting on you, as my brother, do this for me."

With that, I turned around and made my way to the cashier. While settling up, I asked the waitress to bring them two more Heinekens and then I was out the front door.

I got on my bike, put my helmet on, and drove to the motorcycle club. By now it was midafternoon. Fortunately, there was no one else around the club. I unlocked the garage door and parked my bike inside, figuring if I ended up with a broken collarbone, I probably wouldn't be riding it for a while. After covering it up, I headed to the liquor cabinet for some bourbon, thinking, *if Tom does show up, I need to be good and hammered to go through with this*, hoping the alcohol would numb the pain.

After several shots of whiskey, I found myself stumbling around the back workroom of the motorcycle garage, putting up some tools, when I heard a voice yelling from the front door.

"Where the hell are you?"

As I walked through the doorway from the back room into the main garage, I saw Tom and Ski-bo walking toward me, their silhouettes outlined by the sun shining in through the open garage door behind them.

Tom was moving toward me at a quick pace. As he got closer, he reached out and grabbed a crowbar from the workbench on his right. He raised it up over his right shoulder and yelled out, "I'm gonna break your fucking collar bone!"

I walked toward Tom, shortening the distance between us, turned my head as far as I could toward my right shoulder and yelled, "Hit . . . me!"

BAM! Tom hit me right between my neck and left shoulder. I went down to my knees on the concrete floor like a sack of flower.

"Yeeoww! Shit!"

"Is it broken?" asked Tom with a freaked-out look in his eyes.

"Let me see it," Ski-bo said, pulling my dungaree shirt back to check the damage.

"It hurts like hell, but I can still move it."

"It could be a small fracture, or maybe a crack in the bone. But that should be enough, shouldn't it?" said Tom.

"That's not enough. I can still move it. Do it again, Tom."

Tom turned to Ski-bo with a panicked look in his eyes, "I can't do that again—you do it!"

"No. This is between you two, and I'm not doing it. You do it."

"Come on, Tom, do it!" I said as I got to my feet to brace myself for the next blow.

"No, I'm not doing that again!"

"How about a leg?" I said as I pointed to the eight-foot stepladder in the center of the garage. "I'll lay down on the floor and you can jump off the ladder onto my leg. That should be easy."

I sat down on the concrete floor with my left leg stretched out.

Then I put two pieces of scrap two by fours under my leg, below the knee and above the ankle. As Tom climbed to the top of the ladder, I laid back on the concrete and closed my eyes.

Tom landed on my leg with both feet.

"Yeeoww! Shit! That hurt!" I yelled out.

"Let me see," said Tom as he reached to pull up my pant leg checking for damage.

"It's not broken. I can tell," I said, exasperated.

"He's the fucking Iron Man," laughed Ski-bo, "Unbreakable!"

"How about your foot?" asked Tom, "That should be easy; I'll just hit it with a sledgehammer."

"Alright—Let's do it!"

With that Tom picked up a full-size sledgehammer that was lying on the floor by the side of the workbench and wailed it down on my foot.

"OWWW!" I howled. I dropped to the floor.

I heard Ski-bo say, "Come on, help me lift him up. Let's get him to the hospital!"

Next, they shoved me into Ski-bo's car.

My view through the window from the back seat, winding through the narrow roads of the base to the hospital was a blur. They unloaded me at the emergency entrance, piling me into a wheelchair. After explaining to the hospital staff that I had taken a bad fall off a high ladder while working on a light fixture, they left me there to undergo a barrage of x-rays and to sleep it off for the night.

———

The next morning when I woke up, I found myself in a hospital bed in a huge room with rows of at least twenty beds on either side of the room. I felt like shit and was hung over to boot.

Sitting up in bed and propping myself up with a pillow behind my back I looked around. A nurse noticed I was awake and came over with a pitcher of water to check on me.

"That must have been a nasty fall you took, Petty Officer Dorgan," she said. "How are you feeling?"

"Not too good," I replied as I gulped down a glass of water attempting to wash away my cottonmouth. "Sore all over."

"Well, the good news is, you're a little banged up but there's nothing broken," continued the nurse.

"Nothing broken?" I stammered.

"Nope, just a few bruises and the doctor wrapped your foot to immobilize it while the swelling goes down," she continued with a smile, "You'll be on light duty for a few days and luckily you won't have to miss out on your upcoming cruise."

"Oh." I tried to smile and look pleasantly relieved.

"I will bring you some breakfast. After that you should be able to be getting on your way," she said as she turned to leave.

Nothing broken, I thought. *Great plan. Well, I guess I'll be going on this IO* anyway. I laid back down, closed my eyes and tried to relax.

What seemed like just moments later, I heard footsteps approaching my bed.

"Hey Bob, wake up."

I opened my eyes to see Tom standing there at the side of my hospital bed.

"Hey man, you're not gonna believe this shit!" Tom said in a hurried tone, as if he was winded. "They raided your house last night."

"What?" I replied in shock as I sat up.

"The Japanese police raided your house last night and arrested Pic," he replied.

"No! You're shittin' me!" I stammered.

"No shit. They searched your house last night and arrested Pic with some pot."

"I told him to never keep any at the house!"

The Navy was tough on pot, but it was nothing in comparison to the stories we had heard about the treatment of those picked up for pot by the Japanese police.

"Poor Pic. He's gonna be eating fish heads and rice for a long time," said Tom with a look of serious concern—which was unusual for Tom.

As I sat there bewildered, he continued, "Man, you lucked out. You missed getting arrested last night and now you don't have to go on the IO too. You owe me, big time."

"You got half that right. I *will* be making the cruise—nothing broken," I said with a halfhearted smile. "But you're right, I do owe you, Tom. I can't believe that about Pic."

"Nothing broken?" asked Tom, surprised, "After all *that*? Man, I tried."

"Hey, at least I'm not sitting in a Japanese jail right now. I'm glad about that."

"Look at it this way," Tom continued, "Two weeks from now we'll be on liberty in PI having a big time."

"Yeah, you're right."

"Hey, I gotta go. I'm helping Ski-bo pack and I gotta get a few things ready for the cruise. I'll see you later, bro."

"Thanks, Tom," I said. He smiled and left.

I gathered myself up. The nurse gave me a set of crutches and told me, "Try to keep your weight off of it for a few days." Then she put me in a cab with a light duty chit and sent me on my way.

That chain of events left me in deep thought: *It's strange how things turn out sometimes.*

CHAPTER TWENTY-FIVE
ANOTHER IO CRUISE

ONCE AGAIN, the day for us to get underway arrived much too quickly. After saying my goodbyes to Kiyomi back in Zushi, I found myself standing on the starboard catwalk, just outside of the A&O Shop looking down at all the other hundreds of girlfriends and wives waving to us from the pier as the mooring lines were pulled in and the *Midway*'s screws began to turn. I could feel the vibration all the way up at the flight deck level as the speed of the ship's huge propellers increased and she began to churn up the water below the fantail. It wasn't long before we had cleared the end of the pier and the tearful eyes of our sad friends, knowing it would be four and a half months until we would see each other again.

My sea and anchor detail station was still the A&O Shop. I had gotten rid of the crutches by now but was still hobbling around with a black steel toed flight deck boot on one foot and a flip-flop on the other. After we rounded the point and I could no longer see the base, I heard the announcement on the flight deck to assemble at the bow for the FOD walk down. I sure didn't want to get drafted into that event, so I made my way from the catwalk to the shop.

———————

"Hey, Easy Money, how's that foot?" said Hurst as I entered the shop.

"I think it will be all healed up by the morning we pull into Subic Bay, bud," I replied with a grin. "Don't you?"

"It better be, shipmate. We're gonna have some serious partying to catch up on by the time we arrive!" laughed Hurst.

"Yeah, we're going to have our own little Miss PI Contest when we get there," said Fogarty.

The ship was still abuzz from the visit we had on the fourteenth from Miss America 1980 Cheryl Prewitt and the six other beauties of her court who toured the *Midway* and dined with the crew on the aft mess deck.

"Yeah, we'll be judging those little hotties while they're grinding away up on their pedestals at the Florida Club," Hurst said as he sat up on the workbench to claim his spot for muster and receive our work orders for the day.

"Arrr—knock it off!" growled Baski as he came through the doorway from the back of the shop with his clipboard and a handful of work orders. "Listen up!"

"Arrr, arrr, arrr," echoed from several of us around the shop. Everyone mocked Baski, and by now he was used to it.

"Knock it off. We've got work to do," he continued.

"Fogarty, Hurst, V-4 says JP-5 fueling station three is not working. Check it out," said Baski.

"Aye, aye, captain," Fogarty replied as he grabbed his tool belt.

"Kelly, you take Watson with you and check out weapons elevator number four. It's stuck between decks," Baski continued.

"On our way, boss," said Kelly as he motioned to Watkins.

"Dorgan, looks like you're going to be here in the shop assigning these PMS jobs to the rest of these guys," said Baski looking down at my bandaged foot.

"Yeah, and I've got the mid-watch, so I'll be leaving soon for lunch," I replied with a Cheshire-cat grin.

We were on four and eights. I had the 1200 to 1600 watch on Four Board as well as the midnight to 0400 watch. That left me with not much workshop time, as well as not much sleep time in the middle of the night.

Baski then put the new PMS chart, covered in clear plastic, on the workbench and said, "Here you go," and was out the door, as usual. Baski liked to delegate.

After delegating the PMS jobs to Fordyce and the rest of the guys, I made my way down to the chow line at the aft galley.

With a full belly, I got up from the table, dropped my tray off at the scullery window, then headed down to Four Board to relieve the 0800 to 1200 watch, which just happened to be Ski-bo.

———————————

"Hey, hop-a-long, how's that foot healing up?" he asked sarcastically as I hobbled down the couple of stairs from the hatch to the switchboard room, closing the hatch behind me.

"Real well," I replied. "Should be just fine by the morning we get to PI a week from now. What's going on down here?"

"Just counting the days bro. I'm short you know—nine days and a wake up," said Ski-bo.

"Yeah, flying out of PI Stateside, aren't you?" I asked.

"Yup, when you guys are pulling out for the IO, I'll be on a plane for the East Coast."

Pulling up a chair, I sat down next to Ski-bo facing the switchboard. "Bud, I'm sorry about the way things went down."

"Don't worry about it," he replied with that easy going smile. "Sometimes you get the bear, sometimes the bear gets you. It's not your fault. That's just the way it goes sometimes."

Ski-bo was always a man of few words and what he said, he meant. I always trusted Ski-bo and knew I could always count on him without question.

"Thanks Ski-bo. You know it would have been alright with me if it had been the other way around, don't you?" I replied.

"Fuck you. Now you're bullshitting me. I'm the one getting discharged," he said as he got up from his chair, heading for the hatch. "It's getting deep in here. I'm getting out while I still can. See you at midnight." And with that, he was gone.

One thing all electricians standing watch at Four Board liked was that even though you couldn't see the doors from the switchboard, you could always hear the door to the ladder up or the door to the generator room below opening, due to the vacuum created in the space from the exhaust fans in the generator room sucking air out of the space.

Not fifteen minutes after Ski-bo left, I felt the air pressure in the space change. I looked around to see Tom walking in.

"Hey skippy, there's just no way out, is there?" laughed Tom. "When you're scheduled for a cruise, you're going on a cruise!"

"Yeah, we tried, didn't we?" I replied. "But thanks to you, I'm not eating fish heads and rice right now."

"No shit! That's crazy! I think someone wasn't happy about the trial outcome and set you up, bro," said Tom. "They were out to get you one way or another."

We all knew there were some details in the chain of events, which we were not privy to. Unfortunately, Pic was the one caught off guard and now doing time in a Japanese jail cell.

"Well, I'm glad I'm just limping for awhile and not in his shoes!" I said with a sigh.

"Hey, we need to have some kind of send off for Ski-bo in PI before he leaves," said Tom with a smile.

"What do you have in mind?" I asked.

We spent the next half hour or so throwing suggestions back and forth. By the time Tom left, we didn't have anything set in stone but we had agreed on some pretty good ideas.

A week later, July 21, we arrived in Subic, tying up at Cubi Pier, for liberty and to take on provisions. I had my mind on provisions of my own I wanted to get on board prior to departing for the IO.

While changing into my civilian clothes by my rack in preparation for leaving the boat for liberty, I turned to Tom. "I'm going to visit Edna tonight, you want in?"

"No thanks. It's been getting too hot around here and after all you've been through, you've got more balls than me," replied Tom in a whisper.

We headed off base later that day. Ski-bo, Tom, Fogarty, a couple of other shipmates, and I to hit our usual haunts on Magsaysay Drive. By 2200 or so, Ski-bo and I were ready to call it a night, so we headed over to Edna's house.

As usual, she was happy to see us and welcomed us in with open arms.

With Ski-bo leaving for the States in a couple of days, he had no need to stock up for the cruise. I was the only one stocking up and since I didn't have to share my shipping space with anyone, this would be my largest buy ever. Nobody knew what I was carrying, but when I started pulling wads of cash out of every pocket, sock, and shoe I had, she knew I was serious.

"You make me very happy tonight," said Edna with a smile. "Good business night."

"And with your help, I'll be very happy tomorrow, Edna—once I'm back on the boat with this load," I replied.

Ski-bo and I settled in with the girls, hanging out in Edna's living room waiting for her return.

When she came back, we inspected our load, boxed it up, and then caught a little sleep in preparation for our early return to the base in the morning.

The driver came at daybreak as planned and after our normal routine of entering the base, I met up with my buddy from Supply who took over from there.

Following a long cab ride out to Cubi Point, I arrived back on board, changed back into my dungaree uniform, then went to see my shipmate from Supply after lunch.

After my load was stashed safely away, I was able to breath a sigh of relief. Mission accomplished. Now it was party time. We were going to give Ski-bo a send off he would never forget!

"Hey Bob, let's get going." I woke up from a short nap in my rack with Tom shaking my shoulder. "Come on, we're ready."

"Give me a couple of minutes," I replied, knowing it wouldn't take long for me to pull on a shirt and a pair of pants. We were in the tropics. It wasn't like I had to bundle up for winter.

"We'll meet you on the pier," said Tom as he turned to leave.

I jumped up and got dressed quickly. Everyone knows that when a sailor on liberty gets off the boat and onto the pier, he doesn't like to be kept waiting long. The temptation is too strong to just get moving.

When I arrived on the pier there was a small group waiting for me: Tom, Ski-bo, Hurst, Fogarty, as well as Frank, Buckley, and Lucius from the distribution shop.

"It's about time," Tom yelled out. "Let's hit the beach!"

We stopped in a couple of our regular bars for starters to get loosened up. After a couple of drinks and a little entertainment we all pilled into a Jeepney.

"Subic City," Tom told the driver.

It was a wild ride through the streets of Olongapo out to the southwest point and around the huge hilltop cemetery overlooking Subic Bay. The driver zoomed along the cliffside road leading out to Subic City. The night was clear, and the moonlight was bright like daylight. To our left the hillside dropped straight down to the water. We were laughing and carrying on, as drunken sailors do, and didn't have a care in the world.

I could see Tom up front, talking to the driver. Before we knew it, we had stopped in front of a little one-story building that looked like a bar with a large dusty dirt parking lot out front.

"Let's go boys. They've got something inside that will make us all smile," said Tom, waiving us out of the back of the Jeepney.

We all climbed out and headed toward the front door of the club.

Once inside, we were approached by the bargirls, as usual, who were looking to help us spend our US dollars.

The size of our gang caught the attention of the mama-san in charge of the girls. She quickly scurried over to greet us.

"We love all sailors, small and big," she said motioning her hand toward Tom's zipper as she welcomed us into the large, dimly lit bar room.

"And small means you," said Fogarty as he wrapped his arm around Hurst's neck in a headlock and rubbed the top of his head with his knuckles.

"We'll let these fine young ladies be the judge of that," Hurst replied as he struggled to get out of Fogarty's grasp

"Our buddy here is heading back to the States in a couple of days, and we want to send him back with a big smile on his face," said Tom, pointing to Ski-bo.

"Oh, you sailors want smile, yes?" the mama-san asked knowingly.

"Yeah, we all want smile—*a lot*!" Tom enthusiastically replied and we all laughed in agreement.

The mama-san laughed too and said, "Follow me. I have a table for you sailors."

She led us over to a big round table at the side of the room with a large tablecloth over it that hung almost all the way to the ground. We pulled up a few more chairs and sat down. After all eight of us had been seated around the table, a waitress brought us two pitchers of beer and enough glasses for us all. When everyone had been poured a beer, Tom gave a little speech about Ski-bo—how much we were going to miss him and all that shit—and then raised his glass for a toast. He continued, "In honor of Ski-bo, we're going to play a little game tonight called *Smile*."

"That won't be too hard. I'm already smiling!" laughed Hurst sarcastically, taking another swig of his beer and everyone joined in the laugh.

"No, man. You've been up on the flight deck in the sun too long. The object of the game is not to smile," replied Tom. "If you smile, you have to buy another pitcher of beer."

Just then we turned to see the mama-san returning with two hot, young, barely dressed Filipina girls by her side.

"You like these girls?" she asked, looking at Tom.

"Yeah, they look fine to me," laughed Tom, looking around the table at us.

With that, the two girls got down on their knees and crawled under the table.

"Shit, I'm in trouble now!" laughed Hurst. "I'm just gonna put my money up for the next pitcher!" With that he pulled a wad of cash out of his pocket and threw it down on the table.

We spent the rest of the evening telling sea stories, drinking a lot of beer, and busting out laughing at the expressions on the faces of our buddies as the girls did their thing under the table. At one point, Frank was so far gone he just laid all the way back in his chair, with his pants down to his ankles and let his girl bob away on him.

I don't think many of us remembered much about the Jeepney ride back to the base that night. although I do remember us pulling ourselves together when our driver dropped us off at Shit River. After walking the length of the bridge, we had to at least stand up straight as we presented our ID card to the guard at the main gate, hoping we wouldn't be pulled to the side for drunk and disorderly conduct.

Buy the time we arrived back at the boat, it was after midnight. By my rack, as I was changing back into my dungarees, Ski-bo returned from the head. "Where are you going?" he asked.

"Man, I have a lot of bagging to do before we're back at sea again," I replied. "I'll be up in the shop."

"I'll come keep you company. I'm already kicked out, so what's the difference?" he smiled.

"I'll meet you there," I said. Then I headed up the ladder from our berthing compartment to go retrieve my stash and bring it to the shop to spend the rest of the night dividing it into small bags in preparation for our long IO cruise.

When I arrived at the shop, I found Ski-bo already inside, lying on top of the front workbench, asleep. I didn't have the heart to wake him.

After securing the hatch with us inside, I made a pot of coffee in preparation for the long night's work.

Ski-bo slept all the way through the rest of the night. After I was done for the night and had stashed everything away, I woke him at 0600. He still had a smile on his face.

CHAPTER TWENTY-SIX
THE STING OF THE *CACTUS*

FOLLOWING A FEW MORE DAYS of fun in the PI, Ski-bo packed his seabag and checked off the *Midway*, heading Stateside to be discharged. Then on the morning of July 28, 1980, we departed Subic with plans to carry out more GQ drills, NBC drills, Flight ops, PMS, and work before arriving at our next scheduled liberty destination, Singapore.

As we steamed south from Subic Bay through the blue ocean waters toward the Sulu Sea on Monday, it was business as usual. We were to head south in the Sulu Sea, east of Palawan Island, in an effort to avoid detection by Russian Bears out of Vietnam patrolling the South China Sea. I was now switched to One Board as my at-sea watch station to stand the 0800 to 1200 and 2000 to midnight schedule. This was a favorable routine because it got me out of the shop in the morning. There was enough time to lift some weights in the weight room at the bow after dinner and the evening watch was usually quiet. It also gave the opportunity for a good stretch of sleeping hours after midnight in a darkened berthing compartment, as quiet as it could be over two boiler rooms and a generator room. We sailors are grateful for simple pleasures.

That Tuesday evening up on the flight deck, the bow was clear and many of the aircraft were lined up in their normal positions with their tails over the water (TOW) along the port side of the flight deck, aft of the angle deck, in preparation for the next launch cycle. HC-1's SH-3G Sea King Rescue Helicopter "Angel" was sitting at rest in its normal ready position on the angle deck, just forward of the Alert Five F4 Phantom of VF-151.

Drills were a normal part of life at sea on *Midway* and today drills were proceeding as planned.

Part of the evening's exercise was for *Midway* to steam in camouflage. The ship was to be operating in EmCon (with no electronic emissions). The LN-66 (commercial navigation radar) was being used as required for safe navigation. In addition, electricians had rigged a yellow forklift forward on the flight deck with a masthead light strapped atop of it so in the black of the night we would appear to be a destroyer.

A collision alarm drill was scheduled for 2000 and a firefighting training exercise was to be held on the fo'c'sle for all the repair locker officers and flying squad just prior to that.

The line for the aft galley was longer than usual this evening. Barbecue ribs were on the menu, and nobody wanted to miss out. I too waited in line for my share.

After finishing off my meal, I headed down to E Division berthing to stop by my rack before going on watch. Fordyce was in his rack writing a letter to his girlfriend. Some guys were in the berthing's TV lounge shooting the shit, others were just trying to catch a few winks.

Up in the captain's in-port cabin, Edgar Santos was waiting on the 2000 reports to be completed so he could start the movie projector. That night's film was to be *The Wild Geese*.

As we steamed along through the Balabac Strait 450 miles southwest of Subic Bay between Palawan Island and the coast of Northern Borneo and toward the South China Sea, it was at sea life as usual.

The hatch down to One Board was not more than twenty feet from my rack, so I didn't have far to go. I made my way down the ladder, arriving on watch at 1940, relieving the previous watch-stander five minutes early. He updated me on what was going on with the board as well as One Able and One Baker SSTGs then he was out the door, anxious to get his portion of those barbecue ribs.

The time was 1945 and I was looking over all the meters on the face of One Electrical Switchboard control panel, preparing to feel and listen to the space around me hum and vibrate for the next four hours. We were heading closer and closer to the equator, which resulted in all our engineering spaces getting hotter and hotter. It made for an uncomfortable combination.

Up on the flight deck, in the breeze of the dark night's air, Aviation Boatswain's Mate Caesar Quiroz and the V-2 crew were testing the catapults. Looking forward off the bow, in the distance he saw lights. "Hey, we are almost back to Subic!" he yelled out to his buddies.

When Quiroz turned to look again, he noticed the lights straight ahead were getting closer and closer, then his buddies looked up to see it too. A huge ship was headed on a collision course straight for *Midway*. Just then the *Midway* began turning hard to starboard, which caused a list hard to port. Quiroz and his buddies began to run from the bow and as they did, the ship tilted even farther to port. They hit the deck, grabbing onto pad eyes to stable themselves.

AO3 Parker had just completed testing the weapons on the Alert Five F4 (the first aircraft on the angle deck) and was just waiting for the troubleshooters to finish up when the ship's horn began to blow and kept blowing. Parker and another ordie, AO3 Morris, looked out over the water but could only see blackness. As they walked up around the Angel rescue helicopter, the oncoming ship turned on its floodlights.

Parker ran back to the aircraft and gave the shut-down sign across his neck as he pointed to the approaching ship. As the Angel was in the way, the pilot and the radar intercept officer (RIO) seated in the aircraft could not see the oncoming danger.

Looking to the right, seeing the approaching ship passing the bow and heading straight for the angle deck, Parker ran about thirty feet toward the island then dove to the deck grabbing on to a pad eye as the ship listed further to port while making its hard twenty-five degree turn to starboard.

The time was 1948. I was sitting in my chair at One Board when suddenly it felt as if the ship was tipping hard toward to port. Holding onto the wooden handle on the side of the main switchboard to brace myself, I was wondering, *What the hell's going on?* Then the collision alarm sounded over the 1MC.

Next the ship seemed to lift on the port side. My first thought was, *We must have run up along a reef or a sandbar.* Then it lowered back down again.

At that same moment, the bow of the 450-foot 7,717-ton Panamanian merchant ship *Cactus*, heavily laden with logs, had struck the *Midway* at a sixty-degree angle just below the angle deck at frame ninety-one. The closing speed of the two ships was 33.5 knots.

Up on the angle deck, the forward boom of the *Cactus* hit the first aircraft then raked all the birds along the deck as if they were toys.

As the *Cactus* scraped all the way down along *Midway's* port side, it damaged aircraft, ripped away catwalks, smashed sponsons, destroyed the Fresnel lens, and jammed aircraft elevator three in the up position.

Working night shift in the aft jet shop, Charlie Hill opened the hatch to the shop and looked out to see the portholes of the *Cactus* sailing by.

Way down in Engineering, HTC Brackett on duty in Damage Control Central felt the ship lurch and heard a rumbling sound. He thought we had struck a reef since we were transiting the Balabac Strait. Pushing the call button on the bitch box he shouted up to the Bridge, "DC Central to Bridge. What's going on up there?"

A scared voice responded, "We hit a ship! We hit a ship!"

Brackett yelled back at the terrified sailor, "Sound general quarters battle stations!"

"General quarters. General quarters. All hands man your battle stations! This is not a drill! Now set condition zebra throughout the ship except for watertight doors, hatches, and main passageways. All watertight doors, hatches and main passageways will be sealed in four minutes!" *Bong. Bong. Bong.*

The battle station alarm had sounded over the 1MC. I knew something serious had happened, but I had no idea what it was. Standing there waiting for Jojo to arrive to relieve me and assume his battle station at One Board, I pictured the scene playing out on the decks above me, fellow sailors and marines running to get to their assigned battle stations before the four minutes was up and the order was given to seal all watertight doors and hatches. On the second deck all traffic in the starboard passageway went forward and all traffic in the port passageway went in the aft direction. No one dared go against the traffic flow, in fact you could get written up for doing so or run over.

Up on the roof, AO3 Parker got up from the flight deck and noticed the VF-151 troubleshooter was still underneath the Alert Five F4. He had been between the weapons pylon and the centerline fuel tank on the port side of the aircraft the whole time.

AMHAN Potter of VF-151 had been doing an Alert Five turn on the middle F-4 when the boom of the *Cactus* sheared off the tail section of the aircraft, dropping it to the deck. This just happened to be the plane with the carrier air group commander's (CAG) name on it.

Parker and the 151 troubleshooter scrambled toward the top of the Alert Five aircraft to get the pilot and RIO free from the cockpit.

As a result of our intensive *Midway* training and experience, everyone on board instantly took their place and assumed their responsibility as we had been taught to do. All throughout the ship, men went about their duties in an effort to contain the damage and prevent the situation from getting any worse.

"Sorry to keep you waiting. We've been hit!" Jojo yelled out as he burst through the door into One Board. He was out of breath. I could tell he had been running the whole way.

"You've got the watch," I said as I ran past him and out the door, ready to sprint to my GQ station, the A&O Shop. With not much time left, I had to fly.

Up in the hangar bay, the scene was chaotic. The aircraft from Bay One were being pushed as far back as possible into Bay Two. It was a beehive of activity. Bright floodlights from our small boys were shining in through deck-edge elevator three's open door, as they inspected the damage along our port side.

The order sounded over the 1MC to set condition Zebra throughout the ship. If you were not at your GQ station by this point, you were stuck wherever you were, especially if you were below the hangar bay level where the hatches were about to be closed and sealed.

As I reached the top of the starboard ladder up to the 02-level, at the aft end of Bay Two, I turned around briefly to see there was much activity around the port side of Bay One. Next, it was through the hatch, down the passageway, around the corner and into the A&O Shop with the door closed behind me. I had made it to my GQ station, but there were others throughout the ship who had not.

Fordyce quickly stowed away his pad and pen when he heard battle station sound. Startled from the strange rolling movement of the ship and the eerie sound of metal grinding on metal heard all the way down in the E Division berthing compartment on the third deck, he too knew something serious was going on; this was not a drill. Fordyce ran to his GQ station at One-Bravo Repair Locker in Bay One, just across from the forward O2N2 plant, arriving to find activity going on in every direction around him.

Aircraft were being moved. Some of the nuclear bombs that had just come aboard, were quickly being moved aft under Marine guard. Much activity seemed to focus around the forward O2N2 plant.

Fordyce quickly assumed his position as nozzle-man on his hose team as they were ordered to take up their position in front of the O2N2 plant.

Mike Weigel of Repair Locker One-Fox headed up another hose team in front of the O2N2 plant in preparation of what could happen next.

By now the word had spread throughout the ship. The *Midway* had taken a direct hit. The freighter's point of impact was the forward O2N2 plant.

Fordyce and his DC Team looked on as first responders came out of the hatch of the O2N2 plant pale faced and vomiting from the scene inside.

The bow of the *Cactus* had smashed through the steel bulkhead directly into the huge oxygen storage tank and into the LOX production plant itself, ripping it off its steel foundations and spraying liquid oxygen and nitrogen through the air.

Three A Division machinist's mates had taken over the watch at 1945, just before the collision. MM1 Agumata, the watch supervisor, had been writing in the logbook at the watch station over near the main exit hatch to Bay One and managed to escape the space with minor injuries. (Although the experience will certainly haunt him the rest of his life.) MM2 Dan Macey and MM3 Chris Belgum, in that narrow aisle between the port outboard bulkhead, lined with

CO2 cylinders and the huge steel LOX plant (where my buddies and I had sat many times trying to find a little reprieve from the sweltering tropical heat near that air vent), were crushed from the impact. Hopefully they never knew what hit them.

Back down in DC Central, damage reports and updates kept coming in from all over the ship. On the flight deck, crews worked to contain JP-5 leaking from damaged aircraft. A JP-5 fueling station, in the port catwalk near the third F4, had been torn off and was spraying fuel. Ordies worked steadily to disarm missiles attached to aircraft. V-1 crews moved aircraft away from the port side and rechocked and chained all the planes to the deck. Fuel lines, water lines, and fire mains had ruptured. Electrical cables had been torn away. Everyone had a common fear on their minds working near so much spilled fuel.

EM Evangelista assigned to One-Fox Repair Team in Bay One, was busy in the O2N2 plant taping up exposed bare electrical wire ends torn loose from their connections. Having to change his rubber electrical gloves due to his hands becoming wet from sweat on the inside, he told me he had just one thought on his mind, *No sparks, please*!

Standing there surrounding the entrance to the O2N2 plant with his hose team, watching repair and medical team members go in and out, Fordyce said he had thought to himself, *Gee, if this thing goes up, we don't have a chance.*

Down on the second deck, Woody Woodin, who was mess cranking, couldn't get out of the aft galley before the four minutes was up and was immediately assigned to a damage control team in the area. His team had the job of repairing a broken fire main that had flooded the first-class mess. After the main was secured and the water was removed from the space, he was finally able to open the hatch to the JP-5 pump room where two ABFs had been trapped for almost two and a half hours. When they climbed up the ladder from deep down in the ship and out of the hatch, they were as white as sheets.

As the night went on, gradually progress was made in securing the damaged areas. By about 0200 the long-awaited announcement came over the 1MC:

"Attention all hands. Now secure from general quarters. Set the at-sea watch."

While this allowed for all hatches and watertight doors to be opened and the normal traffic pattern to resume, many were still finishing up duties relating to the collision.

I, like many others was glad to get in my rack and get a few hours of sleep before having to be up again to catch breakfast before making my way back to One Board at 0745 for the 0800 to 1200 watch.

July 30 had to be one of the busiest days ever for the boys in V-1 and V-3, as well as everyone else on the flight deck. First thing after daybreak and with the help of the big yellow aircraft crane, crews worked together to lift and move all the damaged planes out of the way. While that was going on, the hanger bay crew sent every aircraft that could fly up to the flight deck on the two working deck-edge elevators.

Aircraft were towed and pushed all over the place to get them in place to be shot off the cats. The goal was to get the entire air wing off the boat today while steaming straight back to Subic Bay for emergency repairs.

Back at NAVST Subic, Aviation Electronics Technician Stacy Wright, who didn't make the cruise, was looking forward to being discharged in a few weeks. He and a couple of buddies who were also TAD to Cubi Point were out on the town taking advantage of having Olongapo all to themselves when they were approached in a bar by MPs and told to get back to Cubi ASAP.

After arriving at the Cubi Point airstrip, the skeleton crew proceeded to recover every air-worthy bird the V-2 cat crew could shoot off the *Midway*. It was a long day. They learned how to secure more than just F-4 Phantoms that day, and in a very short period of time.

We arrived in Subic early the next day and were quickly tied up to Alava Pier. SRF workers quickly swarmed all over the ship, inspecting the damaged areas and making plans on how they could get us back on our way to the IO as quickly as possible.

That morning we received word our commanding officer, Captain Carmichael, would address the crew following assembly on the flight deck, in the dungaree uniform. Proceeding to get ourselves together, we made our way topside.

It took some time for us to all fall in but eventually, there we were, the crew of the *Midway*, assembled on the flight deck, division after division, column after column, standing at attention in the bright tropical morning sun under a clear blue sky, facing the island, waiting for the captain to step out onto the outside bridge.

When Captain Carmichael arrived, we went through our normal military assembly protocol then responded to the command, "Right face!"

In unison, we all turned to our right. Now facing aft, toward the American flag flying from the removable ensign staff attached to the ramp we all stood at attention while the bugler played for our fallen shipmates.

After the formal part of the ceremony was completed, the captain gave us the order to stand at ease and gather in close around the island. He then brought us up to date on the incident, and what our upcoming plans were. In addition, there would be a memorial service in the fo'c'sle for MM2 Daniel Francis Macey and MM3 Christian John Belgum. It was a somber assembly and as we were dismissed, no one had much to say. We all seemed to still be in a bit of shock. All of us knew when we joined the Navy we wrote a blank check on our lives, which could be cashed at any time. This event brought that reality much closer to us all.

The uniform for the memorial service was tropical summer whites. It was rare for we engineers to wear whites. If we were not in our working dungarees (or green fatigues for A&O and flight deck lighting) we were in civilian clothes for liberty. Fortunately, mine were still on the wire hanger, in clear plastic from the last time they were cleaned, hanging in my locker at the end of my rack.

My black leather shoes needed a bit of a shine from sitting packed away so long, so I took a rag and some polish to them for a quick buff up.

Making my way up to the fo'c'sle, I did my best to be careful not to bump into anything that would dirty my fresh white uniform, which is tough to do up ladders, stairs, and over knee knockers.

The space was already filling up with other sailors in their whites by the time I arrived. Chairs were lined up in rows like a theatre, facing forward toward the bow. I quickly grabbed an empty seat near the back.

A Division of the Engineering Department was made up of MMs, ENs, and firemen. They were responsible for auxiliary equipment all throughout the ship: elevators, emergency diesel generators, evaporators, and the O2N2 plants. Their job was to operate and keep the equipment running mechanically. We EMs of E Division were responsible for keeping the electrical side of this vital equipment running. The responsibility for the electrical side of the elevators and O2N2 plants rested in the hands of the EMs of A&O Shop.

Looking around, it seemed that most of the attendees were from A Division. I could see the sorrow in many of their eyes. Unless you've served in the military and have been deployed for extended periods of time, it is difficult to understand the bond created between fellow sailors, marines, soldiers, or airmen through the common hardships endured together. It is a brotherhood, an unquestioning knowledge that "I've got your back and you've got mine." Many of the faces around me were familiar. We had worked together in the middle of the night under pressure, in hot, noisy, and dangerous spaces and conditions to get equipment back up and running.

I knew Chris and Dan, which is to say we worked together in our shared responsibilities of the O2N2 plants. We shot the shit when we could and shared a few meals on the mess decks. We were young and thought we were bulletproof. Nothing like this was ever meant to happen to us.

As the service proceeded, I felt sadness in the tragic loss of these two fine young men, Chris was only twenty-two, Dan was just twenty-one. Looking around me I could see many tearful eyes and lowered heads. The thought came over me of the news reaching the parents of these two sailors, that their sons had paid the ultimate price. There would be no happy homecoming when they finished their tour on the *Midway*. They would never know the happiness of marrying their sweetheart. They would never experience the joy of holding their newborn children or watch them take their first steps or take them to the park. These and a million other events, they would never know. Such a tragedy.

After the chaplain concluded the service, we all got up to leave. Several of us commented to each other on how we would all miss Chris and Dan, but nobody lingered long. The grief throughout the fo'c'sle weighed heavy.

I went up to the flight deck and walked to the stern and back to clear my head in the bright tropical sunshine. Stopping at the bow, I looked out over the calm waters of Subic Bay. Memories of my family and friends, so far away, flooded through my mind. Saying a little prayer for my two shipmates, I thanked God for bestowing me with so much to be grateful for and this beautiful day. Then I continued on my way.

For most of us in the A&O Shop the next two weeks went by way too quickly, just like most any liberty in a tropical port does. We took advantage of all the recreation available to us. There were many activities on base we had not yet experienced. Fogarty, Hurst, and I even played golf at the course on base. One of our favorite meals was filet mignon at the Sampigata Club. One outing we never got tired of was our waterskiing cookout parties at Ski Beach on Cubi Point. We worked hard at sea, and we made damn sure to play hard in port. We learned from the experience on the last IO cruise, our schedule was subject to change, depending on the needs of the Navy.

During our two weeks of R and R in the PI, the SRF workers labored day and night to make *Midway* seaworthy and back to one hundred percent. SRF engineers flew down from Yokosuka to help the local SRF crew put the ship back together.

To get *Midway* up and running to relieve the *Connie* in the IO, the LOX plant from the USS *Enterprise,* which was then in overhaul at Puget Sound Naval Shipyard in Bremerton, Washington, was removed, flown to Cubi Point in a C-5A aircraft and installed in place of the damaged one in just two weeks.

A board of inquiry was convened to review the facts surrounding the collision. Among the findings was that *Midway's* SPS-10 surface search radar was red-tagged as out of service in Combat Information Center (CIC). At the time of the collision, the red tag was still posted and in effect, even though the work on the system had been completed.

The decision of the board was that although the *Cactus* was primarily at fault for the collision because of its port turn, proper action by *Midway*'s bridge team could have prevented the collision. The navigator on the bridge that night, a commander naval flight officer (NFO), who had only just reported aboard in April of 1980 and was not qualified as a command duty officer (CDO) underway, was relieved. The OOD (a lieutenant jg NFO) and navigator both received punitive letters. The commanding officer, Captain Carmichael, was absolved of blame in the incident.

CHAPTER TWENTY-SEVEN
BACK TO GONZO STATION!

FROM AN INTERNATIONAL PERSPECTIVE, this was a critical period. The sixty-three hostages held in Iran had been in captivity over 280 days, with no end of the crisis in sight. Due to our delay, the USS *Constellation* and her battle group had to extend their time operating on GONZO Station with the USS *Dwight D. Eisenhower* (CVN-69) and its task group. Although none of us were looking forward to it, except maybe the newly arrived *boots* who had never been to sea, we could be delayed no longer.

On Thursday morning August 14 we departed Subic Bay. Some of the crew needed to get back to sea to detox from way too much fun in PI, as well as not having any more money to spend on liberty. The rest of us were just following orders.

As soon as we were underway, preparations began up on the flight deck to recover aircraft. All the birds that had spent the past two weeks operating out of Cubi Point were to be flown back on board as quickly as possible so we could make a beeline for the IO to relieve the *Connie*. It wasn't long before we were back into the familiar at-sea routine of work, standing watch, eat, sleep, drills. That would be pretty much it for the next twelve weeks—the joys of an exciting summer IO cruise.

We steamed southwest through the South China Sea just west of Indonesia, toward Singapore. We were all a little disappointed not to be able to stop there for liberty, as was scheduled earlier, but the crew of the *Connie* was anxiously waiting our arrival. She had departed her homeport of San Diego almost six months earlier, February 26, 1980. By now, her crew just wanted to go home.

After passing Singapore to starboard, we transited the Strait of Malacca, between Malaysia and Sumatra, uneventfully reaching the Indian Ocean.

On August 17 we rendezvous with the *Constellation*, relieving her and her battle group from their duties in the IO. By the time they finally reached their long-awaited liberty call in Subic, the crew of the *Connie* had endured a new record of 110 continuous days at sea.

During the next four days it was the same old at-sea work routine as we maneuvered southwest toward the equator for our traditional crossing-the-line ceremony.

Now seeing as how this was our third IO cruise in the past year and a half, and our wog population was very low in comparison to shellbacks, many of us were just not into it as much as we had been in the past.

On August 22 the day began early with the ritual of banging trash can lids in the berthing compartment to get the slimy wogs up and on their feet to begin their initiation. As for me, I got on my feet, dressed, and headed to the aft chow line to get breakfast before assuming my responsibilities standing watch on Four-Board. This time I was resigned to leaving the wog initiation duties to my trusty shellback shipmates.

The day was filled with mayhem as we crossed the equator. Many a good set of dungarees were jettison overboard from the flight deck that day. I was glad not to have clean-up duty on the flight deck.

Being stationed on a carrier, it was comforting to know we were surrounded by the numerous escort ships and submarines of our battle group, whose job it was to protect the carrier. Sometimes we could see our escorts, most of the time we could not—although during flight ops, we always had an escort trailing close behind us, just in case of an emergency.

We felt a bit of distant camaraderie knowing one of our escorts, the USS *Leahy* (CG-16), was crossing the line on the same day we were. Their crew too, held their normal shellback initiation ritual, however after they were done, they headed to the island of Diego Garcia to enjoy four days of liberty. Ahh, the perks of being stationed on a small boy!

For the next week we steamed northeast on a course for the Arabian Sea to rendezvous with Battle Group 8 and the nuclear-powered aircraft carrier USS *Eisenhower* on duty at GONZO Station.

The *Eisenhower* and Battle Group 8 had been conducting operations in the Arabian Sea since relieving the *Nimitz* and her battle group on May 7, 1980. Other than a brief liberty visit to Singapore in July, the crew of the *Ike* had been continuously at sea conducting flight operations and maintaining a constant state of readiness as tensions in the Persian Gulf continued to rise.

In preparation for our arrival on GONZO Station, our days and nights enroute were a constant cycle of flight ops, work, and battle station drills. Not knowing what to expect from the Persian Gulf region, nuclear, biological, and chemical (NBC) warfare drills were held often. These drills involved sealing off the ship into airtight compartments and left us hot, tired, and exhausted.

Shortly after getting off watch at midnight, I was digging through my locker in the shop for a paperback book to take with me when I went back on watch at 0745, when the steel A&O Shop door swung open and in tumbled Hurst and Fogarty.

"Hey, Bob, they've secured from flight ops up on deck," said Hurst. "Lets go to 6-A, burn one down, and check out the stars."

Fogarty turned to me and said, "Come on, you in?"

"Yeah," I replied. "Let's go."

We closed the shop door behind us and made our way out of the closest hatch on the starboard side of the 02 level and out to the catwalk. From the catwalk there was a short set of stairs that took us up to the flight deck. The breeze felt good. We made our way between the parked aircraft, lined up with their tails out over the catwalk. They were all chained down, secured to the steel deck. As always, we had to watch our step.

The center of the deck was clear, and it was much easier to make our way along there. Just a small sliver of a moon was in the night sky. It was very dark. Not a cloud on the horizon either, just stars, lots and lots of stars. More stars than I had ever seen before.

There wasn't much activity on deck other than a few airdales working on aircraft in the dark with their red flashlights on. Trying our best not to trip over the arresting cables, we made our way forward to the angle deck. On the far side of the angle deck, one at a time, we walked over to the edge and climbed down the ladder leading to JP-5 fueling station 6-A. This equipment was another of our shop's responsibilities to maintain and repair, so of course, Fogarty had his tool belt with him, just in case somebody asked what we were up to.

Fueling station 6-A was a small room that contained pumping equipment. It was well hidden away and well ventilated. You just didn't want to get trapped in there during flight ops or you would be waiting a long time to get out.

"Come on, you gonna fire that up or what?" whispered Hurst to Fogarty.

"Easy big fella. You got a hot date waiting on you?" replied Fogarty with a laugh.

He then flicked his lighter and took a long hard draw on the joint, making the ember on the end glow red hot.

"Only date he's gonna have for a long time is with his right hand," I said with a chuckle.

Immediately Fogarty burst out laughing, smoke billowing out of his nose and mouth. We all then laughed so hard it took us a while to get it back together.

"Hey, give me that! You're gonna let it go out!" barked Hurst.

After we passed it around a few times, finishing it off on burnt fingertips, we headed back up the ladder and onto the flight deck.

As we walked back toward the center of the flight deck from the angle, the breeze blowing down the flight deck felt great. We turned to our left and headed toward the bow. There were a couple of guys from V-2 Division working on the port cat. Other than that, the bow was clear.

As we approached the bridle horns at the bow it was so dark it was almost hard to tell where the edge of the flight deck was. We sat down on the steel deck with our legs hanging down over the edge and lay back flat looking straight up at the sky.

"Wow!" exclaimed Hurst.

"Now that's something you don't see every day!" agreed Fogarty.

There were so many thousands and thousands of stars in the night sky it was mesmerizing.

"So, Dorgan, how's it feel being a short-timer?" asked Hurst.

"Feels pretty good," I replied.

"I'll bet he re-ups and stays in Japan," said Fogarty with a laugh.

"No chance of that. I'm headed Stateside boys!" I said with a smile. "I'm ready to get on with my life!"

"Yeah, but you like money; they'll wave that reenlistment bonus in your face, and you'll do it!" laughed Hurst.

"Not enough money to change my mind, bud," I replied. "There's a whole new life out there waiting for me after the Navy and I'm gonna go live it!"

"What about your girl, Kiyomi?" asked Fogarty.

"Well, we'll see what happens. She may want to go with me. But at any rate, I'm short; seven months left and then it's your Navy boys!" I replied.

I had never seen a night sky so clear and never have since. Constellations, the Milky Way, star clusters, planets, we could see it all so clearly. It was an astronomer's dream come true. We counted shooting stars one after another. A lot of shit was shot and many a wish was made that night. The common one we all had was we would not be extended this time in the IO.

———————

On August 31 we arrived on GONZO Station, joining forces with the *Eisenhower* to conduct sustained operations in support of US national interests in the Arabian Sea, Gulf of Oman, and Persian Gulf area.

For the next three weeks in the heat of the Indian Ocean, we did just that twenty-four seven, day in and day out. Work, launch and recover aircraft, stand watch, drill, eat, and catch some shut eye any chance we could. We anxiously crossed off the hot, miserable days one at a time.

The last week in September, we headed south past Somalia to Mombasa for a short liberty call.

After two previous visits to Mombasa, there really was not much of interest in this West African port for me. I decided to spend most of my time during this port visit resting, working out in the weight room, and getting my stash ready for the remainder of our cruise.

It was about this time, following Iran's shelling of Iraqi border towns, that Iraq invaded Iran. For us it meant heaving anchor and heading back to GONZO Station.

Jordan soon offered Iraq total support, including arms bought from the USSR and Western powers. Jordon also gave Iraq access to the Port of Aqaba and land and air facilities for imports and exports. The Iran Iraq War had begun.

Next, Iran issued a notice to mariners, declaring waterways near its coast a war zone. They announced new shipping lanes after ships passed the Strait of Hormuz, absolving themselves of responsibility for what would happen if vessels did not follow the lanes, refused access to Iraqi ports, and warned of retaliation if Gulf nations gave Iraq facilities. This effectively blockaded the Iraqi coast.

On October 5, a United States Notice to Mariners announced that Iran had warned that all coastal waters were battle areas. All transportation of materials to Iraqi ports was prohibited. After passing Hormuz, merchant traffic should stay south of designated points. Mariners were cautioned to be alert to unusual, abnormal, or hostile actions while in the Gulf.

October 7 three foreign freighters were sunk, and two others were damaged by Iranian shells in the Iranian port of Khorramshahr during an exchange of fire with attacking Iraqi forces. At least twenty crewmen were killed.

As tensions escalated in the Gulf, life for us aboard *Midway* back at GONZO Station went on. We were all in need of a break when the announcement came.

October 13 was to be the Navy's 205th birthday and the *Midway* was going to celebrate in a big way with a steel beach picnic. Yes, just what everybody needed—a day off.

Preparations for the big party had to begin days ahead. It was no small task assembling 120 pounds of hot dogs, 420 pounds of chicken, 720 pounds of steak, and 792 pounds of hamburgers and to prepare them to be barbequed on charcoal grills on the flight deck—plus all the fixin's and sides. There were also 270 cases of soft drinks, which needed to be brought up out of storage and put on ice to wash down all that food. Each of the mess cooks worked extra hours to bring this party together.

The bakers in the bake shop too had an extra project on their hands. They were tasked to create what was to be the largest cake ever baked in the fleet. A six-foot- by-seven-foot white birthday cake with white icing.

I also had a job for one of my buddies in the bake shop—make us some brownies for the party.

Just a week earlier, the crew of the *Ike* had celebrated their holiday routine day off with a steel beach picnic. Rear Admiral Fuller, Captain Mauldin, and Command Master Chief Frazier were among the first to toast the occasion with a real beer. For only the second time in sixty years a US Navy ship was allowed to serve beer as a part of a general recreational activity. *Ike* was the first and only *six pack carrier* in the east and west at the time. We would not be outdone.

When I got off the 2000 to midnight watch on the eve of the big party, I stopped along my way to the bake shop to pick up a bag of weed I had stashed. There wasn't much traffic as I made my way along the second deck forward through the starboard passageway. When I turned into the back door of the bake shop, I could see several bakers inside busily working on cake preparations.

I stuck my head through the hatch and motioned to my buddy to come over. With a nod, he headed my way.

"Hey, what's up?" he asked.

"Can you bake us up a pan of brownies for tomorrow's party?" I asked.

"We're working on this big project right now, but I can get 'em done by 0700," he replied.

"That's cool, I know you've got a lot going on," I replied.

"Same deal?" he asked with a grin. "Fifty-fifty split?"

"Of course," I replied. I knew most of his buddies liked brownies too.

I passed him the bag then turned and headed back through the passageway and on down the ladder to E Division berthing and to my rack.

After unlacing and kicking off my black steel toed boots and climbing into my rack to catch a few hours of sleep, I set the alarm on my Seiko digital wristwatch for 0630 so I'd have time to pick up the brownies and stash them away then stop by the aft galley for some breakfast before assuming my watch station at 0745. Then I switched on the small electric fan mounted on the steel bulkhead just to the side of my rack. The breeze gave some relief from the heat in our small corner of the berthing compartment above the boiler room. After putting my earplugs in, I closed my eyes and quickly faded off to sleep to the constant dull hum of the mighty aircraft carrier, thinking of how nice tomorrow would be.

The next day, Hurst and Fogarty were there waiting for me in the A&O Shop as if they knew what I had planned. "Hey Dorgan, whatcha got in the box?"

Closing the hatch, I then walked over to the next hatch leading to the back compartment to check that we were alone.

"Well, we've got lunch waiting for us up on the flight deck; you want desert first?" I asked them with a grin.

Removing the lid of the shoebox size cardboard box I had carried in under my arm, I pulled back the tin foil, revealing its full cargo of evenly cut brownie squares.

"Whoa, who needs lunch?" exclaimed Hurst. "That right there will do me!"

"I'll try one, shipmate," said Fogarty as he reached for the open box.

We each gobbled down a brownie and agreed they did taste pretty good.

With a screwed up look on his face Hurst said, "I don't feel any different. You sure these have something extra in them?"

"I'll have another one just to be sure," said Fogarty reaching into the box.

After we all helped ourselves to a second, I said, "Be careful; it's gonna creep up on you."

Just then the shop hatch opened and Kelly walked in.

"What's up, mon?" he asked in his cool Jamaican accent.

"Want a brownie?" asked Hurst, with a mischievous grin.

Kelly's eyebrows went up with suspicion. "What kind of brownies you got there?"

"Jamaican brownies, bro—your favorite," replied Fogarty.

"Don't mind if I do," said Kelly reaching into the box.

After Kelly grabbed a couple, we stashed away the box in the shop and headed up to the flight deck where the steel beach picnic was already going strong.

Holding up a Frisbee he brought along, Hurst said, "Lets play some Frisbee when we get up there."

"Yeah, and whoever misses it has to go get it!" laughed Fogarty, pointing over the side of the catwalk to the blue ocean below.

We arrived up on deck to the sound of "In the Navy" by the Village People playing over the flight deck PA system. Hundreds of sailors and marines from all departments, most who rarely had an opportunity to venture out onto the flight while underway were already enjoying the day off in the scorching sun of the IO. Many had their shirts off, taking the opportunity to soak in some tropical rays. Most had pale white skin from lack of sun. There would be many cases of sunburn by the day's end.

Smoke rolled off the huge charcoal grills set up at the aft end of the flight deck. The chow line was long, but nobody cared how much time it took. It was just great to be outside.

As we tossed the Frisbee around a few times it began to creep up on me. Then it hit me hard. I was stoned. I noticed my two shipmates had begun to get a little goofier too.

We spent the rest of the day goofing off, sharing our brownies with shipmates, eating, drinking, and enjoying the Navy's 205th birthday.

Of course, the day would not have been complete without Captain Carmichael and Rear Admiral Kirksey performing the traditional first cut of the huge cake.

———

During the next three weeks our normal high tempo operations went on as usual. On October 30 our relief carrier USS *Ranger* and her task force entered the Indian Ocean through the Straits of Malacca, this time without incident.

The addition of *Ranger* brought the number of US naval ships operating in the Indian Ocean to thirty-seven, four of which were in the Persian Gulf. The total number of Russian ships in the IO was twenty-five. Four US Air Force E-3 Sentry airborne warning and control system (AWACS) now operated out of Saudi Arabia, who was also concerned about the conflict in the area.

Tensions continued to rise in the area and have not decreased since.

"Hey, sparky, mind if I join you?"

I turned around in my chair on the aft mess deck to see one of my MM buddies, Troop, standing there with a big grin across his face and holding his full metal tray, looking for a place to sit down and eat.

"Yeah, buddy, I had the maître d' reserve this seat just for you," I replied. "Join me."

We were still operating in the high heat and humidity of the scorching IO, as Troop's sweat-soaked shirt confirmed.

"No point in showering before a meal; I'll be soaked in sweat as soon as I've been out five minutes anyway," Troop said with a smile as he set his dinner tray on the round four-person table where I was sitting and pulled up a chair.

Looking at my own shirt I realized I wasn't much dryer. A long sleeve green turtleneck flight deck shirt with the sleeves pushed up wasn't any cooler than a blue dungaree shirt.

"This heat makes me look forward to getting back on watch so I can sit in front of an air vent and cool off a bit," Troop continued.

"Be careful which vent you're sitting near, bud, that can be hazardous," I replied with a somber face.

"Yeah, you're right," he replied with raised eyebrows. Troop was a third-class petty officer who worked in the O2N2 plants. The memory of the *Cactus* was still fresh for most of us.

Just then our round mess deck table with blue plastic tablecloth begin to tilt to the side, as did the bug juice in our cups. Then we realized the whole aft mess deck was tilting sharply to the side. As we heard other trays and cups hit the deck, we reached for ours, all the time trying to keep our balance. As we looked at each other with disbelief, we both said, "Collision?"

We felt the huge ship continue to list to the side. As it did, we felt it turning at the same time. Next an alarm came over the 1MC and an announcement, "Plane in the water. Plane in the water."

Up on deck an A-7 Corsair piloted by Lt. Cdr. Meyers was unable get up enough speed as it was shot off the bow. As the plane hit the water, he ejected. While the HC-1 Angel helicopter pulled the pilot from the water, the plane sank. Sadly, Lt. Cdr. Meyers did not survive the ejection.

———————

The fall of 1980 was an especially bad season of aircraft crashes, especially for A-7 Corsairs. On October 20 a pilot from the *Eisenhower* was forced to eject from a Corsair. Another Corsair pilot from *Ike* was unable to gain altitude when fired off the catapult on October 26. The air boss called for the pilot to keep it climbing then repeatedly called, "Eject!" The pilot ejected at thirty feet. In addition, there were four other crashes involving Corsairs in November 1980.

The Intruders also had their share of problems. Back on October 2 while piloting a Grumman A-6E Intruder, Lt. McCole of VA-115 lost control of his aircraft during a single engine waive-off and crashed into the ocean near the *Midway*. He and the bombardier/navigator, a Lt. jg, ejected safely and were rescued by the HC-1 Angel. Then, on November 5, the day after our A-7 crashed into the ocean, a KA-6D Grumman Intruder took off from the *Ranger* late at night while enroute to GONZO Station. The aircraft crashed into the dark ocean, but luckily both pilot and navigator safely ejected and were rescued.

Not even the more modern F-14 Tomcat was immune to disaster in the IO.

On September 13, during an air combat maneuver (ACM) engagement with an A-7E Corsair II, an F-14 of VF-143 off *Ike*, entered a flat spin. Unable to recover, the aircraft crashed into the sea a short distance from the *Eisenhower*.

———————

Beginning on November 6, our days began to look brighter with the news Ronald Regan had been elected as the next president of the United States.

The next bright spot was the arrival of the *Ranger* to GONZO Station. Our relief was here at long last! Soon our trek home to Yokosuka would begin.

On November 10 we had a rare photo opportunity while cruising alongside *Ike*. The supply ship *Mars*, and the carriers *Eisenhower* and *Midway* steamed along through the calm waters of the Arabian Sea, side by side, while helicopters ferried men and supplies back and forth. Some sailors were changing duty stations. Most of us were just glad to have mail call.

During the second week in November, we turned over our duties to the *Ranger* and her crew then turned east to begin our return trip to Yokosuka. We had served our time on GONZO Station once again. The responsibility of maintaining a US naval presence in the Arabian Sea was now left to *Ike*, *Ranger*, and their escort ships and subs. Within a week we would be on liberty in the PI.

It was a relief for all of us to be able to slack up from the high pace of operations we had been working under for so long. With each call of the battle station alarm, we never knew what to expect. Now we could all breathe a little easier.

———

When we entered the IO, I had set a cash goal of what I had wanted to make by the time we returned to Japan. I had already met that. However, I still had a few bags of product left and this seemed like a good time to get rid of it.

By this point, I was the member of the A&O Shop who had served the longest in the shop and had the reputation of being able to troubleshoot most everything.

I had just looked at my wristwatch and was thinking to my self, *Switchboard watch is almost over. I wonder what they are serving in the aft galley tonight. Bam*! The door to Four Board swung open and in came Hurst.

"Hey man, number three deck edge won't go down and we can't figure it out!" he said as he walked over to me. "They want you up there right away!"

Hurst had no sooner relayed the orders when my relief came in behind him.

"Good timing," I said. "You've got the watch. I gotta go."

I headed for the door with Hurst close behind me.

After some basic electro-mechanical troubleshooting work with several shipmates looking over my shoulders, watching my every move, and questioning what I was doing, Aircraft Elevator Three was up and running once again. Now I could finally get along down to that chow line.

By now, of course, the line was long and moving slow. It took awhile to finish the process but finally I dropped my tray off at the scullery window, headed past the post office, and down the ladder to E Division berthing.

After a quick change by my rack into shorts, a T-shirt and gym shoes, I cut through the berthing compartment then up the latter to the second-deck starboard passageway and headed forward.

As I made my way to the weight room down on the fourth deck at the bow, anxiously looking forward to my evening workout, I ran into an airdale buddy coming down the passageway from the opposite direction. He pulled me aside into a cross passageway.

"Dude, you got any weed left?" he asked.

I had been keeping him and his buddies stocked for several cruises, so I wasn't surprised.

"Just a few bags," I replied.

"We'll take all you have," he said with a smile.

"Cool," I replied. "After I get done working out, I'll meet up with you."

"Where do you want to meet up?" he asked.

"Bay two conflag, as usual," I said. "In a couple of hours."

"Cool. See you there," he said as he turned to leave, giving me a thumbs up.

I continued on my way to the weight room.

After a good upper-body workout, I made my way back to the berthing compartment for a shower and a fresh change of uniform— green flight deck shirt and green fatigue pants.

Doing my best not to get sidetracked by my shipmates goofing off in the E Division lounge, I cut through the compartment and up again to the starboard second-deck passageway to the A&O Shop to get my tool belt and yellow metal toolbox. I had found the shop toolbox made a great carrying container. Nobody seemed to take a second glance at an electrician walking around the ship with a tool belt and a toolbox, although it did get my heart racing on more than one occasion.

After leaving the shop, empty toolbox in hand, I made my way to the hanger bay. On my way down the ladder, I noticed Hangar Bay Two was closed off by the marines for weapons movement.

Hmmm. I thought. *I will have to find a different way to get across the hangar bay.*

Moving on, I filled my toolbox with the last baggies of reefer from my hiding place in the elevator machinery room. From there it was up the ladders to the 02 level, and a maze of passageways to get to my destination.

While walking along I began to feel nervous thinking, *All I have to do is have someone bump into me and dislodge the latch on this toolbox, and all this pot will fall out on the deck in officer country.*

Just then I turned the corner to the left to begin my trek down the port passageway. Turning to look back over my left shoulder I felt the hair rise on the back of my neck as I saw a master at arms walking at a fast pace, closing in on me from behind, his silver badge reflecting light from the overhead fixtures.

I took off at a full run, leaping through open doorways and over knee knockers at breakneck speed.

"Stop! Stop right there!" I heard a voice yell out from behind me.

With my quick start, I still had a pretty good lead on him. After clearing a few frames and leaping over knee knockers, I made a right turn to a passageway leading to the port catwalk.

As I burst through the hatch leading out to the catwalk, I popped the latch on the side of my toolbox and as I pulled the lid open, let the entire contents fly out over the side of the ship into the pitch-black night. Not waiting to see it all hit the choppy ocean water below, I turned quickly to the AESS control box mounted nearby to the steel frame of the catwalk. Scattering some hand tools on the deck below the control box I turned on my flashlight just as the MA came running out through the open hatch.

The master at arms grabbed my toolbox from the catwalk and pulled open the lid.

"So where are all your tools, sparky?" he asked in a sarcastic tone.

I pointed my flashlight in the direction of his feet where they were all scattered about below the control box.

"Hmmm," he replied in a pissed-off tone.

"You think you're pretty smart, don't you?" he continued.

"No. You want to help me? I replied, pointing my flashlight toward the electrical equipment in front of us.

Setting the toolbox down he gave me an angry look as he turned and walked away.

Whew, that was too close! I thought, still shocked from what had just happened and how quickly.

I gathered up my tools then gazed out over the dark night ocean reflecting on the moment. *That could have gone really bad.* I thought. *I'm short—only five and a half months to go. I don't need this shit; that's it for me!* And just like that, I was done. My last delivery was jettisoned overboard.

CHAPTER TWENTY-EIGHT
LIFE IS FULL OF SURPRISES

WE ARRIVED IN SUBIC BAY on the morning of November 17. We had earned more awards, medals, and commendations during this IO cruise but the only thing most of us were interested in now was stepping off the ship onto NAS Cubi Point's Pier Alpha and dry land.

It had been ninety-five days since our last visit to Subic, minus a couple of days in Mombasa, so it was a wild visit this time in *Po City*. Everyone was in search of a good time.

With Christmas just around the corner and a lot of money saved up while at sea, there were loads of PI furniture bought up and gifts purchased in preparation for our return to Japan. Hurst and Fogarty bought enough furniture to fill their entire house.

By the end of the week the aft section of Hangar Bay Two was piled high with all kinds of PI furniture. Once again it was time to set the special sea and anchor detail in preparation to get underway on our quick cruise back to Japan.

By the second day of our journey, we could begin to feel the change in the air and most of all the temperature. Even below decks it was easy to tell we were no longer in the balmy tropics. It was now late fall in the northern hemisphere and the supply air blowing into the engineering spaces was once again cool and refreshing. We could even sleep with a blanket again in our berthing compartment. What a relief to not wake up sweating.

———————

On the morning of November 26, the day before Thanksgiving, we arrived at our pier in Yokosuka. For the thousands of family members and friends who stood on the pier waiting, we were an overwhelming sight. Many of our shipmates in their dress blues manned the rails, stationed at arm's length apart all the way around the flight deck and at key visible locations about our huge ship. Every sailor wanted to have the opportunity to be the first to see their loved ones on the pier waiting to greet them.

The Seventh Fleet Band, the Japanese Maritime Self Defense Force Band and the Nile C. Kinnick High School Band were all there on the pier, taking turns playing music to welcome us back. Banners were draped everywhere along the pier—on vehicles and held by anxious families straining for a first glimpse of their loved ones.

Since leaving Yokosuka in mid-July, we had steamed over 41,000 miles, launched more than 4,700 aircraft from our flight deck, endured numerous tragedies, and gave our best efforts all throughout this cruise. Now we were finally back home and there was much to be grateful for this Thanksgiving week!

As soon as the brows were set in place by the SRF workers, the floodgates opened as sailors and marines made the dash to the pier.

It was almost an hour until the Engineering Department secured from sea and anchor detail. We engineers who were not on duty could now leave the ship.

By now the crowd on the pier had thinned out. It didn't take long for me to catch a cab to the motorcycle club.

———————

There she was, waiting for me in the club garage under cover, just where I had left her, my Black Yamaha 750 Special. As I looked around, I found myself thinking back to that afternoon with Ski-bo and Tom four and a half months ago. That was a crazy day and one lucky night in the hospital.

When I fired up my bike, she purred like a kitten. It wasn't long before I was on my way out the main gate and not far from Zushi.

Arriving at home I parked my bike out front, unstrapped my flight bag, and walked up the gravel path to my front door.

While fumbling with my keys to get the door lock open, I saw a short shadow pass by the window, then the door opened inward away from me.

As I stepped into the entry, Kiyomi, standing a step above me on the main floor, leaped toward me, wrapping her arms around my neck.

"Boo-Chan! Konichiwa. Welcome home!" she exclaimed, smiling from ear to ear.

"Wow! It's been a long cruise and I'm glad to be home," I replied after a long, passionate greeting.

"I have some bad news," she said next hesitantly with a look of worry in her eyes.

"Pic took your stereo," she continued.

As I looked around the house, I saw it was true.

Apparently, Pic had been released by the Japanese police several months after we left for the IO. Before he left for the States, he came and packed up his stuff from our house and packed up all my electronic equipment too. He took thousands of dollars worth of gear: Bose 901 speakers, Pioneer HPM-100 speakers, tuner, amp, dual cassette decks, reel-to-reel, televisions— everything. This was all top-of-the-line stuff.

I sat down on the couch as the reality of it set in.

"Boo-Chan, you want a beer?" Kiyomi asked.

"Sure," I replied. "But I think I'm going to need more than one."

"Oh, I know how to cheer you up Boo-Chan," she said as she came toward me with a mischievous look in her eyes. No doubt, it had been a long cruise for her too.

Thanksgiving and the next couple of weeks passed by quickly. I spent most of the time off the boat enjoying some well-earned freedom. Immediately following the holiday, I made a visit to the NIS office on base to report the theft, along with all the details, serial numbers, and any other information I could provide on the equipment and the circumstances. They told me they would follow up and see what they could find out.

By the second week in December, we were underway again—this time, just for a short doughnut cruise out a couple of hundred miles or so off the east coast of Japan.

"Hey, Dorgan, how much time you got left aboard?" I heard a voice say over my shoulder.

"Four months," I said as I turned to see Hurst sit down next to me at my table on the aft mess deck.

From across the table Troop asked me, "How long have you been aboard, Dorgan?"

"Since December of seventy-seven," I replied.

"Pass the pepper would you, Bob?" nudged Hurst, pointing across my tray.

"December of seventy-seven?" Troop asked. "That's three years. Are you gonna re-up?"

"No thanks," I replied. "I've done my time. I'm ready to get on with my life."

"Yeah, he's gonna re-up," laughed Hurst.

"Just four months shipmates, and it's your Navy!" I said with a smile looking around at the other three at the table. "You all will have the watch and I'll be Stateside!"

"You know, since you have done all of your sea duty deployed overseas at this command, you should be eligible for a three-month early separation from active duty," said Troop from across the table.

Now, that got my attention.

"What do you mean?" I asked with curiosity.

"I've got a buddy who was in B Division who did it," Troop continued. "He was here for three years, wasn't going to re-up. Went home three months early and got out, just like that."

"What do I have to do?" I asked in amazement.

"Just go down to personnel and tell them you're ready for a three month early out," replied Troop. "They'll take it from there. It's simple."

"Woah, if that works, you'll be really short, bub!" exclaimed Hurst.

"Yeah, then I'll be one month short, shipmates," I said with a grin looking around at the others at the table.

The next day I took a walk to the personnel office and asked for a three-month early out. After they looked at my file and did a little checking, a yeoman came back to the counter and said, "Petty Officer Dorgan, you are eligible for a three-month early separation from active duty. After that you will have two years and three months of reserve duty to complete. With the number of leave days you have saved up, you will be able to check out on leave as soon as we return to Yokosuka."

"No shit?" I exclaimed.

"Yup," the yeoman replied with a straight face despite my obvious excitement.

"What about packing up my household goods and shipping my motorcycle?" I asked.

"The Navy will take care of all of that for you. Just tell them where you want it to go, and they will make sure it gets there. You can make arrangements when we get back to Yokosuka."

Leaving the personnel office and making my way up the passageway, I felt as if I were walking on air. The light at the end of the tunnel suddenly had become much brighter.

The remainder of the doughnut cruise went fairly smooth, although we did lose another A-7E Corsair about 124 miles off the east coast of Japan when the aircraft lost power during takeoff. Fortunately, this time the pilot successfully ejected and was rescued from the water.

When we arrived back in Yokosuka early the week of Christmas, most of the crew had preparations for Christmas Eve on their minds. I was busy with thoughts on my mind of preparations for the beginning of the rest my life.

It was December 23. I had been stationed aboard the *Midway* for exactly three years. Most of the shipmates I had served with when I first arrived had left long ago and I now realized that my time on the *Midway* and in Japan was soon coming to an end. I broke the news to Kiyomi at home that evening. She was inconsolable. We talked about it for a long time and agreed she would obtain a three-month fiancée visa and come to the United States for a visit to see how she liked it. I wasn't sure whether we would end up together, and it turns out, we eventually went our separate ways. But at the time, I was happy to have her with me as I started my next chapter.

The Christmas holiday passed quickly and for us there was much to do.

In Japan, the most important holiday of the year is *Shogatsu*, the ringing in of the New Year. Most businesses shut down from January 1 until at least January 3. The large temples and shrines at the actual turn of the year put on an impressive display with the ringing of the temple bells at midnight. Typically, families gather to spend the days together.

Kiyomi's parents put together a special event for us, a huge dinner with many of her family in attendance. All together there were over twenty family members, young and old. The Tokyo restaurant was first class, and the food was excellent. It was more or less a farewell party.

Finally, with the holidays over, it was time to get moving.

It was early in the morning when the moving truck pulled up to our driveway and four Japanese men jumped out, ready to get started. Two of the men got to it right away, packing each and every dish, cup, and saucer into cardboard boxes while the other two men took to the task of moving out every piece of furniture and loading it all into six huge wooden overseas shipping containers that were sitting on the back of their flat bed semi truck.

They worked all morning then took a break for lunch and finished up in the early afternoon. We thanked them when they completed their job. As they drove away, I thought, *I arrived in Japan with just my seabag. Where did all this stuff come from?*

The next day it was time for a drive to the Yokohama Shipping Terminal, North Pier—just as I had done over two years earlier with Lenny—to ship my bike Stateside.

Thanks to Fogarty, I was not without wheels during the last few days. He was kind enough to lend me his little red pickup truck to tool around in. I still had a few more errands to complete and that sporty little truck was a lifesaver.

Finally, the morning came for me to stand on the pier as the *Midway* pulled out of Yokosuka for its next cruise.

It was 0900 as usual when the brows were lifted away by the towering SRF cranes, and the mooring lines were released from the pier. Black smoke began pouring out of the top of the huge stacks on the island. Water churned up from the stern as her massive propellers began turning. I had never seen the mighty *Midway* from this perspective, and I felt a wave of emotion rush over me.

She began moving forward, her bow pointed toward the mouth of Yokosuka Bay, steadily picking up speed as if she was anxious to get back out on the open ocean water.

Oblivious of anyone else around me, I jumped into the little red truck, fired it up, and followed her. I drove as far as I could toward the water watching her go, then followed the road along, out to the point of the base where Yokosuka Bay opens into the huge Tokyo Bay.

There she was, like a thoroughbred racehorse charging out of the starting gate, making her way into Tokyo Bay.

I jumped out of the truck and walked down to the water's edge. Cutting smoothly through the water, she made the usual starboard turn and headed south toward open water. As she picked up speed, she became smaller and smaller in the distance. *My sailoring days are over,* I thought. *I will never again set foot on the* Midway, *and there are things about the experience I will miss.* As she faded away to a small dot on the horizon, she tugged at my heart.

"Shit! It's time to get on with my life!" I whispered as I turned to get back into the truck. *What am I doing standing here!*

The next couple of days were a whirlwind.

Kiyomi and I spent a night with Steve and Toshi in their high-rise apartment on base. From there, I called and spoke with my parents for the first time in over three years to let them know when our flight home would arrive and confirm they could pick us up at the Philly Airport.

We spent our last night in Japan with Kiyomi's parents at their apartment in Kawasaki. The next morning we boarded a charter bus for Narita International Airport east of Tokyo.

There was much going on in the world that week. On January

14, Ronald Reagan was sworn in as the fortieth president of the United States and immediately the remaining fifty-two American hostages were finally released from captivity in Iran and boarded a plane home.

We, too, were boarding our airplane and getting settled. It wasn't long before we were in the air. Sitting there comfortably in my window seat I looked out to see the many blue roofs of the thousands of homes below us. I thought back to the day I had arrived in Japan over three years earlier. Over that time, I had experienced so much. I had traveled three quarters of the way around the world and the world had changed. I had made friends, lost friends, learned so much, and had come so far!

I was twenty-one now and could legally drink in an American bar.

As our plane gained altitude over the blue Pacific Ocean, I looked out the cabin window, scanning the horizon. There for a moment I thought I caught a glimpse of the *Midway* in the distance, smoke billowing out of her stacks as she cut through the water leaving a wide white wake in her path.

It was at that moment that I realized I was leaving this chapter of my life behind.

My days of sea pay had come to an end.

EPILOGUE

EVERYONE WHO HAS SERVED in the armed forces of our great nation has a story to tell. For better or worse, this is simply my story.

Aboard the USS *Midway* we were well trained and, regardless of how much we grumbled, we took great pride in our duty and our work. We performed flawlessly and our results demonstrated it. "*Midway* magic" was not a phrase we took lightly. There was great truth in those words, demonstrated time and time again.

We were young sailors very far from home, and when given the opportunity, we played hard, often throwing caution, sensibility, and reason to the wind. Over the years since my days in the Navy, I have observed that most people seem to have a common need to get the wildness out of their system. Some do it at an early age, some let it loose later in life. But sooner or later, it will come out in some form.

When recounting sailoring days with shipmates who have gone on to lead successful lives, raised families, and excelled in their chosen fields, we all agree that we are lucky to be alive and to have survived our own stupidity.

It gives my heart great comfort and pride knowing the USS *Midway* is now a floating museum in San Diego, California. There is not a day that goes by that I don't think about my time stationed aboard her and my shipmates with whom I served.

GLOSSARY OF NAVAL ACRONYMS AND TERMS

Accommodation ladder: A stairway suspended over the side of the ship with a platform at the bottom that serves as a landing for boats. It is designed so that as it adjusts up or down, the steps remain level.

ACM: Air combat maneuver.

AESS Cable: Aircraft electrical service station cable. Large service cable with attached head providing 400hz electrical power to aircraft.

AIRPAC: Commander Naval Air Forces Pacific.

Alert Five: The state where fighter aircraft, with crew strapped in, are standing by and ready to be launched in five minutes or less from an aircraft carrier.

Angel: SH-3G Sea King search and rescue helicopter.

ASVAB: Armed Forces Vocational Aptitude Battery Test.

AWOL: Absent without leave.

Bird: Aircraft.

Brow: A form of ramp used when the ship is moored alongside a pier.

Bulkhead: Wall.

CAG: Commander air group

Camel: Large floating platforms used to keep an aircraft carrier away from a pier or wharf so elevators or other overhanging structures will not strike objects on the pier. Also used as a mooring point for liberty boats when secured to an aircraft carrier at anchor.

CDO: Command duty officer.

CIC: Combat Information Center.

COD: Carrier onboard delivery.

CONFLAG: Conflagration station; the elevated hanger bay watch station with windows overlooking hanger bay, for the remote control of firefighting apparatus in the hanger bays, forward and aft.

CV: Carrier version.

CVN: Carrier version nuclear.

CVW-5: Carrier Air Wing Five. Seven squadrons and two Detachments, totaling eighty-five aircraft that were the nucleus of the USS *Midway*'s Strike Force.

Darken ship: Ships may steam at night with all lights out to avoid detection by enemy forces. Only flashlights, lanterns, and lighting with red lenses may be used. All topside door and hatches are closed.

DCC: Damage Control Central.

Deck: Floor.

Dream Sheet: Form used to request future duty station, ship, or command.

EMCON: Emission control. Limited electronic emissions from ship to avoid detection by an enemy ship.

Flight Quarters: The general quarters stations for the air department, air wing, and squadron personnel in preparation to conduct flight operations.

Flying Squad: These sailors, primarily comprised of damage control men, hull technicians, and machinery repairmen, are part of the at-sea fire party and are the first to be called in the event of a damage control emergency.

Fo'c'sle: Short for forecastle; the large covered area at the bow through which the anchor chains also run. Often used as a meeting area.

FOD: Foreign object debris.

Gaiji: Outsider. A derogatory and ethnocentric term used to describe a foreigner in Japan.

GONZO: Gulf of Oman Naval Zone of Operation.

Guidon: A position of honor at the front right of the platoon that carries the unit's flag on a pole, usually the sailor best at executing all the marching commands.

Gun decking: Not doing your work, such as routine maintenance, but claiming that you did.

HTC: Hull technician chief petty officer.

Head: Bathroom.

Hi-Cap Station: High-capacity foam system pumping station. This system delivers firefighting foam to special firefighting equipment and sprinkling systems in the hanger bay.

Island: Aircraft carrier's superstructure rising above the flight deck.

JAG: Judge advocate general.

JG: Junior grade.

JMSDF: Japanese Maritime Self Defense Force.

Ladder: Stairway.

LN-66: Commercial navigational radar.

LSO: Landing signals officer. From the port side of the flight deck, the LSO monitors all aircraft approaches.

MEPS: Military entrance processing station.

Midrats: Midnight rations. On board a US naval vessel there are four meals a day: breakfast, lunch, dinner, and midrats.

MiG: A Soviet military fighter aircraft.

Mooring Ring: An oval hole in the side of a ship two feet high by three feet wide through which mooring lines may be run.

NAS: Naval air station.

NBC: Nuclear, biological or chemical.

NFO: Naval flight officer.

NIS: Naval Investigative Service.

Officers' Country: Includes all staterooms, the wardroom, and living spaces assigned to officers. Enlisted personnel do not enter these areas except on business and do not use their passageways as thoroughfares or short cuts.

OOD: Officer of the day.

Orders: Transfer orders to next duty station, separation to Navy Reserve, or discharge.

ORE: Operational Readiness Examination.

O2N2 Plant: Liquid oxygen and nitrogen production plant.

Pad eye: A device found on the flight deck and hanger bay levels mounted flush in the deck every three feet to which aircraft tie-down chains hook.

Polliwog: A sailor who has not crossed the equator; wog.

PMS: Planned maintenance subsystem.

Rack: Bed.

Rat Guards: Circular metal discs lashed onto mooring lines to keep rats from coming aboard ship.

Removable Ensign Staff: Detachable flagpole affixed to the ramp of the flight deck.

RIO: Radar intercept officer.

ROTC: Reserve Officer Training Corps. Provides preparation and training for a career as an officer in the US military.

SSTG: Ship's service turbo generator.

Separation: A release from active duty including transfer to the Navy Reserve.

Shellback: A sailor or marine who has sailed across the equator and completed the Crossing the Line ceremony transitioning from a slimy pollywog to a trusty noble shellback, a member of King Neptune's Royal Court.

Small boys: Any naval surface ship smaller than an aircraft carrier (destroyer, frigate, cruiser and the like).

SPS-10: Surface search radar; a horizon-range navigational radar.

TAC: Tactical officer; responsible and accountable for the training, leadership, management, and overall supervision of the cadets assigned to their unit.

TAD: Temporary assigned duty.

TOW: Tail over water; positioning of aircraft on flight deck.

UA: Unauthorized absence.

Underway: A vessel is underway when not at anchor or moored to a dock or buoy; to get moving.

UNREP: Underway replenishment at sea.

USO: United Service Organization; non-profit organization that provides programs, services, and live entertainment to United States service members and their families.

MUSIC OF THE ERA

AS YOUNG SAILORS far away from home and all the comforts familiar to us, music was an invaluable component of our lives. Music could be heard in spaces throughout the ship, workshops, berthing compartments, machinery spaces—even at times on the flight deck. Young sailors with the latest bootlegged album recording picked up in the PI or cassette tape of a band's latest recording from back in the States were the center of attention. The request, "Play that song again, shipmate," was often heard to help relieve the stress and monotony of life at sea. Many of these songs helped us get through the deployments. Music was a connection to home and a bit of normalcy to hold on to in an otherwise abnormal way of life.

These songs created a kind of soundtrack to my time in the Navy, so I've included some of my favorites as a soundtrack to this book, organized by the chapter I think best reflects the mood of the song. They aren't all necessarily from the exact dates of my time on the *Midway*, but they are of the general era and help set the tone for each chapter.

The Forge
"The Voice"—Alan Parsons Project
"The Logical Song"—Supertramp
"Locomotive Breath"—Jethro Tull
"Mr. Skin"—Spirit

"Time"—Pink Floyd
"Too Much Time My Hands"—Styx

Boot Camp
"Hell Bound Train"—Savoy Brown
"Cocaine"—Eric Clapton
"La Grange"—ZZ Top
"Low Rider"—War
"Safety Dance"—Men Without Hats
"Get Ready"—Rare Earth
"She's Tight"—Cheap Trick
"Fly Like an Eagle"—Steve Miller Band
"Slip Kid"—The Who

Culture Shock
"No One to Depend On"—Santana
"Highway Star"—Deep Purple
"I'm 18"—Alice Cooper

Power Shop
"Live Wire / High Voltage"—AC / DC
"Heaven's on Fire"—KISS
"Rock and Roll all Night"—KISS

Haze Gray and Underway
"Sweet Leaf"—Black Sabbath
"Calling Dr. Love"—Kiss
"Sweet Talkin' Woman"—ELO
"Long Long Way From Home"—Foreigner

The PI
Planet of Women"—ZZ Top
"Young Lust/Dirty Women"—Pink Floyd
"Use Me"—Sly Stone
"Down to the Waterline"—Dire Straits

ORE
"Lookin' Back"—Bob Seger

"It's Only Rock and Roll"—The Rolling Stones
"Feelin' Alright"—Grand Funk Railroad

Summer in Japan
"I Want You to Want Me"—Cheap Trick

TAD
"30 Days in the Hole"—Humble Pie
"Magic Carpet Ride"—Steppenwolf

Thailand
"Passage to Bangkok"—Rush
"Rudy"—Supertramp
"Snake Charmer"—Ritchie Blackmore's Rainbow
"Slow Ride" – Foghat

Baguio
"Girls, Girls, Girls"—Motley Crüe
"Dirty White Boy"—Foreigner
"Days Gone by Daydreaming"—Joe Walsh
"Ain't Talkin' 'Bout Love"—Van Halen

A&O Shop
"Immigrant Song—Led Zeppelin
"Born to Wander—Rare Earth

Hong Kong
"Cities in Flame With Rock and Roll—Blue Oyster Cult
"So What—Joe Walsh
"Bottoms Up—Van Halen
"Red Hot Women and Ice Cold Beer—New Riders of the Purple
    Sage

Zushi
"Prelude/Nothing to Hide"—Spirit
"Easy Livin'"—Uriah Heap
"Funk #49"—James Gang

Ranger
"Thunderstruck"—AC/DC
"Tell Mama"—Savoy Brown
"You've Got Another Thing Comin'"—Judas Priest

Indian Ocean
"Too Much Time on My Hands"—Styx
"Who do You Love"—Quicksilver Messenger Service
"Lord of your Thighs"—Aerosmith
"Everybody Wants Some"—Van Halen

Summer Fun
"I'm No Angel"—Greg Alman
"Feels Like the First Time"—Foreigner
"Rock the Nation"—Montrose
"Street Worm/Make No Deal"—Spirit
"Rockin' Heaven Down"—Heart
"Break"—Heart

Plan Ahead
"Bad Motor Scooter"—Montrose
"Wango Tango"—Ted Nugent
"Beer Drinkers and Hell Raisers"—ZZ Top
"Eyes of Silver"—Doobie Brothers
"Highway Song"—Blackfoot
"Slippin' into Darkness"—War
"Witch Hunt"—Rush
"Turbo Lover"—Judas Priest

The Original GONZO Station
"Wizard"—Uriah Heap
"War Pigs"—Black Sabbath
"In the Navy"—The Village People
"Get Ready"—Rare Earth
"War Machine"—KISS

Sasebo
"Two Tickets to Paradise"—Eddie Money

"Dust in the Wind"—Kansas

Dry Dock
"Love is the Ritual"—Styx
"Need a Little Taste of Love"—Doobie Brothers

Tip of the Sword
"Tube Steak Boogie"—ZZ Top
"Wango Tango"—Ted Nugent
"Jesus is Just Alright With Me"—Doobie Brothers

General Court Martial
"The Cisco Kid"—War
"Slippin' into Darkness"—War
"Big John is My Name"—Rare Earth

Not Another IO Cruise!
"Problem Child"—AC / DC
"Supernaut"—Black Sabbath
"Flirtin' With Disaster"—Molly Hatchet

Another IO Cruise
"Wheel in the Sky"—Journey
"Same Old Song and Dance"—Aerosmith
"Everybody Wants Some"—Van Halen
"Dirty Women"—Black Sabbath
"Beautiful Loser"—Bob Seger
"Stealin'"—Uriah Heep

The Sting of the Cactus
"Slippin' into Darkness"—War
"Tarus"—Spirit
"Closer to Home/I'm Your Captain"—Grand Funk Railroad
"Long Long Way From Home"—Foreigner
"Crystal Ball"—Styx

Back to GONZO Station
"Fresh Air"—Quicksilver Messenger Service

"Lessons"—Rush
"Miss America"—Styx
"Run Like Hell"—Pink Floyd
"Find Your Way Back"—Jefferson Starship

Life is Full of Surprises
"Hush"—Deep Purple
"Crime of the Century"—Supertramp
"Daughters of the Sea"—Doobie Brothers
"Comfortably Numb"—Pink Floyd
"Long Time"—Boston

ACKNOWLEDGMENTS

A HUGE THANK YOU to all of my shipmates who helped me through the experiences detailed in this book. We are truly lifelong brothers. Additionally, I would like to specifically thank Troy Prince, Buzz Nau, and Ron Pope for their photography assistance and counsel.

Thanks to my family and friends for such great support and motivation throughout the process in bringing this story to print.

Thank you to Becky Hilliker for all of your excellent copy-editing skills and guidance. You have helped improve the vision of an old sailor.

Finally, I am truly grateful to John Koehler, Joe Coccaro, Kellie Emery, designer and artist Danielle Koehler, and all of the wonderfully talented people at Koehler Books for their patience and support in making this book a reality.

Just one more thing. I thank the Lord for watching over me over during those sailoring days and since, guiding me through the maze of challenges in the obstacle course we call life, and helping me to now assist in improving the lives of those around me.

The tragedy of the *Cactus* collision, with the senseless deaths of our two young shipmates, left an indelible impression on all of us aboard *Midway* that day. In an effort to ensure their names and sacrifices are not forgotten, a portion of the proceeds from the sale of this book are dedicated to California Lutheran University's Christian

John Belgum History Scholarship Program and the Shriners Hospitals for Children, in honor of Daniel Macey.

The youngest of five children, Chris Belgum enjoyed fishing, Little League baseball, history, and stories about World War II when he was growing up. After graduating from Thousand Oaks High School, Chris took several classes at CLU, where his father and mother taught and worked. It wasn't long before Chris decided that what he wanted more than anything was to be in the US Navy. And so, he enlisted.

Christian John Belgum was laid to rest in Riverside National Cemetery in August 1980.

Dan Macey enjoyed math and science the most during high school, although he was an all-around honors student. Trigonometry was his favorite class. He belonged to the school's yearbook staff and played on the varsity football team. Dan was very creative and loved to build things. In fact, his favorite hobby was building and flying model airplanes. Working after school at Harv's Amoco Station helped him learn mechanical skills. Dan Macey's dream was to attend college and become an engineer. He enlisted in the US Navy the day after graduating from Olivier High School in 1977.

Daniel Francis Macey was laid to rest in Union Dale Cemetery, across the street from Olivier High School and his childhood home on Brighton Road in August 1980.

Fair winds and following seas, shipmates.